D0845186

*Yale Studies in
the History of
Science and Medicine, 4*

Ernest Rutherford. 1871–1937. Courtesy of the Cambridge University Library.

Bertram Borden Boltwood. 1870–1927. Courtesy of Yale University.

Rutherford, Ernest

RUTHERFORD AND BOLTWOOD

Letters on Radioactivity

edited by

Lawrence Badash

New Haven and London, Yale University Press

1969

INDIANA
UNIVERSITY
LIBRARY

SOUTH BEND

QC16
.R8A43

Published with assistance from the foundation
established in memory of Philip Hamilton McMillan
of the Class of 1894, Yale College.

Copyright © 1969 by Yale University.

All rights reserved. This book may not be
reproduced, in whole or in part, in any form
(except by reviewers for the public press),
without written permission from the publishers.

Library of Congress catalog card number: 78-81411

Standard book number: 300-0-1110-5

Designed by Marvin Howard Simmons,
set in Baskerville type,
and printed in the United States of America by
the Vail-Ballou Press, Binghamton, N.Y.
Distributed in Great Britain, Europe, Asia, and
Africa by Yale University Press Ltd., London; in
Canada by McGill-Queen's University Press, Montreal; and
in Mexico by Centro Interamericano de Libros
Académicos, Mexico City.

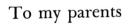

To my parents

Foreword

I have been asked to write a few introductory words for Lawrence Badash's book about the correspondence between Ernest Rutherford and Bertram B. Boltwood. I am happy to do this, since I am probably the only one still living who personally knew both Ernest Rutherford and Bertram Boltwood well.

In the year 1905, Rutherford was already an internationally known scholar, owing to his discovery of the atomic disintegration theory. Bertram B. Boltwood was the leading radiochemist of those years and was a good friend of Rutherford. I myself had discovered radiothorium by a fortunate accident while associated with Sir William Ramsay in London. As a pupil of Ramsay, I had to reckon with some skepticism from Rutherford and Boltwood concerning radiothorium, for they considered Ramsay's later researches somewhat unreliable. This is why Rutherford and Boltwood first regarded the radiothorium I had discovered as a "mixture of thorium X and stupidity." However, I was soon able to win the skeptics over.

After we came to know one another better on a personal basis, we kept in close touch over the years. Rutherford and Boltwood made several trips to Bavaria, and visited the famous Adolf von Baeyer there. From the year 1905 on, Boltwood liked it so well in Germany that he made a trip to Germany every year, mainly to visit Bavaria. By the way, one of the reasons he enjoyed coming to Germany was the good Munich beer!

My discovery of mesothorium was actually due to Boltwood, for discrepancies in my measurements of the half-life of radiothorium led us, Boltwood and myself, to my hypothesis that there must be another as yet undiscovered substance between thorium and radiothorium. When I did discover mesothorium,

Foreword

Dr. Boltwood congratulated me on the fact that my hypothesis of the existence of a new undiscovered substance had been correct after all; and mesothorium, as is known by now, became of considerable importance.

I admired Boltwood especially because of his excellent chemical background.

I am so happy that through Mr. Badash's book another opportunity has arisen to recall the good old days of early radioactivity research, and thereby to remember and revere both of these scientists—Rutherford, the leader in radiophysics, and Boltwood, the leader in radiochemistry.

OTTO HAHN

Göttingen
28 July 1967

Preface

This volume is neither a history of radioactivity nor a biography of Rutherford or Boltwood. Rather, it consists of the source materials upon which such works are built. A scientist's reputation rests largely on the published results of his investigations. If we are interested only in the bare façade of science, its laws and theories, reference to the journals will suffice. However, if we regard science as a very human endeavor and wish to learn not only a man's conclusions but the thought processes and efforts by which he reached that end, recourse must usually be had to unpublished sources.

Such sources, which include correspondence, laboratory notebooks, apparatus, photographs, and interviews, often are too disparate in content and too sketchy in coverage to allow convenient publication. The Rutherford–Boltwood correspondence, fortunately, is an exception, for it consists of a reasonably self-contained and tightly knit group of documents describing certain aspects of the lives of two very capable scientists. It offers the opportunity for an understanding of the motivation behind their work on problems of mutual interest, as well as an explanation of their approaches. Even more, since Rutherford and Boltwood established a warm friendship, their letters contain much professional gossip through which is revealed a strikingly accurate picture of each man's personality.

This last is important, for science is a very personal activity and its practitioners cannot be regarded as cardboard characters. While no one can accuse Rutherford of being two dimensional —the anecdotes still told about him are far too numerous—his personality has never before been revealed full-blown in print. The style of scientific papers, texts, and lectures largely precludes this intimacy and Rutherford's are no exception. Bolt-wood is far less well known today than his friend, which is unfortunate, for the quality of his scientific contributions and spirit deserve recognition. In these letters, then, we can delight in finding the humor, interests, hopes, goals, and idiosyncrasies of both men.

Science does not progress in a figurative vacuum, yet the numerous pressures upon a man's professional life are rarely made public. Again, correspondence furnishes the best source of such information, particularly the attitudes and actions of a man's peers. These factors, as well as university, community, and government developments, help to form a picture of the "state of science" at a given time. Knowledge of this atmosphere in which progress is made is of obvious value in understanding an individual's achievement.

All known letters between Rutherford and Boltwood have been printed here, in their entirety. Those written by Rutherford are preserved in the Yale University Library; those by Boltwood are in the Cambridge University Library. My warmest thanks go to these institutions and their staffs for their kind help, in particular to Miss Jane Hill at Yale and Mr. A. E. B. Owen in Cambridge. My appreciation is also extended to Boltwood's close friend and heir, Dr. Lansing V. Hammond, and to Rutherford's grandchildren, Prof. Peter Fowler, Dr. Elizabeth Taylor, Mr. E. Patrick Fowler, and Dr. Ruth Edwards.

Professor Derek J. de Solla Price first directed my attention to these letters, and to the history of radioactivity, and to him I am deeply grateful. I wish also to express my appreciation to Yale University for several fellowships, to the North Atlantic Treaty Organization for a postdoctoral science fellowship, to the National Science Foundation for a research grant, and to the University of California, Santa Barbara, for research grants from the Academic Senate. Mrs. Dianne Meredith Beyerchen conscientiously typed the letters, becoming expert in deciphering Rutherford's difficult handwriting. Without these sources of aid, completion of this project would have been far more difficult.

The late Professor Otto Hahn, who wrote the foreword to this volume, has also generously helped me on previous occasions. I am conscious of a deep debt to him for all his valuable aid. Other colleagues, students, and friends of both Rutherford and Boltwood, too numerous to name here, deserve more than this brief acknowledgment, for they have enabled me to understand far more about the lives of these two scientists than would be possible from the written record alone.

The kind help of Mrs. Anne Wilde, editor at the Yale University Press, cannot go unmentioned, for she has wisely overseen the evolution of an unruly pile of papers into what may hopefully be considered a scholarly contribution.

Lastly, my gratitude goes to my wife, whose support and encouragement have added to the pleasure of this undertaking.

L.B.

Santa Barbara, California
July 1968

Contents

Notes on Style

Boltwood, from the first, composed his letters on that curious mechanical device that became popular in the late nineteenth century. Except for the correction of a very few, uncharacteristic, spelling errors, the majority of his letters, therefore, are printed here without change from the typed originals. Only the headings, and punctuation in the salutations and closing phrases, have at times been altered for the sake of consistency. Also, closing remarks have been run into the last paragraph. When away from home and his typewriter Boltwood was sometimes forced back to his pen, and the following letters are in longhand:

25 June 1911
15 September 1911
6 October 1912
12 September 1913
11 January 1914

In the transcription of these letters the same rules have been followed as detailed below for Rutherford's letters.

In contrast to Boltwood, Rutherford took to the typewriter much later (probably via dictation to his secretary or wife) and his letters through 22 August 1910 are in his own hand. After this date, they are typed, with the following exceptions:

In Rutherford's hand   15 June 1911
27 January 1914
28 October 1914
22 December 1914 (2)
30 May 1922
16 April 1924

In secretary's hand   27 September 1910
                   1 February 1911
               15 February 1911
                9 January 1915

All letters from Rutherford's wife Mary and daughter Eileen.

Rutherford apparently wrote his letters in haste and proof-read them infrequently. Simple spelling errors sometimes occurred in consequence. Abbreviations and contractions were commonly used and the punctuation marks often fell in the wrong place—or not at all. In this printed edition of his correspondence with Boltwood contractions have rarely been expanded (in brackets when done) and errors have not been rectified, for to have done so would also have altered something of Rutherford's spontaneous style. A list of contractions and abbreviations follows these notes, although most will be understood without reference to it.

Making the rounds in his laboratory, as Sir John Cockcroft fondly recalled, Rutherford would whip out the blunt stub of a pencil he kept in his breast pocket and scrawl calculations for the benefit of his students. Fortunately for those who received his letters, the scrawl at least appeared in ink. In preparing a printed copy of these letters every effort has been made to secure an exact transcription. Deliberate departures from this goal are only as indicated in the following paragraph.

One of Rutherford's idiosyncrasies was to dot only the first of several capital letters in an abbreviation. Thus, R. S stood for Royal Society and J. J T for Rutherford's teacher, Sir Joseph John Thomson. I have supplied dots to all initials. All raised letters have been lowered, their underlinings removed, and the abbreviations closed with dots. Thus, D^r becomes Dr. and exp^t becomes expt. Whether other abbreviations have dots depends on Rutherford's usage—which was inconsistent. Closing remarks have been run into the last paragraph while the headings and punctuation in the salutations and closings have been standardized. All sentences start with capital letters and end with periods or other appropriate marks. Commas, dots, apostrophes, and other marks that are scattered meaninglessly have been silently omitted. Marginal comments that are keyed into the text have been inserted into their proper positions, in brackets, and so indicated. But comments placed in the margins simply because no room was left on the page have been moved to the end of the letter, following the signature. Spelling and other obvious errors in the typed letters have been considered "secretarial" in origin and silently corrected.

Contractions and Abbreviations Used by Rutherford and Boltwood

Ac Sci	Academy of Sciences
Ac, Act	actinium
amt	amount
apptus	apparatus
Ass	association
at	atomic
B A	British Association for the Advancement of Science
bdg	building
c	centimeter
cc	cubic centimeter
contg	containing
C R	*Comptes Rendus* of the Académie des Sciences (Paris)
deflex	deflection
detd	determined
Em, Eman	emanation
expt	experiment
F R S	Fellow of the Royal Society (London)
gm, gr	gram
H	hydrogen
He	helium
mag	magnetic
maxm	maximum
mg, mgr	milligram
minm	minimum
molec	molecular

Contractions and Abbreviations

MS, MSS	manuscript, manuscripts
N C	North Carolina
no	number
Phil Mag	*Philosophical Magazine*
Phys Rev	*Physical Review*
Phys Zeit	*Physikalische Zeitschrift*
ppd	precipitated
ppl	proportional
Ra	radium
RaA, B, C, etc.	radium A, radium B, etc.
RaBr, $RaBr_2$	radium bromide (the latter is the correct formula)
Rad	radium, radioactive
recd	received
R S	Royal Society (London)
sq	square
Th	thorium
ThX	thorium X
U, Ur	uranium
UrOx	uranium oxide
w, wt	weight
α	alpha ray or particle; also proportional
β	beta ray or particle
γ	gamma ray
λ	disintegration constant
$\therefore$	therefore
:: al, :: l	proportional
$\parallel$	parallel

Editor's Abbreviations

BBB	Bertram Borden Boltwood
BCY	Boltwood Collection, Yale University Library
ER	Ernest Rutherford
RCC	Rutherford Collection, Cambridge University Library
Am. J. Phys.	*American Journal of Physics*
Am. J. Sci.	*American Journal of Science*
Arch. Intern. Hist. Sci.	*Archives Internationales d'Histoire des Sciences*
Ber. Deut. Chem. Ges.	*Berichte der Deutschen Chemischen Gesellschaft*
Brit. Assoc. Advance. Sci. Rept.	*British Association for the Advancement of Science, Report of the Annual Meeting*
Centr. Mineral. Geol.	*Centralblatt für Mineralogie, Geologie und Paläeontologie*
Chem. News	*Chemical News*
Comptes Rendus	*Comptes Rendus Hebdomadaires des Séances,* Académie des Sciences (Paris)
J. Am. Chem. Soc.	*Journal of the American Chemical Society*
J. Chim. Phys.	*Journal de Chimie Physique*
Mem. Proc. Manchester Lit. Phil. Soc.	*Memoirs and Proceedings of the Manchester Literary and Philosophical Society*
Phil. Trans.	*Philosophical Transactions* of the Royal Society

Physik. Z.	*Physikalische Zeitschrift*
Proc. Am. Phil. Soc.	*Proceedings of the American Philosophical Society*
Proc. Phys. Soc.	*Proceedings of the Physical Society* (London)
Proc. Roy. Soc.	*Proceedings of the Royal Society*
Sitzber. Akad. Wiss. Wien, Math. Naturw. Kl. Abt. IIa	*Sitzungsberichte der Akademie der Wissenschaften in Wien, Mathematisch-Naturwissenschaftliche Klasse, Abteilung IIa*
Verhandl. Deut. Physik. Ges.	*Verhandlungen der Deutschen Physikalischen Gesellschaft*

Introduction

I. The Second Scientific Revolution

After the scientific revolution of the seventeenth century came another in the 1890s. This second revolution, mirroring the increased pace of life, changed the face of science in little more than a generation, in great contrast to the one hundred and fifty years that spanned the contributions of Copernicus, Kepler, Galileo, Descartes, and Newton.

This upheaval, which replaced the "classical" mechanics of Newton and electromagnetic theory of Maxwell with what is collectively called "modern physics," was largely unexpected. By the late nineteenth century, physics had been brought to such a satisfactory level of explanation that it was seriously argued that little meaningful research in this subject remained. Rather, efforts would be directed toward increased accuracy of the known physical constants—the goal was to be the next decimal place.

Indeed, much was accomplished in this eagerness for accuracy, and not only in measurements and standards of greater precision, which were of value to science and industry alike. Rayleigh, for example, was led to his discovery of the rare gas argon, a discovery shared with Ramsay, because he could not explain away a small bubble of gas remaining from his expended sample of atmospheric air. From his inclination to investigate the next decimal place, where a discrepancy could often be accepted as "within experimental error," emerged an entirely new group in the periodic table of elements.

But twentieth-century physicists were destined to be more than mere adjuncts of an international bureau of standards.

Introduction

Some minor problems that had defied explanation now took on crisis proportions. Einstein's special theory of relativity came, in part, from the failure to find the ether drift that was expected according to the wave theory of light. Only by introducing a quantum hypothesis could Planck derive a formula for black-body radiation that corresponded with the empirical data. And it took the extension of quantum considerations from mechanical systems to electromagnetic radiation for Einstein to explain the photoelectric effect.

Nor was the fuel for the revolutionary fire all theoretical. The subject of cathode rays had been investigated since mid-nineteenth century without agreement as to their nature. Yet these studies of the discharge of electricity in gases led to an epochal series of discoveries, for in 1895 Röntgen found X rays, in 1896 Becquerel chanced upon the phenomenon of radio-activity, and in 1897 J. J. Thomson proved the existence of the electron. Subsequent work, such as Bohr's 1913 elaboration of Rutherford's nuclear atom, served to bring quantum ideas into the stream of atomic physics, while these ideas finally became the mainstay of this field with the quantum mechanics of the 1920s.

Man's view of nature had changed strikingly. No longer did he live among concepts of absolute space and continuum of energy. Even more, numerous atoms were found to transmute spontaneously and matter could have wave, as well as corpuscular, properties. The story of this scientific revolution is many-faceted, but always near its center will be found the subject of radioactivity.

II. Radioactivity [1]

Because Wilhelm Conrad Röntgen's newly discovered X rays were seen to issue from that part of the glass vacuum tube

1. The following sources are recommended for a more detailed discussion of radioactivity:

brought to a bright glow by a cathode ray bombardment, several scientists suspected a connection between phosphorescence and the penetrating radiation. In Paris, Henri Poincaré suggested to Henri Becquerel, an expert on phosphorescence, that he see if various glowing bodies produce radiations similar to X rays. Becquerel happily included some uranium salts among the substances tested (they exhibited a beautiful green glow when stimulated by sunlight) and was delighted to observe that they exposed his photographic plates even through thin sheets of intervening metal. A problem had been posed, a successful experiment had been performed, and the original idea verified: phosphorescent bodies may produce penetrating radiation.

But Becquerel's subsequent thorough investigation of these uranium rays raised some disturbing features. A *non*phosphorescent series of uranium salts also produced this radiation. Even more, the activity was an atomic property, being localized in metallic uranium, which, again, did not phosphoresce. Faced with this dilemma and seeing no other reasonable explanation, Becquerel maintained for several years that the "Becquerel rays," as they came to be called, resulted from a long-lived form of phosphorescence.

In the next few years alternative explanations of the phenomenon were presented by several scientists but none was

T. W. Chalmers, *A Short History of Radio-Activity* (London, *The Engineer*, 1951).

Eve Curie, *Madame Curie* (N.Y., Doubleday, Doran, 1938).

Marie Curie, *Pierre Curie* (N. Y., Macmillan, 1923).

Samuel Glasstone, *Sourcebook on Atomic Energy* (3d ed., Princeton, Van Nostrand, 1967).

Otto Hahn, *A Scientific Autobiography* (N. Y., Scribner's, 1966).

Muriel Howorth, *The Life Story of Frederick Soddy* (London, New World, 1958).

Alfred Romer, *The Restless Atom* (Garden City, N. Y., Doubleday Anchor, 1960).

———, ed., *The Discovery of Radioactivity and Transmutation* (N. Y., Dover, 1964).

widely accepted until the transformation theory of 1902–03. Proposed by Ernest Rutherford and Frederick Soddy, this was an iconoclastic interpretation of radioactivity. Alchemy had long before been placed in disrepute, but here the young physicist and chemist were saying that one atom transmutes into another, with the emission of radiation. And all this was occurring naturally and spontaneously, without the alchemist's incantations and philosopher's stone. Even more surprising than this theory, perhaps, was its rapid acceptance, but the strong evidence in support of it and the circumstance of many scientists growing accustomed to frequent and profound discoveries seem to have eased the way.

In the year following his discovery of radioactivity, Becquerel performed such a complete examination of uranium rays that there seemed to be little room for further study. Indeed, the subject appears to have gone into eclipse in 1897. Early in 1898, however, Gerhard C. Schmidt and Marie Sklodowska Curie independently announced that uranium was not alone in the property of spontaneously emitting a radiation sufficiently powerful to expose a photographic plate or ionize the air in an electroscope or electrometer. Another element, thorium, behaved in similar fashion. When Marie Curie's further work showed that the pitchblende ore, from which uranium had been removed, was more powerful still than the uranium metal itself, her physicist husband, Pierre, dropped his own work and joined her. Together with Gustave Bémont, they soon isolated impure compounds of what they considered to be new elements: polonium and radium.

While work progressed on the isolation and identification of numerous radioelements, a greater effort was expended in the examination of their radiation. Rutherford found in this radiation two varieties of rays which he named, simply, alpha and beta. The former could be stopped by a sheet of foil; the latter showed greater penetrating ability. When Paul Villard, in 1900, discovered a still more penetrating radiation, the obvious name gamma was applied to it.

These rays possessed different properties. The alphas could best ionize the air and, though not until 1903 was Rutherford able to deflect them by electric and magnetic fields, they were long considered to be positively charged particles of atomic dimension. But whether they were hydrogen atoms with half a charge, hydrogen molecules with a single charge, or helium atoms with two charges was not settled until the decisive 1908 experiment by Rutherford and Thomas Royds, described in these letters.

The beta rays yielded more quickly to understanding, for in 1899 Friedrich Giesel and, independently, Stefan Meyer and Egon von Schweidler showed by the direction of their deflection in a magnetic field that the rays bore a negative charge. Immediately thereafter, Becquerel succeeded in deflecting them in both magnetic and electric fields, from which he calculated their charge-to-mass (e/m) ratio, obtaining a value corresponding to e/m for cathode rays or electrons. The beta rays, therefore, consisted of negatively charged particles far smaller than the smallest atom.

The gamma rays were the most intractable in giving up their secrets. Their nature was argued in the first decade of this century, but not as heatedly as that of X rays, which they resembled. And it was not until after the crystal diffraction technique of Max Von Laue, Walter Friedrich, and Paul Knipping had placed X rays in the electromagnetic spectrum, and it had been perfected by William H. and W. Lawrence Bragg, that Rutherford and E. N. da C. Andrade used this method in 1913–14 to show that gamma rays too were electromagnetic.

Those who investigated radioactivity soon learned that while uranium, thorium, and radium showed no apparent decrease in activity, there were other radioelements which lost activity, or decayed, each within a unique interval. The time to reach half the initial value (half-life) became an important means of identifying a particular radioelement. From about 1904, especially with the work of Bertram B. Boltwood, Herbert N. McCoy, William Crookes, Otto Hahn, Frederick Soddy, and Friedrich Giesel, the chemical side of radioactivity came to the fore. Efforts to separate a radioelement had led to the discovery that it was continually being produced as its parent element decayed, and in turn it too was decaying to form a series of daughter elements. Such information had convinced Rutherford and Soddy that their transformation theory of radioactivity was the correct interpretation of the phenomenon. Now the expanded chemical efforts succeeded in uncovering additional radioelements and in placing them in correct sequence in the several decay series: uranium–radium, thorium, and actinium.

This chemical knowledge also raised some problems. Numerous radioelements exhibited remarkably similar chemical properties (they could not be separated when once combined), but quite distinct half-lives. Also, there were far too many radioelements to fit into the periodic table without a major innovation in its structure. The solution came early in 1913, when both Kasimir Fajans and Soddy advanced the group displacement laws and the concept of isotopy. When a radioelement emits an alpha particle, they said, it transforms into another element two boxes to the left in the periodic table. Conversely, a beta emission results in a daughter product one box to the right. If, in a decay series, an alpha particle is followed by two betas, this product is chemically *identical* with its great-grandparent. Thus a new understanding was introduced into chemistry: differences may exist between atoms of the same element. No chemical reaction is capable of separating isotopes, but because they differ in their atomic weights, physical means were later found to effect this separation.

With this explanation for the multitude of radioelements, an insight which allowed the few remaining gaps in the decay

6

series to be identified and filled, radiochemistry effectively
ceased to be an active field of science. Tracer techniques were
devised shortly after World War I, but this constituted an area
of application, not of basic inquiry. It took the discovery of artificial radioactivity in 1934, together with the construction of
large accelerating machines begun in the early 1930s, to resurrect the moribund radiochemistry and transform it into the nuclear chemistry of today.

Both because of radiochemistry's suicidal success and because
of profound advances within itself, physics became the major
vehicle for progress in radioactivity by the middle of this century's second decade. Since the alpha particles were charged,
Rutherford assumed that the scattering observed when a beam
of these particles struck a foil target was due to electrostatic or
Coulomb repulsion by the charge of the target atoms. But the
"plum-pudding" atom models of Lord Kelvin and J. J. Thomson, in which the electron plums were dispersed throughout the
spherical, positively charged pudding, contained no region of
charge density sufficient to turn the alphas about in their tracks.
Nor was a series of small deflections, as the alpha passed by
many atoms, a satisfactory means of obtaining the large scattering observed.

Rutherford then made the inspired suggestion that the
charge of an atom was concentrated in a nucleus far smaller
than the dimensions of the whole atom. Such a nucleus would
have a force field sufficiently powerful to repel an alpha particle
in a single encounter, as his calculations indicated. Thus in
1911 was born an atom consisting largely of empty space.

Two years later, Niels Bohr detailed some of the structure of
this atom. He challenged classical electromagnetic theory by
denying that the orbiting electrons emit radiation, introduced
quantum physics into the sizes of these orbits, and explained
spectral lines as the radiation emitted when electrons jump
from one orbit to another. But notice that this type of inquiry

differs from previous studies of radioactivity, with decay periods, daughter products, isotopes, etc. Radioactivity had, in fact, begun to evolve into atomic physics.

This change was perhaps delayed by World War I, during which many scientists were at the front, while those at home bore additional war duties. Yet even with little laboratory time or assistance, Rutherford performed the essential experiments that led to his 1919 announcement of the artificially induced disintegration of elements. He had bombarded nitrogen gas with alpha particles and produced protons and oxygen isotopes. Postwar efforts, therefore, included a certain amount of traditional studies in radioactivity, but the more exciting and significant investigations had to do with probing the atom. As the subject of radioactivity decayed, that of atomic physics grew.

III. Rutherford [2]

Almost from his very first paper on radioactivity, Ernest Rutherford was the central figure in this science. Not Becquerel, nor the Curies, Soddy, Hahn, Bohr, nor other great names, but Rutherford led the field of talented physicists and chemists in probing that most fundamental question of science: What is the nature of matter? Among the eminent scientists of

2. The following sources are recommended for a more detailed discussion of Rutherford's life:

E. N. da C. Andrade, *Rutherford and the Nature of the Atom* (Garden City, N. Y., Doubleday Anchor, 1964).

A. S. Eve, *Rutherford* (Cambridge, University Press, 1939).

A. S. Eve and James Chadwick, "Lord Rutherford," *Obituary Notices of the Royal Society of London, 2* (1938), 395–423.

Norman Feather, *Lord Rutherford* (London, Blackie, 1940).

Obituary notices in *Nature, 140* (1937), 717, 746–55, 1047–54; and *141* (1938), 841–42.

Rutherford by Those Who Knew Him, Being the collection of the first five Rutherford Lectures of the Physical Society. Reprinted from the *Proceedings of the Physical Society,* between 1943 and 1951 (London, Physical Society).

the first half of the twentieth century few, if any, achieved a success comparable to Rutherford's in scientific discovery, teaching, and what we may call the politics of science.

The man who became Lord Rutherford of Nelson, member of the exclusive Order of Merit, President of the Royal Society, Cavendish Professor of Experimental Physics in Cambridge University, Nobel Prize winner, and recipient of dozens of other medals and honors was born 30 August 1871, the son of a poor New Zealander farmer. His youthful experiences stamped upon him the lifelong characteristics of robust good humor, enthusiasm, directness, and simplicity. Indeed, simplicity of experiment became his trademark, for he possessed unusual ability to design his apparatus free from the complications that more readily permit extraneous influences on experimental data.

Rutherford's schooling in New Zealand was capped by attendance at Canterbury College, Christchurch. From there a scholarship enabled him to enter Cambridge University which had just opened its doors to graduates of other institutions. England was far closer to the world's scientific "center of gravity" and his teacher in the Cavendish Laboratory, J. J. Thomson, was one of the reasons for Britain's scientific eminence. When Rutherford arrived there in 1895 he carried with him a research project on radio waves begun at Canterbury. Soon, however, "J.J." had his brilliant student helping him investigate the ionization of gases. Various means were employed to ionize the gases, including exposure to X rays and ultraviolet radiation. Inevitably, the newly discovered uranium rays also were tried and, with his uncanny knack for pursuing the significant, Rutherford saw more than just another way to create electrical effects among gas molecules. Instead, he saw a profound physical phenomenon, which from that time occupied the remaining four decades of his life.

In 1898 the young but already noteworthy physicist was appointed to a professorship at McGill University, Montreal. Quickly creating a powerful research group, an impressive number of papers on radioactivity flowed from his laboratory. Well aware that he was competent himself to investigate physical phenomena, but needed skilled help in the chemical study of the radioelements, Rutherford was quite receptive to offers of such assistance. Soddy joined him in 1900, Hahn in 1905, and Boltwood began their correspondence in 1904. Although relatively unknown at these dates, each man soon proved his genius, but these achievements were due in no small part to the association with Rutherford. During his nine years at McGill, Rutherford's own most memorable accomplishments were the 1902–03 transformation theory of radioactivity (with Soddy), and his proof in 1903, from their electric and magnetic deflections, that the alpha rays are positively charged particles.

Yet Montreal seemed to be on the outskirts of the scientific map and Rutherford longed for the chance to return to Europe. This occurred in 1907, when Sir Arthur Schuster chose to retire early from his chair in the University of Manchester if Rutherford would fill it. This he did, with distinction, for the next dozen years, until he was called upon to replace J. J. Thomson as Cavendish Professor in 1919.

Some scientists are remembered for a single outstanding discovery. It is a measure of Rutherford's greatness that he may be credited with at least three. The transformation theory was born during his stay in Canada, but two others emerged from Manchester. These were the concept of the nuclear atom (1911) and the artificial transmutation of elements (1919). Further, it may be argued seriously that in Manchester Rutherford made equally great discoveries in human talent, for among his students and colleagues were Hans Geiger, Niels Bohr, Henry Moseley, James Chadwick, Kasimir Fajans, Charles G. Darwin, and George von Hevesy.

In the game of musical professorial chairs that followed World War I, J. J. Thomson became Master of Trinity College, Cambridge, and resigned the Cavendish Professorship. The obvious successor was his most distinguished pupil and, thus, to no one's surprise, Rutherford was selected. During his nearly two decades as director of this world-famous laboratory, Rutherford presided over the transition from little science to big science. Not only was his physical plant greatly enlarged, but the number of students, research workers and funds to support them increased measurably. Even more, the tenor of science changed— from a man working alone in a room on apparatus he himself had constructed to research teams using large pieces of engineered equipment. Though Rutherford's own research activities diminished as his administrative responsibilities increased, and he personally found the large machines uncongenial, he appreciated their usefulness and admired those capable of designing them. Similarly, he recognized the power of quantum mechanics and was willing to use its results, but did not himself become expert in its intricacies.

In other respects, the Cavendish carried on the tradition, established in Rutherford's Manchester and McGill laboratories, of great accomplishments and outstanding scientists. John Cockcroft and E. T. S. Walton in 1932 succeeded in disintegrating elements with artificially accelerated protons, while Chadwick in the same year discovered the neutron. In addition, fundamental work in the electronic counting of radiation and in cosmic rays, wireless, intense magnetic fields, and low temperatures, as well as in atomic and nuclear physics, was pursued in Cambridge, and such names as P. M. S. Blackett, Peter Kapitza, Mark Oliphant, G. I. Taylor, and E. V. Appleton are prominent.

With Rutherford's death in 1937, an era of British leadership in physics ended. That the role passed to the United States is in some degree a result of World War II and the circumstance that big science costs big money. That Rutherford and his school accomplished as much as they did with the resources available is yet another tribute to his genius as scientist, teacher, and administrator. James Jeans has called him the Isaac Newton of atomic physics. Newton discovered the laws that govern the universe; Rutherford did the same for the realm of the infinitely small.

IV. BOLTWOOD [3]

The year before he was asked to become director of the Physical Laboratory at the University of Manchester, Rutherford had received a similar proposal from Yale University. However, he saw little reason for a move that would not take him back to England and he declined the post which then went to Henry A. Bumstead, who was already at Yale. Concerning this matter, the following letter was sent by the president to the secretary of Yale University on 8 February 1906:

> After leaving the matter open until the last minute, Rutherford finally decided that he could not come here for the Sloane Laboratory. The position is to go to Bumstead. Bumstead has during the last year been doing really distinguished work. We are going to associate Boltwood with him as his assistant in the Laboratory. I think that this will make a good combination. Boltwood is a man of great mechanical ingenuity, and an untiring experimenter. His vivacity will counteract the effects of Bumstead's seriousness, and Bumstead's concentration will prevent Boltwood from scattering his brains loose around the table. It is delightful to see the enthusiasm and ambition with which the two men are going into the work. I predict great things for them.

3. No book-length biography of Boltwood exists. However, further details of his life may be obtained from the following obituary notices:
A. F. Kovarik, *American Journal of Science, 15* (1928), 188–98.
————, *Biographical Memoirs of the National Academy of Sciences, 14* (1930), 69–96.
E. Rutherford, *Nature, 121* (1928), 64–65.

Introduction

President Hadley was a shrewd judge of both personalities and professional talent. Boltwood and Bumstead formed a most happy team and each enjoyed a distinguished career.

Bertram Borden Boltwood was born on 27 July 1870 into a family that had been among the early settlers of New England and New York. Whereas Rutherford's parents, coming from a similar pioneering tradition, were still tied to the land, Boltwood's grandfather and father had become lawyers and the boy grew up in comfortable surroundings. After preparatory school, Boltwood entered Yale's Sheffield Scientific School in 1889, majoring in chemistry. Despite his irrepressible good humor, bordering on practical joking, and his great interest in fine foods and wines and the theater, Boltwood took highest honors in his subject. After graduation in 1892, he departed for two years of advanced study at the Ludwig-Maximilian University of Munich, where the training he received in analytical methods and in the rare earths was to prove valuable in later years.

The autumn of 1894 saw him back at Yale pursuing graduate research, which terminated with the award of his doctoral degree in 1897. Although he began an academic career, as instructor of both analytical and physical chemistry, Boltwood in 1900 established a private laboratory as a consulting chemist in New Haven, Connecticut. By this time he had become a master of experimental technique, ever interested in new procedures and apparatus.

In his commercial venture, Boltwood joined in partnership with a mining engineer who sent him ore samples for analysis. As many of these samples contained rare earth elements, Boltwood also became familiar with uranium and thorium, which are commonly associated with the rare earths. With this specific knowledge of their chemical properties, his inclination toward analytical and physical chemistry, the challenge offered to his laboratory skill, and the current exciting work being done in radioactivity, it is not surprising that Boltwood should decide to investigate problems in this field.

His interest had been captured by the transformation theory, and although the evidence in its support already was impressive, Boltwood felt he could more strongly confirm it by showing a constant ratio between the amounts of radium and uranium in unaltered minerals. Such uniformity in composition would have to be accepted as proof of a genetic relationship, wherein the uranium decayed in several steps to form radium, which in turn decayed to form a series of several daughter products.

Beginning his work in 1904, Boltwood quickly saw that the minute traces of radium, with chemical properties of its own, would be difficult to separate and test quantitatively. He therefore chose to measure radium's first daughter product, emanation, as an indication of the amount of radium present. Emanation, being chemically inert and a gas, required only mechanical separation; its activity thus was easier to measure. Within a few months, Boltwood's gas-tight gold-leaf electroscope yielded the data showing that the activity of radium emanation was directly proportional to the amount of uranium in each of his samples. Rutherford, delighted with this news, encouraged Boltwood to perform the same tests on minerals with much smaller percentages of uranium. Yet even with this further confirmation in hand, Boltwood decided that *direct* proof that uranium decays into radium was desirable—he would try to "grow" radium.

One of the first steps in this effort was to determine more precisely the equilibrium amount of radium. Since Boltwood's heavy correspondence with Rutherford had ripened into warm friendship and professional respect, the two collaborated, by mail, in the 1906 announcement that "the quantity of radium associated with one gram of uranium in a radio-active mineral is equal to approximately 3.8×10^{-7} gram." (The figure accepted today is 3.42×10^{-7} gram.) Still, Boltwood's attempts to grow radium were unsuccessful. At that time only one product between uranium and radium was known to exist; this was uranium X, whose short half-life should allow detectable quantities of radium to form within reasonable time limits. Yet, even after more than a year, he was unable to observe any radium emanation in his uranium solution. Refusing to question the validity of the disintegration theory, Boltwood concluded that there must be a long-lived decay product between uranium X and radium which was preventing the rapid accumulation of the daughter product.

His search for the "parent of radium" was interrupted by his appointment as assistant professor of physics at Yale College. This post in physics came about because radioactivity was a hybrid science, straddling both chemistry and physics, and could therefore be placed in either department. In addition, he was welcomed to the physics department by his friend Bumstead, whereas the position of the chemistry department, beset by campus politics and vested interests, was uncertain. During the summer of 1906 Boltwood moved his apparatus into Sloane Physics Laboratory and prepared to undertake his new academic duties. Because of Bumstead's absence, these responsibilities proved greater than anticipated and Boltwood was left in charge of extensive renovations in the old building. Resumption of his research, however, led him to Debierne's actinium, and Boltwood indeed believed for a while that he had properly placed actinium in the decay series. Among others, Soddy in Glasgow was working on the same problem and the two carried on a heated controversy in the pages of *Nature*. Rutherford also was disinclined to accept actinium as the parent of radium and based his objection on the relative activities of actinium's products, a field in which Boltwood and McCoy had done basic work. The activities of many radioelements had been determined, relative to that of uranium, and if those of actinium and its products were added to those of uranium, uranium X, radium, radium emanation, radium A, B, etc., the total would be far greater than that of the mineral which supposedly contained them all in secular equilibrium.

Further investigation now showed Boltwood that his difficulty lay in accepting as correct Debierne's work on actinium.

In fact, there were other constituents in the Frenchman's radio-element, one of them having similar chemical properties to thorium. It was this product, named "ionium" by Boltwood in 1907, that was the immediate parent of radium. He had now proven that ionium grows radium; still to be shown was that uranium grows ionium. Tests a few years later were unsuccessful, owing to the small quantity of ionium accumulated. Soddy finally, in 1919, conclusively proved the uranium–radium relationship, using uranium purified many years earlier.

One outgrowth of this work was a superior method for the determination of the half-life of radium, a most important constant in radioactivity as many other values were based upon it. Under Boltwood's direction during the 1913–14 academic year, a Norwegian chemist, Ellen Gleditsch, who previously had worked in Madame Curie's laboratory, obtained a value slightly under 1,700 years. Another result of this intensive study of the chemistry of the radioelements was the realization that many of these bodies, which differed in type and intensity of radiation, nevertheless could not be separated chemically. Beginning about 1907, Boltwood, as well as Hahn, McCoy, and most other radiochemists, recognized the inseparability of, for example, thorium, radiothorium, ionium, and uranium X. But it was not until 1913 that Fajans and Soddy declared them chemically identical, isotopes, and explained the decay sequence by the group displacement laws.

Not strictly speaking, radioelements, but nevertheless of great interest to radiochemists, were the inactive end products of the decay series. Boltwood soon recognized that lead invariably appeared with the uranium. Between 1905 and 1907 he extended these early observations and noted further that the geologically older minerals contained higher proportions of lead, as would be expected if this end product was accumulating over the ages. The thorium series was less well understood and Boltwood at first doubted that it ended in lead, while actinium was not then recognized as forming part of a distinct series.

Introduction

Science often makes its greatest impact upon the layman through its applications. The bone pictures achieved with X rays and the medical uses of radium are notable examples. Boltwood pioneered in yet another striking application of science, the method of radioactive dating of rocks. If the rate of formation of an inactive decay product could be determined, the total amount found in a mineral would immediately yield its age. Lead and helium (believed by most to be the alpha particle) both were seen as suitable elements and, indeed, both served in radioactive dating techniques. The helium method, pioneered in England by R. J. Strutt, later the fourth Lord Rayleigh, could not, however, give more than a minimum age, since a variable portion of the gas would have escaped from the rock. But the lead method, developed by Boltwood in 1907, proved satisfactory and is still in use today. In effect, he reversed his procedure of confirming the accuracy of lead:uranium ratios by the accepted geological ages of the source rocks and used these ratios to date the rocks. Because most geologists, under the influence of Lord Kelvin's nineteenth-century pronouncements, inclined toward an age of the earth measured in tens of millions of years, Boltwood's claim for a billion-year span was met with some skepticism. However, the subsequent work of Arthur Holmes, an understanding of isotopes, and the increasing accuracy of decay constants and analyses, finally brought widespread acceptance of this method in the 1930s.

While Boltwood's major contributions lay in the understanding of the uranium decay series, his work was not confined to this chain. With Rutherford in 1905, he suggested that actinium is genetically related to uranium, but not in the same series as radium, while in the thorium series he almost beat Hahn to the discovery of mesothorium in 1907. His other significant service to the subject of radioactivity was to bring greater precision and advanced techniques into the laboratory, as in his insistence that only by complete dissolution of the mineral and boiling could all the emanation be extracted from radioactive bodies.

17

Introduction

Boltwood remained at Yale the rest of his life, except for the academic year 1909–10 when he accepted an invitation to Rutherford's laboratory at the University of Manchester. Yale, fearing that he would remain in England indefinitely, offered Boltwood a full professorship in radiochemistry. This appointment brought him back to New Haven, but it also marked the end of his research career. Heavy academic duties, including supervision of construction of a new physics laboratory and unsuccessful efforts to obtain large quantities of radioactive materials for research, seem to have taken all his time and energy. His stature as the foremost authority on radioactivity in the United States brought him membership in the National Academy of Sciences, the American Philosophical Society, and other organizations, but it also brought him numerous requests from prospectors, mine owners, speculators, chemical refiners, and wholesalers to analyze samples, devise separations processes, and find financial backing (from wealthy Yale alumni) for various projects. These efforts probably helped stimulate the production of radium, in which the United States led the world by about 1915, though they did not appreciably aid the progress of science.

In 1918 Boltwood was appointed director of the Yale College chemical laboratory and he presided over the consolidation of the Y.C. and "Sheff" chemistry departments. To cement this union, a new university laboratory was proposed and Boltwood was placed in charge of its design. This he completed successfully, but the strain of this effort caused a breakdown in his health from which he never fully recovered. Severe periods of depression alternated with the more customary cheerful spirits and resulted finally in his suicide during the summer of 1927.

Boltwood's influence in radioactivity was widespread, but effected largely through his published papers, correspondence, and personal contacts, for he trained surprisingly few research students. Part of his success stemmed from his close association with Rutherford, but like Rutherford's other chemical collaborators, Soddy and Hahn, he was eminently capable of major contributions in his own right.

V. The Correspondence

> These numbers agree so closely that it makes me strongly suspect that there is something *wrong* somewhere . . . I have a brand new theory in embryo . . . I wish that you would comment on the following scheme . . . I think that the deductions which can be made from this assumption will make even the metaphysicians dizzy . . . Your results are very striking . . . Why doesn't Ramsay have one of his students rediscover radium?

Such comments are the substance and the spice of this correspondence. Rutherford and Boltwood, both intensely serious about their scientific research, still retained the ability to question their own results with good humor (and the results of others sometimes with skepticism). Their actions, and the motivations behind them, emerge clearly from these letters. The random comments above typify further the intimate and extensive exchange of information and ideas between the American and the New Zealander. Each frankly respected the other's competence, as testified by the numerous questions asked, data requested, and hypotheses offered for criticism.

During Boltwood's active years (roughly 1904-10) these letters sparkle, as a superb physicist and a brilliant chemist throw scientific fact and fancy at each other. Even during Boltwood's later inactive period the letters continue to effervesce, though the contents are less about science and more about the scientific community.

Rutherford always had need for a chemist upon whom he could rely, and in 1904, so soon after the transformation theory was proposed, naturally was interested in the work of a man determined to uncover confirmatory relationships between the radioelements. The correspondence documents Boltwood's work on the radium:uranium ratio and then his concern with the final, inactive products of the decay series. Throughout there is constant speculation about the position of both known and yet undiscovered radioelements in the decay chains, coupled with their probable chemical properties. Numerous cases of chemical similarity are noted, but, without the additional information contained in the group displacement laws, it is too early to anticipate the existence of isotopes.

Boltwood's discovery of ionium is a good example of the trial and error procedures followed by the early radioactivity scientists. He first proved a genetic relationship between uranium and radium by the constancy of their ratio. Then, assuming a direct descent through known radioelements with known half-lives, he found he could not "grow" the calculated quantity of radium in a given time. Only two explanations were possible: the transformation theory was wrong, that is, one element did *not* decay into another, or there was a long-lived unknown product between uranium and radium. Boltwood had had no doubts about the transformation theory in 1904, and nothing since had occurred to change his mind. His search, therefore, was for the intermediary radioelement. The ever-perplexing actinium, whose sequence in different possible decay series was long a problem, seemed a prime candidate as the parent of radium. Yet other evidence seemed to contradict the choice. Finally Boltwood decided once more to question the analyses of other chemists and discovered that the "standard" actinium contained at least one other product. In this fashion he separated ionium, whose chemical properties corresponded to those of thorium, not actinium. The development of his ideas and his application of various techniques and arguments are typical of the skilled scientist's method of work not only in radioactivity but in all sciences.

Despite its rich content, it need scarcely be emphasized that all of modern physics and chemistry will not be mirrored in this volume. Because Boltwood died in 1927, these letters contain virtually no information about nuclear physics. The correspondence is even more than chronologically circumscribed, however, for the scientific subject matter is bounded largely by the limits of Boltwood's own interests, which were mostly chemical. Thus, these letters reflect the single major concern of the chemist and but one of the many areas of intense interest to the physicist. In this field the two could meet on equal footing, for Boltwood was as good a radiochemist as any. But with the physical side of radioactivity and atomic science, where Rutherford was a master, Boltwood had little real familiarity and even less interest.

True, Boltwood occasionally ventures a remark to share Rutherford's excitement about, for example, particle energies or charges. His perfunctory comments regarding the 1911 nuclear atom and the 1919 announcement of induced transformations may also be seen as efforts at least to acknowledge important steps concerning which he has little competence. Rutherford, for his part, seems not to expect Boltwood to contribute to this conversation and rarely describes much physical detail. When the positions are reversed, however, Rutherford continually appears interested in Boltwood's chemical procedures. The explanation is utilitarian: he practiced some of the more simple tasks himself and he could also assign a repetition to one of his chemically inclined students.

Yet even on the chemical side of radioactivity there are significant omissions. The correspondence begins after the Rutherford–Soddy transformation theory and we are thereby denied an insight into the gestation of this accepted explanation of radioactivity. Such information would be highly interesting, for there is some question concerning the authorship of the idea, Soddy's biographer claiming it solely for him.[4]

More serious, since it falls within the time period covered, is

4. Muriel Howorth, *The Life Story of Frederick Soddy* (London, New World, 1958), pp. 83–84, 91.

the lack of comment by Boltwood on the 1913 group displacement laws and concept of isotopy. While Boltwood was not fond of Soddy, he seems to have had nothing against Fajans, the other author of these advances, so disinclination to discuss a "competitor's" success is probably not the explanation for his surprising silence. More likely, as indicated earlier, Boltwood had completely lost contact with current research efforts and even if he were aware of this particular work he may not have felt competent to comment on it. Science had passed him by and he could be little more than a spectator. This had a further adverse effect upon his correspondence with Rutherford for, without interesting discoveries to report, he took to his typewriter less frequently.

In addition, Boltwood's initial pro-German sympathies during World War I, coupled with a few unfortunate remarks in his attempts to secure the services of Rutherford's interned glassblower, caused the friendship some strain. Even after the war, when warm relations were reestablished, the correspondence remains thin and rather barren of scientific content. Both men had grown older and it was not possible to recapture the excitement and intimacy of earlier days when they could share the hopes, joys, frustrations, and successes of their work. Boltwood was now completely involved with administrative chores and beginning to suffer from periods of mental depression, while Rutherford's increasing administrative duties slowly began to supplant his research activities. By the time of Boltwood's death in 1927, the period of active collaboration, complete frankness, mutual respect, and hearty fellowship was but a fond memory.

Another aspect of the correspondence worthy of mention is the quantitative nature of radioactivity in these years. While the early work was qualitative to a large extent, as the science matured numerical data became the key to progress. In the cases, for example, of relative activities and the equilibrium quantity of radium, note how such data are first obtained, then used repeatedly to argue out other uncertainties.

For the most part, Rutherford's letters are filled less with scientific data than with scientific gossip. A man of honest character, he could not understand devious practices by other men of ability. Sir William Ramsay emerges as something of a villain, more anxious for scientific notoriety than accuracy, while Frederick Soddy is occasionally chastised for his belligerence. Rutherford's laboratory was always filled with colleagues and students from around the world, and the news he forwards to Boltwood often contains capsule commentaries about these individuals. As Boltwood had visited both Montreal and Manchester, he was personally familiar with many of them.

In addition to such biographical information, which fills in the characters of those discussed as well as of Rutherford and Boltwood, the correspondence is a valuable source for the fragments that help to paint a picture of the times. In this category we find material about attitudes toward patenting scientific processes and toward priority, about institutional support of research, public recognition, teaching and other academic duties, the sources and prices of radioactive materials, periodicals, scientific congresses, the effect of wartime upon scientific activity, and so forth. The result is a greater awareness of the external conditions of science early in the twentieth century, conditions as different from our own as is the science itself.

THE CORRESPONDENCE BEGINS

Although Americans were quick to dabble in radioactivity (one early investigator found granulated sugar more active than uranium), little significant work was done in the period immediately following Becquerel's discovery. Then in 1901 the Germans Elster and Geitel observed that atmospheric air contains radioactive matter, and the ensuing years saw this discovery confirmed throughout the world and extended to soil, ground water, rain, snow, and even the mist at the base of Niagara Falls. This widespread distribution of radioactivity, coupled with the relative ease of observing it, made such studies popular. When in 1903 J. J. Thomson voyaged to Yale University to inaugurate the now traditional Silliman Lectures, he urged his physicist-hosts to examine the waters around New Haven for radioactivity. Henry Bumstead and Lynde Phelps Wheeler, both friends of Boltwood, made such an investigation, being among the first in the United States to undertake a serious study in this science.

This activity among his colleagues may have served to bring radioactivity once more to Boltwood's attention. He had, in fact, begun research in 1898 or 1899, but no publication resulted from this and the details of the work are unknown.[1] Boltwood also was adviser to a student who, for his bachelor's thesis in 1899, repeated the chemical separations of the Curies and came to the conclusion that there existed in the pitchblende another radioelement differing from uranium, radium, and polonium.[2] However, the work was dropped upon the student's graduation in June, and in October 1899 Debierne announced from Paris the discovery of what was later called actinium.

These threads of interest apparently converged upon Boltwood when he learned that Rutherford, the most exciting figure in radioactivity, would lecture at Yale in the spring of 1904.

1. BBB—ER, 23 Sept. 1907.
2. Untitled thesis prepared by Clifford Langley, June 1899, BCY.

25

Boltwood began his study of the relative proportions of uranium and radium in natural minerals, a subject bearing great significance for the transformation theory, and was able to discuss preliminary results when Rutherford visited New Haven. Boltwood's humble "You will perhaps recall meeting me when you were here," which opens their correspondence, masks the fact that Rutherford called upon him in his private laboratory on Orange Street and, presumably, was impressed with the chemist's plans. During the first year of their acquaintance a certain formality was maintained, and their letters begin "Dear Prof. Rutherford," and "Dear Mr. Boltwood." This gave way, however, to warm friendship and salutations of "My dear Rutherford," and "My dear Boltwood," after Rutherford's return to Yale in the spring of 1905 to deliver the Silliman Lectures. Within this short time Boltwood's work had commanded international attention and signaled the shift of interest from the physical to the chemical side of radioactivity.

11 MAY 1904

139 Orange Street
New Haven, Connecticut

Dear Prof. Rutherford,

You will perhaps recall meeting me when you were here in New Haven and talking over the question of the determination of the relative proportions of uranium and radium in natural minerals, a subject on which I was at that time working.

Within the last ten days I have succeeded in obtaining a series of results which seem to throw considerable light on that question and which lead to conclusions which seem to me to be of very great importance. As a brief preliminary notice of the results of my work will appear in the Engineering and Mining Journal,[1] which is published tomorrow, and since these results so strongly support your theory of the production of radium from uranium, I am taking the liberty of sending you a brief account of what I have accomplished.

A piece of apparatus constructed entirely of glass was first prepared [Fig. 1]. This consisted of a bulb (A) of about 50 cc capacity which was joined by a short tube to a smaller bulb (B), the latter being in turn connected with a smaller bulb (C). An accurately weighed quantity of the very finely powdered mineral was introduced into the bulb B and in the bulb C was placed a sufficient quantity of a suitable acid, its actual quantity and nature depending on the character of the particular mineral under investigation. The whole apparatus was then

27

sealed up air-tight at a slightly diminished pressure and, by tilt-
ing, the acid was transferred to the bulb containing the mineral.
The mineral was then decomposed by gentle warming and the
apparatus was allowed to stand for several days (about 3). The
bulb A was then sealed off from the rest of the apparatus and
allowed to stand for two hours, and then after washing the interior walls with a strong sodium hydroxide solution to com-

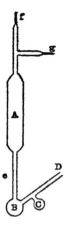

Figure 1. Boltwood's glass apparatus for dissolving uranium minerals in acid and collecting radium emanation. From "On the ratio
of radium to uranium in some minerals," *Am. J. Sci., 18* (Aug. 1904),
100.

pletely remove acid fumes, the air and radium emanation were
transferred to an air-tight electroscope [Fig. 2] and the rate of
leak measured. In comparing results obtained with different
minerals the rate of leak at the end of three hours was chosen,
since at this time the rate was at its maximum and was fairly
constant over a considerable period. The actual quantity of
uranium in the solution in bulb B was determined by analysis
and the relative proportion of the emanation measured to the

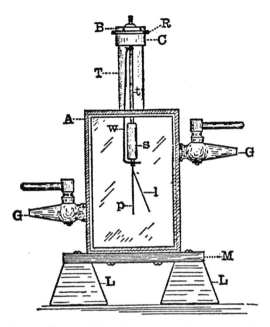

Figure 2. Boltwood's air-tight electroscope for measuring activity of radium emanation.

A	brass case 15 x 10 x 4.5 cm	T	glass tube
B	brass cap	l	gold leaf
C	brass ring	p	brass plate
G	brass stopcocks	s	cast sulphur rod
L	lead ingots	t	brass rod
M	iron base plate	w	soft iron wire
R	rubber washer		

From "On the ratio of radium to uranium in some minerals," *Am. J. Sci., 18* (Aug. 1904), 98.

entire amount produced was calculated from the measurement of the capacities of the two final parts of the apparatus.

The results which have been obtained from those minerals thus far examined are as follows:

No.	Substance	Per cent. Uranium contained	Taken Uranium gram	Leak Divisions per min.	Ratio Leak to Uran.
1	Uraninite	82.5	0.1067	22.5	211
2	Gummite	66.1	0.0982	20.8	212
3	Uranophane	46.6	0.0671	12.1	181
4	Uraninite	83.9	0.1017	18.7	184
4	Repeated	83.9	0.0994	20.6	207.2
5	Samarskite	9.8	0.0299	6.4	214.2

(Nos. 1, 2, 3 and 5 from North Carolina; No. 4 from Branchville, Conn.)

The slightly low value of the ratio in the case of No. 3 can be explained by the fact that this mineral gives a small amount of emanation at ordinary temperatures. I am going to repeat this measurement under somewhat different conditions which will overcome this difficulty. In the first result given with No. 4 the low value is due to the fact that a small portion of the emanation was accidentally allowed to escape. I believe that any variation observed in the ratio can be explained from the fact that the analytical determination of the uranium is not accurate beyond the first two figures of the constant.

From the extreme sensitiveness of this method I am inclined to believe that it may be possible to actually measure the rate of formation of radium from uranium. The normal air leak of the electroscope was only about 0.01 of one division per minute and as will be noted the actual quantity of uranium taken was only about 0.1 gram. With about 500 grams of uranium in solution it ought to be possible to get some idea of the rate of production. I am preparing to carry out some experiments in that direction.

You will also probably be interested to learn that a preliminary experiment on the variation of the polonium, or at least that portion of it which is deposited on a bismuth button, looks very much as if this element varies also with the per cent. of uranium in the mineral.

I hope that you will find this information of interest.

With very sincere regards, I am, Very truly yours,

BERTRAM B. BOLTWOOD

P.S. I sent off a communication to Nature [2] last Saturday on the above subject. I hope that they will think it worth publishing.

1. BBB, "Radium in uranium compounds," *Eng. Mining J.,* 77 (12 May 1904), 756. A preliminary notice also appeared as "Relation between uranium and radium in some minerals," *Nature, 70* (26 May 1904), 80.
2. Ibid.

20 JUNE 1904

The Macdonald Physics Building
McGill University, Montreal

Dear Mr. Boltwood,

Your letter reached Montreal while I was absent in England [1] and has awaited my return. I was very pleased to see that you had attacked the problem of the relative amounts of radium and uranium. Your results are very striking and I hope that you are continuing your analysis of as many kinds of pitchblende as you can obtain. The results of most importance would be obtained from analysis of radioactive minerals with a small quantity of uranium. I have found, for example, that orangite & thorite both contain radium in moderate quantities, although they are supposed to contain only a trace of uranium. I wish you would examine them with the other minerals. I quite agree with your criticism of Strutt's [2] heating method,[3] in fact, I had raised the same objection to him myself when I saw him in England and

31

he promised to amend his method in that particular. I would not lay any especial stress on negative results of attempts to grow radium as in Soddy's [4] letter to Nature.[5] It is quite likely that products (possibly non-radioactive) of very slow rate of change may intervene between uranium and radium. I would go ahead steadily with the line you have taken as it appears to me to be the only method of definitely attacking the question within a limited space of time. If you have time, let me know how your research progresses. Wishing you every success. Believe me, Yours very sincerely,

E. RUTHERFORD

1. Rutherford was in England to deliver the prestigious Bakerian Lecture to the Royal Society, which was published as "The succession of changes in radioactive bodies," *Phil. Trans., 204A* (1904), 169–219.

2. Robert John Strutt, son of the famous physicist Lord Rayleigh, and successor to that title himself in 1919, was at this time a fellow of Trinity College, Cambridge, and engaged in research in the Cavendish Laboratory. In 1908 he was appointed professor of physics at Imperial College of Science and Technology, South Kensington.

3. In his published reports Boltwood criticized the similar work of Strutt, who had collected the radium emanation by heating uranium minerals. Boltwood pointed out that heating drives off only a small and variable fraction of the emanation contained in the mineral, whereas complete dissolution in acid releases all the entrained gas.

4. Frederick Soddy graduated from Oxford, then served as a demonstrator in chemistry at McGill University between 1900 and 1902. There he accomplished much brilliant work in radiochemistry, capped by publication of the disintegration theory of radioactivity with Rutherford. Next, he spent a year in Ramsay's laboratory in London, then accepted a position as lecturer at the University of Glasgow. Soddy remained there until 1914 when he took a similar job at Aberdeen. In 1919 he was appointed professor of chemistry at Oxford, but his productive career had ended. He was awarded the 1921 Nobel Prize for his contributions to radiochemistry, particularly the work leading to an understanding of isotopes.

5. F. Soddy, "The life-history of radium," *Nature,* 70 (12 May 1904), 30.

8 AUGUST 1904

139 Orange Street
New Haven, Connecticut

My dear Prof. Rutherford,

The receipt of your letter of the twentieth of June afforded me very great pleasure and I was very glad to learn that you had found the results obtained with the uranium minerals interesting. I sent you a few days ago a reprint of my article in the Am. Jour. Science [1] and presume that it has already reached you. You will notice in it that I have extended the examination to a number of different minerals with similar results in all cases. I have recently tested a sample of Joachimsthaler pitchblende and find that it gives the same results as the others examined. I note with much interest what you state about radium in orangite and thorite. Before the receipt of your letter I had made a test of a sample of Connecticut monazite and found that it contained radium equivalent to about 0.06% uranium. I unfortunately have not enough of this material for an analytical determination of uranium.

I am planning to extend the examination to include minerals containing small percents of uranium, as suggested in your letter, and have already made arrangements to secure some samples of material. One decided difficulty, however, is going to be the analytical separation of the uranium when present in very small amounts. One has to take a lot of material to begin with and it is difficult to separate the uranium precipitates completely from other things which persist in coming down with it. I have recently tried to determine the uranium in North Carolina monazite. There is certainly *some* uranium in it, but *just* how much it is difficult to determine accurately.

I have started my experiments on growing radium from uranium, but the result thus far obtained is not very encouraging. I sealed up about 200 grams of very carefully purified uranium nitrate in a glass bulb. The salt was dissolved in water and there was a small air space at the top of the container from which the air, and any accumulated emanation, could be removed and tested. At the end of 60 days the emanation present was not more than the quantity of emanation associated with 8×10^{-6} gram of uranium in pitchblende. However, I have a number of different tests going in which I am going to separate the emanation by boiling the solutions and any results obtained will be of interest if not conclusive. I am also going to take about 100 grams of pure N. C. pitchblende, dissolve it in nitric acid, remove as much of the radium as possible, leave all of the other constituents and watch for any increase of emanation from this solution. If there are any "dead changes"[2] or other intermediate products between the uranium and the radium they might be expected to stay in the solution and keep on working.

Apropos of this last experiment I am planning to carry out some work on which I should find your opinion most valuable. It is on the radio-active constituent of thorium, if there really is a special radio-active constituent.[3] I am fairly familiar with your work on thorium, the thorium emanation and thorium X, but my knowledge is not sufficiently extensive to convince me that it is not possible for ordinary thorium to contain some special radio-active constituent. Please do not think that I make any reference to the work of Baskerville,[4] but I am thinking of the apparent analytical complexity of the element, and the persistent assertions of Hofmann[5] that he has obtained thorium salts of very low radio-activity from certain minerals. What I am planning to do is to obtain a considerable number of samples of thorium nitrate from a variety of different minerals and prepared by different methods, dissolve equal weights of the samples in equal volumes of water and test the radio-activities of these different solutions by introducing them into the same vessel separately, allowing the emanation X to accumulate for equal periods of time on a negatively charged plate, and then measuring the activity of this plate as accurately as possible with the instruments at my disposal. If there is anything on the face of this investigation which makes it hopeless at the start, or if it interferes in any way with anything you have done or planning to do, please let me know and I will think no more about it.

The thing which started me on this matter was something you said while in my laboratory about the very possible interrelationship between all the different radio-active substances, and I have been thinking how it would simplify matters if thorium, which seems to occur so persistently with uranium minerals, could only be fitted in with the uranium and radium. I have just been examining a sample of carnotite, that peculiar uranium-vanadium mineral which occurs so abundantly in Colorado. It has been analysed by Hillebrand, a very reliable analyst, who reported no thorium present. He has personally assured me that he would not have failed to have found it if it were present. But on working up several grams of it I have been able to separate a slight precipitate which corresponds to thorium and the solution of which gives off measurable quantities of thorium emanation. I have also found thorium in two other minerals, gummite and uranophane, not generally supposed to contain it. I am therefore somewhat skeptical about any uranium mineral without *some* thorium in it.

Another matter which may interest you is that I have prepared several grams of radio-lead in a metallic form by fusing the lead salts obtained from pitchblende with potassium cyanide. The peculiar thing is that it gives off no radium emanation (which would of course not be expected, since radium would not be reduced to metal by the cyanide), but the radiations which it sends out have a much higher ratio of penetration than those produced by the radium salts obtained from the same mineral. The proportion of radiation passing through an alu-

35

minium plate 0.1 mm in thickness is about 10 times as great in the case of the lead as in the case of the radium salt. This seems to me to point strongly to the actual individual existence of radio-lead. I hope to investigate the matter more carefully when I obtain an opportunity.

Just at present I am very busily occupied with an examination of the waters of the hot springs on the Government Reservation at Hot Springs, Arkansas, undertaken at the request of the Department of the Interior.[6] The work is not as exciting or interesting as it might be, but one has to do a little "pot boiling" occasionally. There are 48 separate sources to be tested and the samples of water are sent on to me here by express where I examine them for radium salts and radium emanation. So far I have examined samples from 18 of the springs and have found that they all contain radium emanation in varying proportions. The highest proportion of radium emanation found was in a *cold spring* water, which contained per liter emanation equal to that associated with 23×10^{-4} gram uranium in pitchblende; the highest in a hot spring was 14×10^{-4}. The first was measured 10 days from the time of collection of the sample, the second 7 days. The others varied down to 0.3×10^{-4} (eight days from time of collection). The New Haven tap water examined by Bumstead is about 0.06×10^{-4} as drawn from the pipes.

I have received several grams of thorium X residue from the chemist of the Welsbach Light Co. This which I have was prepared about 4 months ago from 50 kilos of thoria precipitated as hydroxide from a solution of the nitrate. It is still quite radioactive and gives off large quantities of thorium emanation. Mr. Miner, the chemist, has further offered to prepare additional quantities of this for me if I desire them. I am going to examine this residue carefully and see if I can discover anything further as to its (ThX) chemical properties.

I got a very interesting letter from Bumstead a few days ago. He was in Paris and had just been to call on M. Curie [7] at his laboratory. Bumstead described wild scientific orgies in which

280 MILLIGRAMS OF PURE RADIUM BROMIDE figured conspicuously, and appeared to have had altogether a very interesting and amusing time of it.

I have just noted with apprehension the length to which this letter has grown. I beg to assure you of my high appreciation of your kind letter and remain, Sincerely yours,

BERTRAM B. BOLTWOOD

1. BBB, "On the ratio of radium to uranium in some minerals," *Am. J. Sci.*, *18* (Aug. 1904), 97–103.

2. Presumably, by "dead changes" Boltwood meant what were more commonly called "rayless transformations." These were steps in the decay series undetectable (at that time) by measurement of ionization. Hence it was felt that no alpha or beta particle was emitted in such a step. Since the products that decayed in this fashion could make their presence known only in a roundabout way they were more difficult to identify.

3. After the discovery of thorium's radioactivity in 1898 there were numerous attempts to show that the activity resided not in elemental thorium but in a constituent that was difficult to separate from thorium.

4. Charles Baskerville, formerly professor of chemistry at the University of North Carolina, in 1904 became director of the chemical laboratory at the City College of New York. Although he claimed to have discovered a new element in thorium (not necessarily radioactive) and investigated some inconsequential topics in radioactivity for a time, his substantial reputation seems to have derived most from industrial consulting work.

5. Karl Andreas Hofmann, at this time a chemistry professor at the University of Munich, studied the radioelements for a number of years, particularly the properties of radiolead.

6. BBB, "On the radio-active properties of the waters of the springs on the Hot Springs Reservation, Hot Springs, Ark.," *Am. J. Sci.*, *20* (Aug. 1905), 128–32.

7. Pierre Curie, a brilliant physicist who discovered the phenomenon of piezoelectricity (with his brother) and who did basic work on the magnetic properties of matter at different temperatures, was for many years head of physics laboratory teaching, then professor, at the School of Industrial Physics and Chemistry of the City of Paris. Not until shortly before his death in a traffic accident in 1906 was he appointed to a chair worthy of his abilities, at the Sorbonne. His Polish-born wife, Marie, undertook an investigation of radioactivity for her doctoral thesis topic, and soon discovered that thorium, in addition to uranium, emitted "Becquerel rays."

Pierre realized that her work was of the greatest significance when she detected radioactivity in the pitchblende ore from which the uranium had been *removed,* and dropped his own studies to help her. This initial effort led to the discovery of two new elements in 1898: polonium and radium. Both husband and wife now pursued radioactivity relentlessly, Pierre devoting himself to physical investigations and Marie largely to the chemical extraction and purification of the new elements. This work was rewarded with the 1903 Nobel Prize in physics, which they shared with Henri Becquerel. After Pierre's death, Marie was appointed to his professorship, the first woman to hold such a position in France. Her later work was not of major significance, although she did receive the Nobel Prize in chemistry in 1911. More important were the scientists she trained in her Radium Institute after World War I, particularly her daughter Irène and Irène's husband, Frédéric Joliot, themselves Nobel Prize winners.

11 AUGUST 1904

139 Orange Street
New Haven, Connecticut

My dear Professor Rutherford,

Since writing my long letter to you a few days ago I have had a brief interval between the receipt of additional samples of Hot Springs water which I could devote to other purposes and I have devoted it to a hasty examination of some of the chemical properties of thorium X. I have reason to hope that you will find the results interesting.

It has always seemed to me that it was very curious that thorium X should be so readily precipitated from a solution with the thorium present, except when the thorium is precipitated as hydroxide by ammonia. This would suggest that it had marked chemical characteristics and affinity, while the investigation conducted by yourself and Mr. Soddy showed that, when the thorium was once removed, none of the reagents which you used would precipitate the thorium X from the solution. This suggested to me that the thorium X might have the properties

of an alkali metal of high atomic weight, with a tendency, therefore, to form difficultly soluble double salts especially with thorium. With this idea in mind I have prepared a small quantity
of thorium X from a couple of ounces of thorium nitrate (all
that I had at disposal), and after evaporating the filtrate to dryness, igniting the residue to remove ammonium salts, dissolving
the residue in water and filtering, I treated the solution thus obtained with hydrochlorplatinic acid, exactly as in the case of
the determination of potassium. No visible precipitate was
formed and so a drop of ammonium chloride solution was
added, and the precipitate of ammonium platinic chloride was
filtered off and washed with dilute alcohol. The precipitate was
tested in the electroscope and found to be quite active but the
residue obtained by evaporating the filtrate to dryness was only
very slightly active. The precipitate was then ignited to bright
redness and again tested. It was about as active as before. It was
washed with a small quantity of hot water. It retained its activity and the filtrate when evaporated was scarcely active at all.
The residue was then treated with a few drops of concentrated
hydrochloric acid, warmed and washed with water. The platinum residue, after being again ignited, had an activity 4 times
as great as that of the residue from the hydrochloric acid with
which it had been treated. The active constituent therefore behaved exactly as would be expected if it was an alkali metal of
high atomic weight. This would explain why it is removed
when thorium oxide is treated with water.

These are the results as far as I have obtained any. It would
certainly be very interesting if thorium X proved to be the first
member of the radium-thorium-uranium group in the periodic
system, falling in the same vertical row as the alkali metals.

I shall be immensely interested to learn your opinion of this
whole matter. Very sincerely yours,

BERTRAM B. BOLTWOOD

16 AUGUST 1904

McGill University, Montreal

Dear Boltwood,

I have been much interested in the account of your experiments on thorium and radio-lead. I have just done some work which I think throws a good deal of light on the subject of radio-lead. An account of my experiments will be given to the Congress at St Louis,[1] but as for the present suffice to say that I have got two more products of radium of slow rate of change one of which gives out *initially only β rays*. This product must be present in pitchblende & I have no doubt you have got it mixed with the lead. If you could spare some of your radio-lead, I think I could settle the matter pretty quickly.

In regard to thorium, I am quite prepared to believe that its radioactivity may be due to an impurity but the position I take at present is that the published results to the contrary do not appear to me conclusive. I think that your line of attack by comparing different specimens would be useful but it would be still better to get some of Hoffmanns gadolinite & repeat his experiments with decent radioactive measurements.

Your investigation on ThX is interesting. I have no doubt that ultimately all the radioactive products will have to find a place in the periodic table.[2] Of course ThX is an unstable element with a very limited life. I cannot speak with knowledge to the chemical side of your experiments but there is one point that I think that must be borne in mind in dealing with such minute traces of matter viz that the precipitation of the active matter may not depend on its chemical properties but be due to an adherence of the matter to the precipitate. I think experiments along the line of attack you mention to me ought to throw light on its chemical constitution. I am much obliged for

the copy of your paper which I have read with much interest.
Wishing you all success in your experiments. Yours sincerely,

E. RUTHERFORD

1. This was the International Electrical Congress, held in September
1904 as part of the St. Louis Universal Exposition, which marked the centennial of the Louisiana Purchase. See ER, "Slow transformation products
of radium," *Phil. Mag., 8* (Nov. 1904), 636–50.

2. This attitude, while widespread, was still perhaps surprising. Whether
one believed that the periodic table was a superficial construct of transi-
tory value, or an enduring tool based on a real, physical ordering of the
elements, both were agreed that the numerous new radioelements had to
be fitted into this table. In other words, with little argument to the contrary, these unstable products were accepted as full-fledged elements.

18 AUGUST 1904

139 Orange Street
New Haven, Connecticut

My dear Prof. Rutherford,
Your very kind letter of the 16th, inst., has just reached me
and I am very much interested in what you state about radio-
lead and the other matters. It gives me great pleasure to send
you herewith a piece of my lead, which is one-half of the quantity which I have prepared, and represents material obtained
from about 30 grams of uranium minerals (uraninite, gummite
and uranophane), equivalent to about 20 grams of uranium.
The material was separated as chloride (recrystallized) and
sulphate (from H_2S precipitates) and was reduced to the metallic state by fusing with potassium cyanide. It was prepared
about four months ago. If you care for more I shall be pleased
to send you the other half and can readily prepare more of it.
In regard to thorium X I have already been impressed with
the fact that the *apparent* chemical reactions are not always to
be relied on. If the residue obtained after the precipitation of

41

the thorium is dissolved in hydrochloric acid and an excess of ammonia added to this solution, a very slight, but highly radioactive precipitate is obtained. The active constituent in the filtrate from this precipitate, after the removal of ammonium salts, is *not* completely precipitated by hydrochlorplatinic acid. The active precipitate with ammonia when redissolved in acid and again precipitated is less active, showing that the active constituent has probably been simply entrained (just as you suggest) by the ammonia precipitate. One point, however, which my results seem to show, is that the rate of decay of the activities of some of these precipitates is different from that of thorium X, but all of the work thus far done is very rough and I have no confidence in the results. I hope to continue the work later with larger quantities of thorium X which are promised me by the chemist of the Welsbach Company.

I suppose that you have seen that article by McCoy [1] in the July 9th number of the Berichte, in which he states that he has found that the actual activity of a number of different uranium minerals is proportional to the per cent of uranium in the minerals. His conclusion that the radium is proportional to the uranium does not seem to be well founded, but if his results mean anything, it seems to me that they mean that the entire content of radioactive constituents is proportional to the uranium.

Wheeler [2] and I are getting quite hopeless about ever being able to buy a copy of your book.[3] We have had our orders in with the bookseller for several months and are still waiting. We wish very much that a little "induced activity" could be imparted to the publishers!

With best regards. Very sincerely yours,

BERTRAM B. BOLTWOOD

1. Herbert Newby McCoy, after Boltwood the leading American radiochemist, rose from instructor to professor of chemistry at the University of Chicago between the years 1901 and 1911. Although he resigned his chair in 1917 to become an executive of a chemical company, he continued re-

search in his private laboratory and achieved notable success in several areas besides radioactivity.

2. After three decades on the staff of the physics department of Yale's Sheffield Scientific School, Lynde Phelps Wheeler in 1926 began a new career in electronics and radio, working for government agencies and private companies. He is known also as the author of a biography of Josiah Willard Gibbs.

3. ER, *Radio-Activity* (Cambridge, University Press, 1904). While not the first book on radioactivity published, it was the first real text to appear.

9 SEPTEMBER 1904

McGill University, Montreal

Dear Mr. Boltwood,

I am very much obliged to you for the radio-lead you sent me. I think there is little doubt that it is the product I have separated from radium but further experiments are necessary to make sure.

I took the liberty of mentioning that you had sent me a specimen of radio-lead in my paper [1] on the subject. I trust that you have no objection to such a statement. It does not commit you in any way.

I have been very busy preparing for the Scientific Congress at St Louis and leave for St Louis on Sept 13. Possibly you may be thinking of going, in which case I would see you. I will stay at the Epworth Hotel. Yours very sincerely,

E. RUTHERFORD

1. ER, "Slow transformation products of radium," *Phil. Mag., 8* (Nov. 1904), 636–50.

12 DECEMBER 1904

The Macdonald Physics Building
McGill University, Montreal

Dear Mr. Boltwood,

I think I told you about the radio-lead you sent me & you will probably have seen a note to that effect in the Phil Mag of last month. You mentioned in one of your letters that you could send me some more radio-lead if I wanted it. I am already using what you sent me in order to see the variation of its activity with time and would be obliged if you could let me have about the same amount which you forwarded me last time, as I wish to try another experiment or two with it. I hope your work is progressing satisfactorily. I am writing a second edition of my book & would be glad to receive any results you have obtained in your experiments if you feel so inclined. Could you forward me a gram or so of pitchblende of which you have determined the percentage content of uranium? [1] It would be useful to me in some work I am doing. Yours very sincerely,

E. RUTHERFORD

1. At the top of this letter Boltwood inscribed "74.70 Uranium."

23 DECEMBER 1904

139 Orange Street
New Haven, Connecticut

Dear Prof. Rutherford,

Your kind letter of the 12th instant was duly received and I have delayed answering it until the present in order that I might at the same time be able to send you the materials which you requested. I am enclosing herewith two samples of radio-lead, the one (marked No. 1) being the other half of the piece which I originally sent you, and the other (marked No. 2) being a fresh preparation recently reduced to metal from the carefully purified sulphate. The latter sample is prepared wholly from uranium minerals other than pitchblende, chiefly gummite and uranophane. I am also enclosing a paper containing 5 grams of North Carolina pitchblende, which is essentially pure uraninite. This material is almost completely soluble in dilute nitric acid (on warming), the slight flocculent residue which remains consisting of silica only.

In conducting any experiments with this uraninite it is important to note that its emanating power at ordinary temperatures is quite high and that in the finely pulverized condition in which it is sent it contains only about 89.5 per cent of the equilibrium quantity of radium emanation. This factor has been determined by sealing up a quantity of it in a glass tube and measuring the quantity of radium emanation which accumulates in the tube at the end of 40 days. I have observed that this emanating power of the cold minerals differs considerably with different minerals and with different samples of the same mineral. For example, a sample of Saxon pitchblende which I have tested loses only 2.6 per cent of its total emanation. A matter which has interested me not a little is the fact that this spontaneous loss of emanation appears to decrease slightly as time passes, just as if the minute, inter-molecular crevices through which the emanation escapes became clogged by the formation of the active deposit. I have quite a number of samples under observation for the determination of this matter.

I have recently been making a re-determination of the radium-uranium ratio for a number of the minerals containing higher per cents of uranium, employing a method which is different and somewhat more accurate than the method originally employed. The method consists in dissolving or com-

pletely decomposing the mineral in a suitable reagent and dis-
placing the emanation set free by a current of steam which is
conducted through the solution. The emanation is then collected in the Reichhardt apparatus (described in my paper in
the November Journal of Science),[1] and introduced, through a
drying tube, into the electroscope. To the activity of the emanation as measured is added the activity of the emanation lost by
the mineral on standing at ordinary temperatures. This, of
course, gives the equilibrium activity of the emanation, and this
activity divided by the quantity of uranium gives the constant
used in the comparisons. I have in this manner examined: N.C.
Uraninite, Gummite, two varieties of Uranophane, Saxon Pitchblende, Joachimsthal Pitchblende, and N.C. Samarskite. The
ratio obtained in all cases was quite constant in value. I have
also examined three different varieties of Thorite; i.e., Thorite,
Orangite and Urano-Thorite, and find that the ratio in this substance corresponds with that in the others. A mineral purchased
for Aeschynite, but differing from the described varieties of this
species and containing 4.6% of Uranium, also gives a similar
ratio. Fergusonite and Euxenite, the former containing radium
equivalent to 3.09% of uranium, the latter radium equivalent to
9.26% of uranium, both appear to correspond to the published
analyses of these minerals, although I have not yet determined
the uranium in these particular samples. A sample of North
Carolina Allanite, which is quite noticeably radio-active, gives
radium equivalent to only 0.007% uranium, and as the quantity
taken was small and the results uncertain, I should not be surprised if it contained even less radium or perhaps none at all. I
mean to examine it more carefully shortly. In the case of
Monazite and the mineral Xenotime, closely related to it, I
have been obtaining a series of rather surprising results. From a
series of carefully conducted experiments, in the results of
which I have every confidence, I find radium equivalent to
0.41% uranium in N.C. Monazite (sand), radium equivalent to
0.35% uranium in Brazilian Monazite (sand), radium equiva-

lent to 0.39% uranium in Norwegian Monazite (crystals), radium equivalent to 0.29% of uranium in Connecticut Monazite (massive), and radium equivalent to 0.61% uranium in Norwegian Xenotime. These results were at first quite startling, owing to the fact that none of the published analyses of these minerals show the presence of *any* uranium, and owing to the present controversy between Zerban [2] and others as to the presence of even the small per cent of uranium which the former claimed to have found present. As I have already written to you in an earlier letter, I have found no serious difficulty in detecting the presence of *some* uranium in the N.C. monazite, but the routine methods of detecting this element either fail altogether in giving even a qualitative test or else result in the separation of only a few hundredths of a per cent. These results were very disconcerting until I found that when I added 0.4% of uranium to the original mixture the analytical results came out just as before, that is, only a few hundredths of a per cent of the uranium present could be separated. I have therefore been employing a new method of analysis which depends on the separation of the greater portion of the rare earths by simple recrystallization from a solution containing a large excess of sulphuric acid and the chemical separation of the uranium from the residual solution. By this method I have succeeded in getting out as much as 0.2% of uranium, with strong evidence of the presence of more uranium in some of the supposed uranium-free precipitates which had been separated. I have also succeeded in obtaining strong qualitative proof of the presence of notable quantities of uranium in the crystallized Norwegian monazite, although I have as yet devoted but little time to this mineral. I attribute the difficulty of separating the uranium in the monazite either to the presence of some rare element in the monazite which combines with the uranium and changes its ordinary chemical behavior, or else to the possibility that the large quantity of phosphoric acid in the mineral is the disturbing factor. As a matter of fact the chief difficulty which I have encountered has been in separating the uranium *completely* from the great excess of phosphoric acid which remains in the solution after the removal of the other constituents. As you are perhaps aware the affinity between phosphoric acid and uranium is one of the strongest, and monazite is practically a pure phosphate. I am perfectly confident that the monazites contain the indicated quantities of uranium.

I have found this problem of the separation of the uranium from monazite a most difficult one and have already devoted weeks to it. It is, however, most fascinating to me since I believe that it is the first case where quite positive indications (You will note my conviction!) of a quantitative physical character have demonstrated the pitiful crudity of established chemical methods. When I have established the presence of the indicated quantities of uranium in monazite, which I mean to do even if it takes years to accomplish it, I am going to drop this line of research right there and rest on the assumption that the radium-uranium ratio is constant in ALL MINERALS, leaving it for others, who may so desire, to attempt to PROVE the opposite.

Of the *direct* formation of radium from uranium I am very skeptical. I have just recently tested a solution of 100 grams of uranium nitrate which had been sealed up for five months without being able to detect the presence of a measurable quantity of radium emanation. My electroscopes are of course comparatively quite crude and insensitive.[3] If you should care to have this solution under observation with the more sensitive instruments at your command, I shall be very pleased to send it to you. It has the advantage of being quite radium-free at any rate. The nitrate from which it was prepared was purified by recrystallization.

I have not had a chance to do anything with thorium-X since I last wrote to you. I have noted one interesting fact, however, and that is that the fresh quantities of the "X" which are formed in the precipitated hydroxide pass into solution if the hydroxide is suspended in water. By suspending the washed hydroxide in water and filtering off occasionally it is possible to get the active "X" residue free from ammonium salts, which is a great convenience in preparing any (comparatively) considerable quantity of it. I have also in every case when I have prepared the residue (either by direct precipitation or from the suspended hydroxide) found that the residue consisted chiefly of ordinary thorium, although I have noted that in your book, as well as in the original paper,[4] it is stated that the residue is free from thorium. Now I can not make this statement agree with the fact that I have found the thorium repeatedly and moreover that the hydroxide *must be somewhat* soluble in a dilute solution of ammonium nitrate containing an excess of ammonia as well as in plain water. Now in precipitating 100 grams of thorium nitrate in say about 500 cc of water and washing the precipitate thoroughly, the final volume of the filtrate would be about 1,000 cc. If 1 part of the hydroxide was soluble in 1,000,000 parts of the liquid this would leave about 1 mg. of the hydroxide in the final residue. I think that the hydroxide is if anything, more soluble than above assumed, and that when pure thorium nitrate, free from alkali metals, is used that the residue consists *chiefly* of thoria. This connection is borne out by the fact that a quantity of the thorium-X residue prepared for me by the chemist of the Welsbach Light Co. from 50 kilos of fairly pure thorium nitrate contains about 60 per cent of thoria. Baskerville has also stated in a paper (Jour. Am. Chem. Soc., 26, 922 (1904) that the residue was free from thorium, but in answer to a letter which I wrote him on the subject he seems rather inclined to doubt his own conclusion. I am therefore inclined to believe that Mr. Soddy must have overlooked the thorium or else that he worked with such small quantities and volumes that the thorium in the residue escaped him.

I was intensely interested in your paper on "radio-lead" in the Phil. Mag.[5] and much complimented by your courtesy in mentioning my name in it. One thing which puzzled me, however, was the statement that you found the "radium-D" soluble in sulphuric acid. Since the radio-lead which I have prepared has all been separated as sulphate it would at first sight seem that it could not contain any of the "D" product. Have you made any experiments to see whether the "D" product is carried down by lead sulphate precipitated in its solution? If you could spare a reprint of your article I should be greatly pleased to receive one of them.

I am conducting some further experiments on the relative quantities of polonium in uranium minerals and am wondering what effect the natural emanating powers of the minerals will have on the polonium in them. If the polonium is one of the decomposition products of the emanation, and a portion of the emanation continuously escapes from some of the minerals, then I should expect that these minerals would contain a smaller proportion of polonium than another which lost little or no emanation. Am I correct in this conclusion?

I trust that you will pardon me for having again afflicted you with such a long letter, and by way of apology I can only state that there is no one here with whom I can talk over these matters with any satisfaction.

It is impossible for me to express the delight and satisfaction which I feel at the prospect of your giving the Silliman lectures here next spring.

With best wishes and Christmas greetings, I am, Very sincerely yours,

BERTRAM B. BOLTWOOD

1. BBB, "On the radio-activity of natural waters," *Am. J. Sci., 18* (Nov. 1904), 378–87.

2. Fritz Zerban, born and educated in Germany, came to the United States in 1904 as a Carnegie Research Assistant, and worked on radioactivity under Baskerville at City College of New York. Two years later he accepted a position as chemist at a sugar experiment station in this country, and remained in this field for the rest of his career.

3. In general, it seems that chemists preferred to use gold-leaf electroscopes while physicists chose the (supposedly) more accurate electrometers. This was probably due to the chemists' lack of familiarity with the

electrical measuring instruments of physics; the electroscope was easiest to comprehend. It must be understood, however, that in the hands of a skilled chemist the electroscope could yield superior results, for construction and condition of the devices, as well as technique, permitted wide ranges of sensitivity for both instruments.

4. ER and F. Soddy, "The cause and nature of radioactivity. Part I," *Phil. Mag., 4* (Sept. 1902), 370–96.

5. ER, "Slow transformation products of radium," *Phil. Mag., 8* (Nov. 1904), 636–50.

1 JANUARY 1905

139 Orange Street
New Haven, Connecticut

Dear Professor Rutherford,

With reference to the matter of the content of uranium in monazite, mentioned in my letter of Dec. 23d, I feel sure that you will be interested to learn that I have succeeded in separating uranium equivalent to 0.38 per cent from N.C. monazite. I do not believe that there can be any doubt as to the accuracy of the analytical method employed or any question as to the identity of the substance separated.

Uranium is most certainly the parent of radium. Very sincerely yours,

BERTRAM B. BOLTWOOD

29 JANUARY 1905

The Macdonald Physics Building
McGill University, Montreal

Dear Mr. Boltwood,

I am very much obliged for the long letter you sent me giving an account of your work and results, and I congratulate you on your success in proving the relation between Ra and Ur. It is quite dramatic to discover from other data that Ur must be present in substances and then to prove it. I am much obliged for your specimens of radio-lead & pitchblende with which I am now working. Your method of separation of ThX in a water solution is quite interesting and will prove very useful when large quantities of ThX are required for any experiment. I can quite believe that thorium is present with ThX. Soddy usually worked up 5 or 10 grams and he might easily have overlooked it. In fact I suppose that no separation of that character can ever be completely freed from traces of the main substance. You are quite right in believing that the amount of polonium must depend on whether the radium mineral is emanating or not. The amount must be sensibly less for an emanating mineral. I have sent off a letter to Nature [1] in which I have given a synopsis of recent work. Radio-tellurium and radium E,[2] as I expected, decay at the same rate viz $\frac{1}{2}$ value in 150 days. My calculated period is of the right order. I did'nt have active polonium to compare with it as mine had reached its final small limiting value. However, I am pretty confident it will decay at the same rate, and we will thus put the three substances in line. I am now quite sure that radio-lead contains radium D—at any rate your radio-lead does. It may interest you to know that I find radium D is a twin. The true radium D (40 years period) is a rayless change. Then follows a β ray change radium E; period 6 days; and then radium F (polonium). I missed it in my first experiments as I did'nt start measurements early enough. It is rather interesting the way the subject is working out, but I trust no more letters of the alphabet will be required for some time. Let me have copies of your papers as soon as they come out. Did I send you my Bakerian lecture? [3] I intended to. Yours very sincerely,

E. RUTHERFORD

1. ER, "Slow transformation products of radium," *Nature, 71* (9 Feb. 1905), 341–42.

2. The name has since been changed to radium F.
3. ER, "The succession of changes in radioactive bodies," *Phil. Trans.*, *204A* (1904), 169–219.

30 JANUARY 1905

139 Orange Street
New Haven, Connecticut

Dear Prof. Rutherford,

You will find below a table of the results which I have obtained from an examination of 22 different samples of uranium minerals. Column I gives the activity of the total emanation from 1 gram of material, Column II the emanating power of the cold samples (per cent. of the total emanation lost by 1 gram at ordinary temperatures), Column III the weight in grams of uranium contained in 1 gram, and Column IV the ratio obtained by dividing the activity by the quantity of uranium.

No.	Substance	Locality	I	II	III	IV
1.	Uraninite	North Carolina	170.0	11.3	0.7465	228
2.	Uraninite	Colorado	155.1	5.2	0.6961	223
3.	Gummite	North Carolina	147.0	13.7	0.6538	225
4.	Uraninite	Joachimsthal	139.6	5.6	0.6174	226
5.	Uranophane	North Carolina	117.7	8.2	0.5168	228
6.	Uraninite	Saxony	115.6	2.7	0.5064	228
7.	Uranophane	North Carolina	113.5	22.8	0.4984	228
8.	Thorogummite	North Carolina	72.9	16.2	0.3317	220
9.	Carnotite	Colorado	49.7	16.3	0.2261	220
10.	Uranothorite	Norway	25.2	1.3	0.1138	221
11.	Samarskite	North Carolina	23.4	0.7	0.1044	224
12.	Orangite	Norway	23.1	1.1	0.1034	223
13.	Euxenite	Norway	19.9	0.5	0.0871	228
14.	Thorite	Norway	16.6	6.2	0.0754	220
15.	Fergusonite	Norway	12.0	0.5	0.0557	215

No.	Substance	Locality	I	II	III	IV
16.	Aeschynite	Norway	10.0	0.2	0.0452	221
17.	Xenotime	Norway	1.54	26.0	0.0070	220
18.	Monazite (sand)	North Carolina	0.88	—	0.0043	205
19.	Monazite (crys)	Norway	0.84	1.2	0.0041	207
20.	Monazite (sand)	Brazil	0.76	—	0.0031	245
21.	Monazite (massive)	Connecticut	0.63	—	0.0030	210
22.	Allanite	North Carolina	0.014	—	0.00007	(est.)

In the above, the determination of the uranium in monazite was made with only 1 gram of the material. Using 10 grams of material No. 18 I separated 0.0399 gram of uranium which corresponds to the ratio 221. The analytical method used for the analysis of monazite tends to give a slightly high result, which explains the slightly low average of the ratios in nearly all of the minerals containing small percentages of uranium. I feel that this ought to definitely settle any question as to the radium-uranium ratio and the non-participation of thorium in the production of radium.

I have just finished and sent off for publication a paper in which these results are embodied.[1]

I have discovered in looking over a copy of my letter of Dec. 23d that I omitted to mention the per cent. of uranium in the sample of uraninite which I sent you. I have a faint impression that I did put it on the paper in which the sample was wrapped, which I hope was the case. If not, let me state that it was a portion of sample No. 1 mentioned in the table and contained 74.65% of uranium. I hope that it reached you safely together with the two samples of radio-lead which were sent at the same time. I wish very much that you could determine the actual per cent. of radium in it by comparison with a known quantity of pure radium bromide, since the actual molecular proportions in which the radium and uranium occur together would seem to be quite important.

I am greatly obliged for the printed copy of your Bakerian Lecture and also the reprint of the article in the November Phil. Mag. which you were so kind as to send me. Sincerely yours,

BERTRAM B. BOLTWOOD

1. BBB, "The origin of radium," *Phil. Mag.*, 9 (Apr. 1905), 599–613.

A Radioactive Friendship

In memory of their mother, the children of Mrs. Hepsa Ely Silliman in 1883 left to Yale the sum of eighty thousand dollars to establish an annual course of lectures. Not until 1902, however, did the university come into possession of the fund, and then immediate steps were taken to implement its provisions. The lectures were to be designed to "illustrate the presence and providence, the wisdom and goodness of God, as manifested in the natural and moral world." Science, not theology, was intended, and the eminence of the first lecturers (J. J. Thomson, C. S. Sherrington, Rutherford, and Walther Nernst) assured successful compliance with the benefactors' wishes.

Rutherford presented a series of eleven lectures in March 1905. His topic, and the title of the book they subsequently formed, was radioactive transformations. Much of the physics of radioactivity, the nature of the radiations, was only surveyed, to provide background information. Rutherford dealt mostly with the transformations, discussing the physical and chemical properties of the many decay products. This was symptomatic of the current shift of interest from the alpha, beta, and gamma rays to the emitters of these rays. It also marked the rise of curiosity about the chemical nature of these radioelements and serious efforts to understand them.

Not only was Rutherford renewing old acquaintances on this visit to New Haven, and being scrutinized by his hosts with an eye towards offering him a professorship, he was solidifying his professional liaison with Boltwood with a genuine friendship. The two got along famously. Rutherford's boisterous good humor meshed well with Boltwood's high spirits and a new tone now entered their letters: their salutations to each other became less formal (the common usage of given names comes after their time) and far more professional gossip was exchanged.

9 APRIL 1905

The Macdonald Physics Building
McGill University, Montreal

My dear Boltwood,

I got through to Montreal the same evening I left New Haven & have been busy since correcting papers for publication and revising proofs. You all gave me a thundering good time in New Haven and I have a very pleasant recollection of the same.

Strutt has just sent me an early proof of his paper. As I know you are very anxious to see it, I forward it to you in *confidence* for a few days. I would like to have it back in a few days after you have soaked it in. What do you think of the thorium-helium argument? It does'nt appear to me very strong but of course thorium does produce He as it gives out α particles. After seeing Strutt's paper, I appreciate how good your results are. He fell through on monazite in great style.

Strutt tells me that Ramsay [1] has a substance (new element) which gives out Th Emanation (probably R.S. paper announcement we saw).[2] He hazards that it may be ThX—I'll back 10 dollars it is. If it proves so, we shall have a good laugh on Ramsay. Ramsay says it is a substance like aluminium! He gets it from thorianite.

I hope you can read this scrawl. Yours ever,

E. RUTHERFORD

1. Sir William Ramsay was perhaps the most famous British chemist of his day, having made his reputation by the discovery of a number of the so-called inert gases. His interest in radioactivity arose from Rutherford and Soddy's belief that the emanations also were inert gases. In 1903, Soddy moved from McGill to Ramsay's laboratory in University College, London, and the two soon discovered helium "growing" in a radium preparation. This was interpreted as strong confirmation for the disintegration theory and was also a good example of the fruits obtainable through the collaboration of specialists—in this case a radiochemist and an expert in the isolation of minute quantities of gases and their spectroscopic study. Unfortunately, Ramsay never became skilled in radioactivity and, when Soddy departed after a year, his work in this field was for the most part undistinguished. Such a series of "discoveries" that never stood the test of time issued from his laboratory that the competent workers in radioactivity disbelieved *all* announcements and were dismayed when scientists in other fields, cognizant of Ramsay's earlier achievements, quite naturally accepted his pronouncements on radioactivity as accurate. Ramsay was a controversial figure and these letters point to a detracting side of his personality and career. For a defensive biography, see Morris W. Travers, *A Life of Sir William Ramsay* (London, Edward Arnold, 1956).

2. O. Hahn, "A new radio-active element, which evolves thorium emanation. Preliminary communication," *Proc. Roy. Soc., 76A* (24 May 1905), 115–17. Ramsay communicated the paper to the Royal Society, where it was read on 16 March 1905.

11 APRIL 1905

139 Orange Street
New Haven, Connecticut

My dear Rutherford,

I was very glad to get your letter of the 9th and to learn that you had gotten back safely. It is a great pleasure to know that you had a good time here, for I am sure that we fellows enjoyed your visit immensely.

It was very good of you to send on the proof of Strutt's paper,[1] which I read with the greatest possible interest. To be frank, though, I must say that the paper is very disappointing. I don't see how he could have had the nerve to publish his results on the uranium-radium ratio, and then consider them as confirming any conclusion except that uranium was *not* the parent of radium. In Sec. 4 he states "The ratio of radium to uranium is given in the last column of the table, and varies very little for the different minerals." I don't see how it could possibly vary very much more! And then his method of standardizing with radium bromide strikes me as being *terribly* crude. You have probably noticed that the value which he gets for the relative quantities of radium and uranium is almost one-half that which I found by comparison with your radium bromide solution.

I think that the thorium-helium part of the paper is all rot, both the methods and the conclusions. I notice that Sec. 5 was "Amended March 6" which was just three days after he had talked with J.J. and Bumstead at the Cavendish. What it was before that heaven only knows, for it is bad enough as it stands. If I felt any confidence in any of the figures given in the table on page 7 I could perhaps rationally discuss his conclusions as to the occurrence of thorium and helium together, but as it is I don't find much basis for an argument either way. It so happens that all three of his pitchblendes, his cuprouranite and his carnotite are secondary uranium minerals, and all of them are probably quite highly emanating. So the fact that he found no helium in them is of no significance so far as the alleged absence of thorium is concerned. But I do note that several of these are stated to contain as much helium as is shown to be present in his 48.5% ThO_2 orangite. If conclusive experiments ever do show that thorium and helium are coexistent in minerals I shall interpret it as evidence that thorium is a disintegration product of uranium, unless you yourself find a better explanation.[2]

I hope that you wont mind my being so "square toed" in my comments on this paper, for I know that you are a friend of Strutt's and I appreciate that I am perhaps somewhat prejudiced in this matter. But after all that you have said about Hoffman [3] and Baskerville, to have a physicist come out with a paper like this—to quote Josh Billings—is "two mutch"!

My own work is moving along pretty slowly at present. The determination of the relative proportion of the actinium present in the minerals is not going to be as easy as at first sight appeared. The effect due to the actinium is going to be so small that it will be necessary to take a lot of material in order to get large enough effects to measure with accuracy.

The experiment with the uraninite, observing the rise of the activity of the residue after dissolving and evaporating 0.1 gram to dryness, has been going for 5 days now. The first time that I tried it, I found that I could not rely on the accuracy of the readings that I was getting, so I began all over again, first constructing a new electroscope for this special purpose. The plan of this electroscope is shown in the accompanying sketch. The sample was dissolved in a small quantity of nitric acid, rapidly evaporated to dryness in a platinum dish and quickly introduced into the electroscope. The readings were begun about 15 minutes after the mineral was first dissolved and are given in the following list. The readings are expressed in the terms of divisions of the scale per minute. The time is reckoned from the time of solution.

Time	Reading	Time	Reading
15 m.	12.5	2 days	14.0
30 m.	12.6	2 d. 3 hrs.	14.3
35 m.	12.4	2 d. 4 hrs.	14.4
45 m.	12.3	2 d. 6 hrs.	14.6
50 m.	12.3	3 days	15.3
1 hr. 20 m.	11.8	3 d. 4 hrs.	15.4
4 hr. 20 m.	11.5	4 days	15.9
5 hr. 40 m.	11.6	4 d. 5 hrs.	16.0
1 day	12.8	5 days	16.7

As I calculate it this points to a maximum of about 1.8 as compared with the 1.6 which you obtained.[4] I am going to try the same experiment later with other minerals, and will send you the results.

I have held up this letter somewhat, hoping to find some details of the R.S. paper on the new (?) element "which gives off thorium emanation" in the Nature which came last night.[5] Now that I know that it comes from thorianite, I also am willing to bet that it is Th-X. Why doesn't Ramsay have one of his

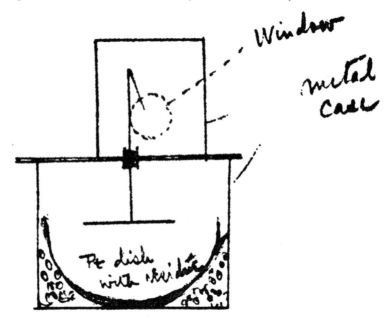

students rediscover radium? It offers lots of interesting possibilities!

I got a letter from Bumstead a few days ago which worried me a good deal. He is up for reappointment as assistant professor this year and has been informed by the "Director"[6] that his appointment for the next five years must be at the same salary as he has been getting in the past, viz., $1,800 per year. Bumstead writes that he can't possibly live on that with his growing family, and that he will be forced to take an appointment elsewhere if he can possibly get one. Chittenden's policy is to grind everyone down to the lowest possible limit, and he has succeeded in antagonizing all of the younger members of his faculty. Of course he thinks that Bumstead won't have the courage to leave, but if he does it will be a great loss to the institution and a calamity for his friends. If you could possibly encourage anybody to make him an offer it would undoubtedly have the effect of bringing "the little Boss" to terms. I feel sure that you appreciate what a first rate man Bumstead is.

Please don't think that I have entirely forgotten about that note on the genesis of radioactive minerals, which I shall certainly send to you in a couple of days. I want to thank you for that reprint from the Archives which came yesterday.

With best regards, Sincerely yours,

BERTRAM B. BOLTWOOD

1. Strutt, "On the radio-active minerals," *Proc. Roy. Soc., 76A* (24 May 1905), 88–101.

2. Thorium was not yet pictured as starting an independent decay series, and efforts were made to insert it into the uranium series. Strutt (ibid.) suggested that thorium is the parent of uranium, for all thorium minerals contain uranium, but not all uranium minerals contain thorium. This, he explained, could occur if the parent thorium had completely decayed into uranium. Boltwood faulted this argument by reinterpreting Strutt's evidence and by pointing out the unlikelihood of thorium's atomic weight being greater than that of uranium. If anything, he felt that uranium is the parent of thorium. As for the helium, Boltwood was not alone in believing that this gas resulted from the alpha particles emitted by uranium, radium, and some other radioelements. But he and many colleagues saw no reason why all alphas had to be helium ions. This equality was finally proven conclusively by Rutherford and Royds in 1908, but until then many believed that some alphas could be hydrogen ions. Boltwood's statement that the presence of helium merely proves thorium's connection to uranium is part of his position that the alpha emitted from thorium may be hydrogen. See BBB, "On the ultimate disintegration products of the radio-active elements," *Am. J. Sci., 20* (Oct. 1905), 253–67.

3. Karl Andreas Hofmann. See note 5 to Boltwood's letter of 8 Aug. 1904.

4. In the process of dissolving the uranium mineral and then evaporating it to dryness the radium emanation is removed. The increase in activity shown in Boltwood's data occurs as more emanation is generated from the radium in the sample and this emanation begins to decay. In time the emanation will reach its equilibrium value, meaning that it is decaying into its daughter products as fast as it is itself being produced. Boltwood was interested in calculating the ratio of the sample's equilibrium activity to its activity with the emanation removed. In this manner he could determine the relative activity of a single constituent of a decay series. Such information was invaluable in piecing these series together.

5. Hahn, "A new radio-active element, which evolves thorium emanation," *Nature, 71* (13 Apr. 1905), 574. Judging from the date of publication, the date of this letter, and the fact that the journal had to make its way across the Atlantic, Boltwood held up his letter for a considerable time and/or *Nature* was dated later than it actually appeared.

6. Russell H. Chittenden, a leader in the field of physiological chemistry, was director of Yale's Sheffield Scientific School.

15 APRIL [1905]

The Macdonald Physics Building
McGill University, Montreal

My dear Boltwood,

I was glad to hear from you and to hear how the recovery curve of the activity was going. You are quite right, the maxm. should be 1.8 times the minimum. I have examined my residue & find it 1.6 as I told you. Either my compound is emanating or all the Ra is not dissolved. Now in regard to the conclusions we can draw from the experiments. Comparison of relative activity of uraninite in rad[ioactive] equilib[rium] with black Ur oxide. Ratio 5.56. I intend to repeat this.

Let Ur = activ[ity] due to Ur

Ra = activ[ity] (maxm.) due to new radium
includes Ra, Em, Rad A, B & C *but not F*

X = activ[ity] due to other active matter including RaF, actin[ium], thor[ium] &c.

Then supposing black oxide & uraninite have about the same density & content of Ur

$$Ur + X + Ra = 5.55 \, Ur \qquad [1]$$

From your result, since **Ra** at minm. has ¼ of maxm. activity

$$Ur + X + Ra = 1.80 \, \{Ur + X + \tfrac{1}{4} \, Ra\} \qquad [2]$$
$$\therefore .80 \, (Ur + X) = .55 \, Ra$$
$$\therefore Ur + X = .69 \, Ra$$
$$.69 \, Ra - X = Ur \qquad [3]$$
$$\text{But from } [1] \; X + Ra = 4.55 \, Ur \qquad [4]$$
$$\text{Adding } 1.69 \, Ra = 5.55 \, Ur$$
$$\therefore Ra = 3.3 \, Ur$$
$$\therefore X = 1.25 \, Ur.$$

These are of right order & indicate that X is RaF alone. Actinium cannot in consequence come in as a direct product.[1]

Ra = 3.3.Ur is too small for a direct product if there is only *one* α ray change in Uranium, for the α rays from Ra are on an average 1.80 times as penetrating as those from Ur ie their ionization is 1.8 times as great for equal number of α particles. Thus if Ur and Ra are [in] *direct* succession

$$Ra = 1.8 \times 4 \, Ur \,^2$$
$$= 7.2 \, Ur.$$

But only 3.3 times observed *or almost half* ∴ possibly 2 α ray changes in Ur. This too is supported by your expts. on amount of *Ra* in *Ur* since only about half of theoretical amount is obtained. [*Added in margin:* Rather contradicted later.] Let us calculate the activity of pure Ra compared with Ur to fit in amt of Ra in 1 gram Ur = $1/1.25 \times 10^{-6}$ gr.[3]

Let X = activity

$$10^{-6}/1.25 \times X = 3.3 \, Ur \text{ (ordinary)}$$
$$X = 4.1 \times 10^6 \, Ur.[4]$$

I think I shall try & calculate activity for pure RaBr more accurately to see how [?] it fits in.

If activity of Ra = 4 × 10⁶ Ur, Then since the average α ray product produces 1.8 times ioniz[ation], no. of atoms of Ra compared with Ur = 4/4 × 10⁶ × 1/1.8 = 5.6/10⁷ or too small from our estimate of Ra in Ur. If however two changes in Ur giving α rays, amt. compared with true Ur (one change) should be twice as great or 1.12/10⁶. The true value derived .8 × 10⁻⁶ is intermediate between these two, so not much light is thrown on the question.

I believe, however, results will fit in pretty well (considering uncertainty attaching to data) if

1. There are two α ray changes in Ur instead of 1.
2. That activity of Ra is nearer 4 million than 2 million.

The above is rather muddled, but I think you can see that this method of attack is likely to yield very valuable results.

I agree with your remarks re Strutt. I don't think his paper is worth much. Let me hear how things are going with you. Yours sincerely,

E. RUTHERFORD

Sorry to hear what you say of Bumstead. Hope all will finally be well.

1. This is a good example of the information that may be extracted from an investigation of relative activities. Since the activity of actinium and its products relative to the activity of uranium was approximately known, it could be seen that the actinium family was not in the main line of decay of the uranium series; the total activity would be far greater than actually observed.

2. There were four known alpha decays in the radium chain (excluding RaF), hence, if there were only one alpha from uranium, the total radium activity would be 4 × 1.8 Ur.

3. This value, of the amount of radium associated with one gram of uranium, was revised to 7.4 × 10⁻⁷ gram before publication. For its derivation, see ER and BBB, "The relative proportion of radium and uranium in radio-active minerals," *Am. J. Sci.*, 20 (July 1905), 55–56. This was one of the few times, however, that Rutherford published results he

would later retract. The source of the error involved is discussed in subsequent letters in this collection.

4. This means that, weight for weight, radium is of the order of four million times more active than uranium.

18 APRIL 1905

139 Orange Street
New Haven, Connecticut

My dear Rutherford,

I was very much interested in your letter of the fifteenth and in the deductions which you make from the experiment with uraninite. The later readings which I have obtained are the following: 6 days 16.9; 7 days 17.4; 8 days 17.9; 9 days 18.3; 10 days 18.6.

I am particularly interested in your conclusion that the activity of the thorium and actinium present in the sample is too small to figure prominently in the total activity, since this is borne out by my experiments attempting to measure the quantity of actinium and thorium actually present. I haven't yet been able to get enough thorium and actinium emanation from ten grams of material to measure with any accuracy. The excited activity which accumulates on a negatively charged plate suspended over a solution containing 0.1 gram uraninite for 24 hours is only equal to about 0.12 div. per min. at the start and in six hours falls to 0.0055 div. per min. This does not look as if very much thorium was present.

I have been working a lot over that question as to whether lead is a disintegration product of radium (Radium G in fact) and am extremely impressed by the data that I find in support of this hypothesis. Taking some of Hillebrand's [1] figures for example, I find that the relative proportions of lead and "nitrogen" [2] are as follows:

Boltwood   18 April 1905

	Glastonbury	Branchville	Colorado	N.C.	Anneröd	Elvestad
PbO	3.08	4.35	0.7	4.2	9.0	10.06
N	2.41	2.63	0.15	0.37	1.17	1.28
Uran.	72	74	72	77	66	66
Sp. G.	9.62	9.35	8.07	9.09	8.89	9.15
	(1)	(2)	(3)	(4)	(5)	(6)

also include

	Elvestad	Skraatorp	Huggensak.	Arendal	Texas	Thorianite
PbO	8.58	9.46	9.44	10.95	10.08	2.50
N	1.08	1.03	1.08	1.24	0.54	He— 10 cc per gm
Uran.	57	65	68	61	55	10
Sp. G.	8.32	8.97	8.93	?	8.29	9.32
	(7)	(8)	(9)	(10)	(11)	(12)

You will notice the following interesting relations:

1. That in the specimens from the same general locality, the variations of the lead and "nitrogen" (helium) are in the same direction, i.e., when the lead is higher, the helium is higher (Nos. 1 and 2) (No. 5, 6, 7, 8, 9 and 10). The lead and helium both increase with higher specific gravity in the mineral, i.e., with greater density and therefore lower emanating power.

2. The proportion of both lead and helium is smaller in the youngest (secondary) specimen (No. 3). The specific gravity of this sample is also quite low, so that both Pb and He may be lower than would be required by the actual age of the mineral; the ratio of Pb to He, however, is of the same order as in samples 5 to 10.

3. The ratio of lead to uranium is highest in the oldest mineral, thorianite, and lowest in the youngest, No. 3. The thorianite is undoubtedly *very* much older than any of the other minerals, with the possible exception of No. 4. This variety is however highly emanating, while No. 12 is *very* dense as is shown by its high Sp. Gr.

4. The relative quantities of lead and helium in the very dense minerals are in the proportion which would be expected

if the helium was produced *only* by the 5 alpha particles given off in the change Ra-Pb, if it is assumed that the gas measured and calculated as nitrogen was actually all helium. This would of course give a maximum value for the helium, and it is interesting to note that even in thorianite, with the large content of thorium, this proportion is not exceeded. I know that you will resent my confining the production of helium to the change Ra-Pb, but it seems to me that everything points in that direction.

5. Danne's[3] radioactive pyromorphite may be the residue of radium salts which have been transported by the waters and deposited for countless ages where they are still being deposited.

6. If lead can be shown to be a disintegration product of uranium, will it not necessarily follow that all of the lead existing on the globe originated in this way?[4] I think that the deductions which can be made from this assumption will make even the metaphysicians dizzy.

There is every evidence that all of the primary uranium minerals contain lead. A present difficulty will however be encountered in the case of monazite with its high content of helium and its very low proportion of lead.

I am enclosing the promised note on radioactive minerals and hope that you will find it what you wanted. It is pretty well boiled down, but I hope not too much so. Sincerely yours,

BERTRAM B. BOLTWOOD

1. William F. Hillebrand was a chemist for the U.S. Geological Survey from 1880 to 1908, at which time he became chief chemist of the Bureau of Standards. He received many honors, including election as president of the American Chemical Society in 1906.

2. Hillebrand's analyses, dating from the late nineteenth century, were made before the presence of helium was detected on earth. Apparently he was more interested in the minerals' solid constituents than in the gases and merely assumed the gases he extracted were, in all cases, nitrogen.

3. Jacques Danne, assistant to Pierre Curie, was editor of the newly founded (1904) journal, *Le Radium*.

4. Modern values for the percent abundance of the stable lead isotopes are as follows: uranium series, $U^{238} \rightarrow Pb^{206}$, 26%; thorium series, Th^{232}

→ Pb^{208}, 52%; actinium series, U^{235} → Pb^{207}, 21%; original lead, Pb^{204}, 1.3%. Thus, while Boltwood could envisage two different types of alpha particles, he could not foresee different means of lead production. The "law" of economy in scientific hypotheses (Occam's razor) was being invoked inconsistently.

28 April 1905

The Macdonald Physics Building
McGill University, Montreal

My dear Boltwood,

Just a line at midnight to thank you for your kindness in forwarding me the MSS on radioactive minerals. I think it is very good and, if you will allow me, I will place it as an appendix in my book. I may possibly have to abbreviate it a little.

I have been busy with the help of Bronson [1] in trying to get the activity of pure Ra & found a mare's nest which will react on the conclusions of the recovery of activity of uraninite after solution. I was trying to find activity indirectly by adding RaBr solution to known weight of Ur as nitrate solution & then evaporating to dryness. One can get any value one likes within limits as the Ur deposits first & leaves the Ra on top. I am trying after drying to thoroughly mix deposit and escape difficulty that way. The results at present appear more probable. You will at once see the objection to our recovery expt. The difference in your rise 1.8 & mine 1.6 is probably merely due to the fact that you had more Ra at the surface of your deposit. Could you try another experiment of a similar character but after evaporation thoroughly mix the deposit together & *then* note rise. I feel very uncertain about the first results. It shows how very careful one has to be in radioactive work. I smelt brown when your rise & mine went different and expected to get what we did in the Ur + Ra expts. I have been trying. I am hoping tomorrow to settle whether the α particle is helium. Things look mighty promising. Have got over difficulties of electrostatic deflection.[2] Remember me to Wheeler & all my kind friends. Yours ever,

E. RUTHERFORD

Am working like a slave over proofs & writing up papers. Leave Frisco May 18. Probably leave here on May 9 or 10.[3]

1. Howard L. Bronson received his Ph.D. degree from Yale in 1904, having written his dissertation under Bumstead. He then went to McGill, where he worked on radioactivity in Rutherford's laboratory. In 1910, he was appointed to a chair in physics at Dalhousie and remained there for the rest of his career.

2. Rutherford was too optimistic, for he was unable to determine the electric deviation with the accuracy required. See ER, "Some properties of the α rays from radium," *Phil. Mag., 10* (July 1905), 163–76.

3. Rutherford spent the summer of 1905 at his family home in New Zealand, joining his wife, Mary, and three-year-old daughter, Eileen, who had gone there several months earlier to take advantage of the warm season in the southern hemisphere.

4 MAY 1905

139 Orange Street
New Haven, Connecticut

My dear Rutherford,

I was much interested in your letter of April 28th, particularly in your conclusions as to the uncertainty of data obtained from the measurements of the recovery of the activity of uraninite after solution. I became convinced that there was something decidedly wrong somewhere, just as soon as I attempted to repeat the experiment, and I tried to get around it by using very thin films of material (0.01 gram of substance evaporated on a ground-glass surface of 15 sq. cm. area). In this way I found it possible to get a better agreement between my activities, but the variations are still altogether too large for any definite deductions. For example, two such films of pure uranium

nitrate equivalent to the uranium present in 0.01 gram of uraninite gave activities of 0.36 and 0.42 div. per min., a variation
of over 16 per cent., although the conditions under which they
were prepared were as nearly identical as possible.

I wish that you would comment on the following scheme:
The uraninite to be ground as fine as possible in an agate mor-
tar with chloroform and then flowed over a platinum plate,
where the chloroform is allowed to evaporate, leaving the
uraninite in a very thin, uniform film (McCoy—Jour. Am.
Chem. Soc., April, p. 391). The activity of the plate is measured, and the plate is heated to a white heat (over a blast
lamp). The activity is again measured and the difference is of
course equal to the emanation expelled. The recovery of the activity of the plate with time can then be observed, and if the
activity finally rises to the initial value it can be definitely concluded that the only thing expelled is the emanation. By determining the emanation in such a film before ignition it will be
possible to find out what proportion of the total emanation is
present at the start, and by determining the emanation contained in the film after igniting (until the activity has attained a
constant value) it will be possible to find out whether the entire emanation is expelled.

I have tried this experiment in the following rough way: A
film of uraninite was prepared with chloroform in a shallow
platinum crucible-cover, the uraninite being in the same condition as that which I sent you (a portion of the same material).
After the chloroform had completely evaporated (at ordinary
temperature) the uraninite adhered tightly to the cover and
none of it fell off when the cover was inverted over a white
paper. The activity of this film was equal to 2.8 divisions per
minute.

The crucible-cover was heated to a bright red heat over a
bunsen burner and the activity again measured. It was equal to
2.73 div. per min. It was again heated for several minutes and
again measured and the activity was 2.66 div. per min.

The cover was heated over a small blast-lamp. The activity was equal to 2.31 div. per min.

The cover was heated for 5 minutes over a large blast-lamp to a white heat. After heating the activity was equal to 1.96 div. per min. and after standing for three hours had fallen to 1.70 div. per min., after which the activity rose steadily.

The crucible-cover has stood for 12 days and the activity is now 2.7 div. per min. It would appear from this that nothing but the emanation was driven off on heating, and that our old friend Ra-F behaves like a respectable chemical element with a non-volatile oxide.

And now as to what this rough experiment would seem to indicate. The total activity at start was 2.8 div., the minimum after heating was 1.7 div.—the difference 1.1 div., which corresponds to 90% of the total emanation (and products of rapid change). One hundred per cent. would equal 1.2 div., which with the minimum = 2.9 div. per min. as the activity if all of the emanation were retained by the mineral. But 2.9/1.7 = 1.7, and the value you give for the activity of the mineral as compared with uranium (=5.56), corrected for the same loss of emanation gives 5.75 Ur. Solving by your equations this gives Ra = 3.16 Ur; x = 1.59.

Now if it is assumed that the activity of ordinary radium is 4 million times ordinary uranium, and that 1 weight of radium is associated with 1,275,000 weights of uranium (my value), then the activity of the radium associated with a unit quantity of uranium is 3.14 or Ra = 3.14 Ur; and the value of x = 1.61 Ur.

These numbers agree so closely that it makes me strongly suspect that there is something *wrong* somewhere, or that the agreement is purely accidental. I am going to try over the experiment of heating the uraninite with the checks on the method which I have described and find out what there is in it. One of the great objections to the solution method is that the residue obtained on evaporation is a hydrated salt which can take up or give off moisture, and this alone would seem to explain some of the variations in activity noticed. The ignited mineral is a good stable mixture of oxides, and should give concordant results under proper precautions.

Another interesting point in this matter is that the activity of a deposit of radio-tellurium on bismuth, obtained from 1 gram of uraninite corresponds to about 0.70 Ur, which is not far from one-half of the calculated value of x (1.6).

I wonder if you saw that foolish article by Kohlschütter and Vogdt [1] in the April 15th Berichte, p. 1419. Also the latest bay of the Hound of the Baskervilles,[2] in the same number. The former have probably got a nitride of uranium or some other similar compound, and their statement as to the presence of water in helium bearing minerals is entirely contrary to analytical results, at least there is no proportionality shown between them. I wish that some rough proportionality did exist, for it would indicate that hydrogen was one of the disintegration products.

After that synopsis of Hahn's paper "On a new element etc." in Nature [3] I am positive that the substance he got was Th-X mixed with a little radium. If he made any experiments of the rate of decay he was thrown off the track by the activity of the radium rising, as the Th-X fell off. I have obtained exactly similar precipitates in working with other minerals. They give off thorium emanation when fresh and radium emanation when old. I am surprised that Ramsay has not yet named his "new element."

I hope that your alpha particle experiments have turned out satisfactorily. I shall be much interested in your conclusions. Very sincerely yours,

BERTRAM B. BOLTWOOD

1. V. Kohlschütter and K. Vogdt, "Ueber feste Lösungen indifferenter Gase in Uranoxyden," *Ber. Deut. Chem. Ges., 38* (1905), 1419–30, 2992–3002. Kohlschütter was on the staff of the chemical institute of the

University of Strassburg, and later was professor at Berne. Vodgt was his student or assistant.

2. Since Arthur Conan Doyle's *The Hound of the Baskervilles* was published in 1902, Charles Baskerville must have encountered a certain amount of joking about his name. His paper was "Zur Klarstellung der Thoriumfrage," *Ber. Deut. Chem. Ges., 38* (1905), 1444.

3. Hahn, "A new radio-active element, which evolves thorium emanation," *Nature, 71* (13 Apr. 1905), 574. Otto Hahn originally had in mind a career as an industrial chemist. To qualify for a certain position he needed a command of the English language; to acquire this facility, in 1904 he obtained permission to work in Ramsay's laboratory in London. Upon his arrival, Sir William handed him a bowl of active salts and requested that Hahn extract the radium. Hahn, an organic chemist, failed in this effort, but instead discovered a new radioelement, radiothorium. Such ability should not be wasted and Ramsay suggested that when Hahn returned to Germany he consider an academic career with research in radioactivity. First, however, Hahn decided to spend a year in Rutherford's laboratory, for he needed more training in this field and Montreal was the center of activity. Hahn pursued his research at McGill University during the 1905–06 academic year and then began his academic lifework in Berlin. His long and distinguished career as the world's leading radiochemist, a career notable also for his thirty-year collaboration with the physicist Lise Meitner, was culminated by the discovery of nuclear fission in 1938.

18 May 1905

San Francisco, California

My dear Boltwood,

I had such a rush to finish up before my departure from Montreal, that I could not attend to those numbers you sent me. I intended to write up a rough draft of a paper for your consideration before I left but I had'nt time to look round.

I did some more experiments on the recovery curve of uraninite, evaporating it to dryness & then mixing it up again & got a mean value of two specimens of increase *1.63* which is pretty close to my old value. You will be able to compare this with your values & it will probably be best to take a mean. The difficulty lies in the escape of emanation. Your method seems a good one & the results obtained are in pretty good agreement with yours. There is a difficulty of publishing these results just at present, as some more work ought to be done to settle some of the points. I think, however, the content of Ra in one gram of Ur ought to be published soon and the other might wait till my return in September.

If you are agreeable, we might publish a short note in the Amer Journal Sci [1] & then expand things in the later paper. I shall endeavour to enclose a rough draft of the MSS before I leave.

I did not have time to read the papers you mentioned re water in radioactive minerals or Baskerville.

I have not Bumstead's address or I would write and tell him that I have today declined the Yale position. I tell you this *in confidence* but I should be glad if you would at once write Bumstead & tell him that the way is now clear. It would be just as well to be ignorant on this matter until you hear from the others. I have written to Hastings [2] on the matter today. I shall be very glad to see Bumstead get the post. With the best wishes for the success of your work. Au revoir,

E. RUTHERFORD

P.S. Am sending MSS at the same time.

Address in New Zealand—Prof. E. Rutherford Pangarehu Taranake New Zealand.

1. ER and BBB, "The relative proportion of radium and uranium in radio-active minerals," *Am. J. Sci.*, 20 (July 1905), 55–56.
2. Charles S. Hastings, professor of physics in Yale's Sheffield Scientific School.

18 JUNE 1905

139 Orange Street
New Haven, Connecticut

My dear Rutherford,

Your very kind letter of May 18th, before sailing from San Francisco, reached me in due time, as did also the rough draft of the paper mailed with it. It was very good of you to tell me of your decision as to the Yale offer, for I was naturally greatly interested in the matter. I was of course disappointed to know positively that you were not coming, since it would have afforded me the greatest personal satisfaction and pleasure to have had you here, but I do believe sincerely that while it would have been a fine thing for the University, you yourself would have lost rather than gained by the change suggested. I feel sure that you would have been disappointed with many things here in New Haven.[1]

I was pleased, however, at your reference to Bumstead, and I wrote[2] to him immediately as you had requested. We who know him best had all hoped that he might have a chance at the position if you decided not to accept it, but we had obtained no direct information that he was being seriously considered. He is one of the best of men, and the opportunities afforded by such a position are just the ones which he requires at present.

From your rough draft I made up a paper for the American Journal of Science, the proof of which I am enclosing in this letter. The article will appear in the July number.[3] I hope that you will approve of it. For the quantity of radium with one gram of uranium I took the number obtained from the measurement of the total (equilibrium quantity) of emanation, i.e., 7.4×10^{-7}, instead of the round number 8.0. I did this because the first determination, made while you were here, gave the value 7.7 when closely calculated, and further because any impurity in the original radium bromide used would raise the value of the final number.

The other work on determining the relative proportion of the total activity of the minerals due to the separate constituents present is going along slowly. My modification of your method, depending on the heating of the uraninite, is not as simple as it first appeared, because among other disturbing factors the mineral after heating does not retain all of the emanation produced within it. All of the numbers which I have obtained, however, indicate a value of about 1.6 for the ratio, which is in agreement with the numbers which you got from your measurements. I think that I shall have the matter in shape by the time that you get back in September.

I hope that you are in good health and that you are enjoying your vacation. With best wishes, Sincerely yours,

BERTRAM B. BOLTWOOD

1. Boltwood was probably referring both to the relatively poor facilities and equipment at Yale (McGill had one of the best laboratories on the continent) and to the wasteful duplication of science departments in Yale College and the Sheffield Scientific School.

2. Bumstead was then spending a term at the Cavendish Laboratory, engaged in research on X rays.

3. ER and BBB, "The relative proportion of radium and uranium in radio-active minerals," *Am. J. Sci.,* 20 (July 1905), 55–56.

16 SEPTEMBER 1905

The Macdonald Physics Building
McGill University, Montreal

My dear Boltwood,
I have just returned from New Zealand where I had a very pleasant time although I was moving about most of the time.

They gave me a very hearty reception in N.Z.—including a reception by the Mayor of Christchurch & Council!

I recd. a copy of our joint paper in New Zealand & have just read your papers you sent me. You have rather run a tilt at Soddy [1] and I do not think it undeserved considering the uncertainty attaching to his methods & accuracy of experiment. There is, however, always the possibility that he *may* have observed an increase, since the method used by you to remove the radium may have removed all trace of the intermediate product whilst his methods only removed a fraction.

The subject is rather replete with uncertainties but I have no doubt some solid bed rock will be struck before long.

How have your experiments on actinium been prospering? & also the experiments on uniform films? I understand my book (second edition) is to be on the market at once if it is not already out.

Remember me to Wheeler and Bumstead & my numerous friends in New Haven. Yours ever,

E. RUTHERFORD

1. Both Boltwood and Soddy, now a lecturer at the University of Glasgow, tried to measure the rate of growth of radium in a sample of purified uranium. Soddy felt he had detected the appearance of a minute quantity of radium during eighteen months of experimentation, but Boltwood's simultaneous investigation seemed to indicate otherwise. Because he found no growth of radium in his solution, Boltwood suspected the existence of a long-lived radioelement between uranium and radium in the decay series. Such a product would delay considerably the accumulation of radium. The story of Boltwood's discovery of ionium, the parent of radium, appears in these letters. Rutherford's remark that Boltwood had "run a tilt at Soddy" refers to the paper in which Boltwood concluded that "the results obtained by Mr. Soddy are without significance." Besides questioning Soddy's data and methods, Boltwood suggested that the Englishman's observed increase in activity was due to a radioactive impurity which he had inadvertently introduced into his solution. Though Soddy had himself implied this possibility, he was a highly contentious individual and did not take it kindly that someone else would accuse him of sloppiness. See BBB, "The production of radium from uranium," *Am J. Sci.*, 20 (Sept. 1905),

239–44. Soddy waited almost two years to return the criticism: "The origin of radium," *Nature, 76* (13 June 1907), 150. See also the tables of the radioactive decay series which are printed in the appendix to this volume.

22 SEPTEMBER 1905

139 Orange Street
New Haven, Connecticut

My dear Rutherford,

Your letter of the sixteenth reached New Haven promptly but as it was addressed to the Club [1] I did not happen to get hold of it until last evening. I was very glad to learn that you had gotten back safely.

As to the Soddy paper, I quite agree with you that there *may* have been a growth of radium in his solution, and as a matter of fact I really believe that there was, but I don't think that he proved that there was or that it *necessarily* followed from his results that uranium was the parent. For example, with the crude material which he used there might have been any number of substances present at the start, and if radium *was* produced it would not *necessarily* follow that it had been formed from an intermediate uranium product. It seems to me that the only way in which the legitimacy of the offspring can be proven is by starting with a *pure* uranium compound and then waiting patiently for the radium to appear. That it will be formed ultimately I have not the slightest doubt, but I am absolutely certain that it is not generated at anything like the theoretical rate at the commencement.

One of my chief objections to Soddy's papers was that he took a position entirely on the fence and could jump in all directions with equal facility. While he suggests the existence of an intermediate product, he at the same time insinuates that the change uranium–radium may be a direct one, and that the theoretical quantity of radium *may* have been formed but that he *may* have

78

failed to detect it. I was fully conscious that the intermediate product may well have been present in his solution at the beginning, but I was not going to suggest this as an explanation of his results and to thus offer him a hole to crawl into. I am quite willing to acknowledge that I was considerably irritated by his assumption that my results on minerals confirmed these rotten experiments of his.

I wonder if you have noticed one interesting detail in connection with his paper. In his May 12, 1904 (Nature)[2] communication he states distinctly that his solution was 12 months old when last tested. In the Phil. Mag.[3] article he states that the solution had stood 9 months after that before being again tested. There was an additional period of 23 days before the end of his experiments was reached. He gives the total period as 18 months, but 12 mos. + 9 mos. + 23 days = 21 mos. 23 days, or, in other words, he apparently experienced as much difficulty in attempting to measure time as he did in attempting to measure emanation. He is undoubtedly suffering from Ramsamania.[4]

I have not been able to accomplish very much along the lines of work undertaken at your suggestion. It has been so infernally humid here all summer that work of that character has been almost impossible. Residues of nitrates and similar salts have liquified almost instantly on exposure to the air and everything has been so wet and sticky that accurate measurements with an open electroscope have been quite out of the question ever since the middle of July. One point of considerable interest which I was able to settle before conditions became so bad was that the relative activity of uraninite and pure uranium can not possibly be so high as 5.56 (the number you used in your calculation), but lies between 4.0 and 4.5 for uraninites containing little or no thorium, when the activities are calculated on the basis of equal quantities of uranium. This lower ratio is obtained on comparing the maximum activity per unit weight of substance, the latter being determined by measuring extremely thin films[5] of both the minerals and pure U_3O_8. I notice that McCoy in a review of his own paper[6] on the origin of radium

states (Journ. Am Chem. Soc., July, Abstracts page 382) [7] that
he has arrived at the number 4.17 by a series of similar measurements. If the ratio U + Ra + x = 1.6 (Ur + 1/4Ra + x) is
correct, and I am confident that it is not very far off, this will
give something not far from Ra = 2U.

I am preparing to carry out a further experiment with a bearing on the above. I am going to prepare a mixture of uranium
and radium in the same proportions as they occur in minerals
and bring this finally into the form of the double oxide, U_3O_8,
corresponding to uraninite. By comparing the activity of this
mixture with pure U_3O_8 it will be possible to obtain the value of
the ratio (U + Ra): U and (U + 1/4Ra): U.

With the object of obtaining a closer insight into the occurrence of actinium I have worked up a kilogram of carnotite ore
containing about 200 grams of the pure carnotite. I found that
if any thorium or other rare earths were present their quantity
was too small to make it possible to separate them by the ordinary analytical methods, while the quantity of actinium present
(as determined by its activity) was approximately proportional to the uranium, that is, was approximately equal to the
actinium separated from equivalent quantities of other minerals (uranophane and uraninite). In order to get the actinium
out of the solution of the carnotite it is necessary to add a small
quantity of some rare earth in solution. On treating the mixture with oxalic acid the rare earth added is precipitated as an
oxalate and the actinium comes down with it. It does not make
any difference whether the added rare earth is thorium, cerium
or lanthanum, but if a mixture of all three is added the
actinium remains with the thorium when the earths are afterwards separated. In the absence of thorium the actinium sticks
with the lanthanum. This explains Giesel's "emanating substance" [8] which was undoubtedly separated from a uranium
mineral containing no thorium but only cerium and lanthanum.

Apropos of Ramsay's "new element which evolves thorium
emanation" you will perhaps be interested to know that I have

worked up 5 grams of thorianite, following the method described by Hahn, except of course, that I did not attempt to
fractionally crystalize the barium-radium chloride, but simply
treated the solution with ammonium hydroxide, and examined
the precipitate thus obtained. This precipitate when fresh gave
off large quantities of thorium emanation but its emanating
power has steadily decreased and its activity now, after 7 days, is
less than a third of what it was at the commencement. Miner,
the chemist of the Welsbach Light Co., is working up a kilogram of thorianite for me, and is going to send me the insoluble
residue left after fusing with sodium bisulphate. This should
furnish enough material to throw a definite light on the nature
of this new ? element. I am confident still that it is only a new
compound of Th-X and stupidity, and if perchance I can prove
that such is the case . . . well, there will be something doing.

Speaking of Sir William reminds me of Baskerville, and I am
wondering whether you have seen his new book on "Radium
and Radio-Active Substances." [9] The book has been sent to me
for review in the Journ. Am. Chem. Soc., and I am having a terrible time in deciding how much I shall damn him. I can in-
dorse only a single statement in the book and that is the dedication, but I would like that better if he said "a much higher"
rather than simply "a higher." [10] I wonder whether you have
already discovered that he has simply cribbed page after page of
your book.[11] Compare, for example, page 36 ff of his book with
page 91 of yours. Notice the order in which the subjects are presented, the references to the literature, the identical sentences
used in innumerable cases. Really, it is the most extraordinary
case of scientific plagiarism that has ever come to my notice.
What he has put in of his own is absolute rubbish, and he has
destroyed the value of most of that which he has taken from you
through his ignorance as to what it was all about, anyway. In his
preface he says, referring to your book and Soddy's: [12] "The
appearance of these works has made it necessary to alter this
book somewhat"!! "Alter" is a mild word under the circumstances. If he had altered it a little more the fact that he had

stolen it would not be quite so evident. I used to think that Baskerville was an ass but now I believe that he is a rascal.

Bumstead got back to New Haven on the 19th. He had a fine time and succeeded in finishing up a splendid piece of research work. We are all delighted to have him back and to have had his work turn out so satisfactorily. He is looking very well and wishes to be particularly remembered to you.

I am enclosing the proof of an article which will appear in the October Journal of Science.[13] I am afraid that it is awfully hypothetical but still I think that there are a good many points in it which ought to be brought out now in the hope that they may help some of the people who are working on the chemical side of the problems. A further point in favor of the production of hydrogen is the fact that Moss (Nature 72, 167) finds that hydrogen constitutes 45% by volume of the gases which he gets from monazite on pulverizing in a vacuum. I believe that nitrogen may well be another of the products, but the quantitative data on this point are so meager that I refrained from mentioning it. Don't bother about returning the proof, but, if it isn't too much trouble, let me know what you think of the paper.

I earnestly hope that if you are down in this part of the country at any time you will arrange to stop over in New Haven and give us all the pleasure of again seeing you.

With best wishes, Sincerely yours,

BERTRAM B. BOLTWOOD

P.S. I have been very much interested in your papers which have appeared during the summer. I hope that you will be able to spare me reprints of them.

B.B.B.

1. Faculty Club.
2. Soddy, "The life-history of radium," *Nature*, 70 (12 May 1904), 30.
3. Soddy, "The production of radium from uranium," *Phil. Mag.*, 9 (June 1905), 768–79.

4. A reference to the inaccuracies in Ramsay's work.

5. The activity of thin films was measured to avoid, as much as possible, the absorption of radiation within the mass of radioactive material. In this fashion a more accurate value of activity could be obtained.

6. McCoy, "Ueber das Entstehen des Radiums," *Ber. Deut. Chem. Ges.*, *37* (1904), 2641–56. This appeared translated as "The origin of radium," *Chem. News, 90* (14 and 21 Oct. 1904), 187–89, 199–201.

7. McCoy, "Review of American chemical research," *J. Am. Chem. Soc.*, 27 (July 1905), 381–82.

8. Friedrich Giesel was a Ph.D. chemist employed by a quinine factory in Braunschweig, Germany. As something of a hobby, he purified and sold radioactive materials, and was the only source for concentrated preparations at a time when the Curies released for sale only moderately active materials. In addition, Giesel was one of the major, early investigators of radioactivity, discovering the magnetic deflection of beta rays, extracting radium from ores other than pitchblende and by a process different from that of the Curies, discovering the physiological effects of radium (a sample, held before a closed eye, produced the sensation of light), and discovering a radioelement which he first called "emanating substance" and then "emanium" (and which later was shown to be identical with Debierne's actinium).

9. Baskerville, *Radium and Radio-Active Substances. Their Application Especially to Medicine* (Philadelphia, Williams, Brown and Earle, 1905).

10. The book was dedicated "To Ernest Rutherford whose investigations on radio-activity are worthier of a higher tribute."

11. ER, *Radio-Activity* (Cambridge, University Press, 1904).

12. Soddy, *Radio-Activity: An Elementary Treatise, From the Standpoint of the Disintegration Theory* (London, *Electrician*, 1904).

13. BBB, "On the ultimate disintegration products of the radio-active elements," *Am. J. Sci., 20* (Oct. 1905), 253–67.

28 SEPTEMBER 1905

The Macdonald Physics Building
McGill University, Montreal

My dear Boltwood,

I was very glad to get your interesting letter and to hear your views on things radioactive and non-radioactive. In regard to

Baskervilles' book, I was interested in your statement. I have not yet seen the book but I presume he will send me a copy some time. From B.s remarks on radioactivity at various times, I did not anticipate a particularly accurate account of things because I know he has not the faintest idea of the disintegration theory or rather had not. I am getting quite accustomed to have my views and remarks and sections copied wholesale without even a Thankyou. If you read Duncan's [1] book, you will find many of my paragraphs reproduced & ideas & everything else including even tables of radioelements. I think, however, that the time has arrived that these plagiarists should be jumped on. There is no room for another book with Soddy's & Strutts [2] not to mention my own in the field. It is a cheap way of gaining notoriety without doing any work except reading to a typewriter.

In regard to the compound of "ThX and stupidity"—very neatly put. You may be interested to know that Hahn is coming over to work with me this year. I think he wants to know how to measure things radioactive so as to be able to prove his elements. In fact, I think he will *"take physic and throw up his element."* He arrives in a few days and I will be able to see how the subject stands in his eyes. I am also expecting another PhD from Göttingen a little later.[3]

I cannot lay my hands on my results of the measurement of activity of uraninite and do not remember the number I gave you. I compared the uraninite with the black oxide (composition unknown) as I have no metallic uranium.[4] $Ra = 2$ Ur and $X = 1.1$ Ur excludes actinium as true offspring. I hope your expts. on mixtures of Ur_3O_8 & Ra will work out. I think I told you Bronson tried some expts. for me on mixtures of Ur Nit-[rate] & RaBr—evaporating to dryness & sometimes mixing resulting powder. The results, however, were entirely variable, the activity of Ra varying between 2 and 6 million. In addition, the emanation escaped in large quantity. He came to the conclusion that the method was useless. I think you will have to be

mighty careful even in your expts. to prevent unequal distribution of the Ra. I expect, however, if the powder is ground up
fine, the results ought to be good and settle the question. I
think the experiments are well worth doing, as they will give
the most direct *quantitative* proof of the succession of Ur and
Ra & also throw light on whether Ur gives off more than one set
of α particles.

I was much interested in your general survey of possible constituents of disintegration in minerals. I quite agree with you
that some of them will undoubtedly prove to be products but
it is a terrible business to more than suggest the *probability* unless we discover some method of getting further on the question.
I think you put the matter as well and pushed it as far as it can
be done at present. I am hoping when e/m for the α particle is
settled to see my way clear to a few deductions. I am hard at
work on that subject at present. I do not think it likely that the
α particles differ in mass, although such a consideration cannot
be lightly dismissed. I have, however, a brand new theory in
embryo which I think offers a much wider scope of possible disintegration products than the usual view. I shall be glad to hear
your opinion on it but please keep it *private* as I am not prepared for the moment to put it forward. You remember that
most astounding property of the α particle of losing all its properties of ioniz[ation], phosphor[escence] & photog[raphy] when
still travelling at a very high speed. Now we know from other
data (Townsend) [5] that the + ion produces new ions by collision at a velocity much below the critical velocity of the α particle. I think that the only explanation lies in the fact that the α
particle is *entrapped* in the atom & forms an integral part of it.
The resulting atom may be stable but generally unstable and it
may then break up again, after an interval (possibly in some
cases long) & form new substances. In this way, every substance
originally present in pitchblende may suffer disintegration &
even ordinarily *inactive* matter, for there is no necessity to suppose that the atom only throws out the intruding α particle. It

may break up in plenty of other ways.[6] I think you will see that the basis of this theory is experimental to some extent & it would offer a reasonable explanation of the numerous substances found in radioactive minerals.

Your remarks re Strutt quite agree with my own views on the question. Let me hear from you directly. What has Bumstead been doing? I have'nt heard of the direction he has been working at the Cavendish. Let me hear from you soon. Yours ever,

E. RUTHERFORD

I will forward you reprints in a day on this.

1. Robert Kennedy Duncan, *The New Knowledge; A Popular Account of the New Physics and the New Chemistry in Their Relation to the New Theory of Matter* (New York, Barnes, 1905). Duncan, after several years as an instructor in private secondary schools, became professor of chemistry at Washington and Jefferson College, Washington, Pennsylvania, in 1901. An interest in interpreting science for the lay public developed about this time and he became a contributor to some of the better known magazines of the day, as well as the author of a few widely read books. He later served as professor at both the University of Kansas and the University of Pittsburgh, where he was instrumental in establishing close ties with industrial research. Out of these efforts came the Mellon Institute.

2. Strutt, *The Becquerel Rays and the Properties of Radium* (London, Edward Arnold, 1904).

3. This was Max Levin, whose work in science and career as a professor at Göttingen ended early, when he was forced to take over his father's cloth factory.

4. Rutherford's achievements are all the more remarkable when one considers the paucity and weakness of his radioactive sources.

5. J. S. E. Townsend entered the Cavendish Laboratory as a research student in 1895 only moments after Rutherford's arrival. The abilities of these two men confirmed the wisdom of the new policy under which Cambridge University accepted as research students graduates of other universities. At first, a special type of degree was awarded to those who completed the program, which included an original research project. Later, to make its graduates more competitive with holders of doctoral degrees from the German universities, Cambridge began to award its own doctorates. Townsend became an expert on the discharge of electricity in gases, a

topic not surprising considering the interests of J. J. Thomson, his teacher, and served many years as professor of physics at Oxford.

6. Such a view would encompass the type of fission found in 1938. Rutherford was not being especially prescient here, for in the early years of radioactivity no one was willing to state dogmatically that an atom can decay only by the emission of alpha, beta, and gamma rays. It was only after decades of observing no other forms of decay that the idea of fission seemed so unlikely.

4 OCTOBER 1905

139 Orange Street
New Haven, Connecticut

My dear Rutherford,

I was very much interested in your letter of September the 28th. My position as a reviewer of Baskerville's book was a somewhat delicate one, since B. is a Councilor of the Am. Chem. Soc. and is highly esteemed by the majority of the members. As it is, I think that I wrote a stronger criticism than has appeared in the Journal [1] for some time, although I omitted any reference to the obvious plagiarism. In my letter to the Editor, W. A. Noyes. I took the opportunity to tell him, "that a large number of pages show unmistakable evidence of having been transcribed almost directly from Rutherford's 'Radio-activity.' "

As to Duncan's book—The New Ignorance—, it simply passes the limit. The publishers sent me a complimentary copy early in July, asking me for an expression of opinion in regard to it and stating at the same time that the book had "been most favorably endorsed by Sir William Ramsay, Becquerel, Prof. Thomson of Cambridge, Prof. McLennan [2] and others." I wrote them that I did not approve of the book, that I saw no reason why such a book should ever have been written, and that I found less reason why it should ever have been printed. I don't anticipate any further favors on their part. You can imagine my chagrin and sorrow when I came across that very fulsome review signed "W.R." in Nature.[3] Verily, "One touch of Ramsay makes the whole game skin."

I have recently had an opportunity of pumping a young man named Gutmann,[4] a former colleague of your Dr. Hahn, just fresh from Ramsay's laboratory and about to occupy a position at the feet of The Great Baskerville. Gutmann spent Sunday here in New Haven and I had a good opportunity of seeing him. From what I could get out of him, which was not very definite, there seems to be more reason than I had supposed for assuming that Hahn may really have found something. You will have undoubtedly sized up the situation by this time, and I should be extremely interested to learn your conclusions. I suppose that it is not impossible that there may be an intermediate radio-active product between thorium and Th-X, and that thorium itself, like actinium may undergo a rayless change and be itself nonradio-active. If the intermediate product had a fairly long average life, then this would explain Hahn's results.

As to the matter of the maximum activity of uraninite, etc., I am sending you some oxide of uranium, U_3O_8, carefully prepared from very pure, radium free, uranium nitrate. It contains 85.5% of uranium. I thought you might like to have it as a standard. As to the Ur + Ra mixture, I was planning to obtain a homogeneous, non-emanating and non-hygroscopic mixture, if possible. The difficulties which Bronson experienced could thus be obviated. I haven't completed the work yet.

Your new theory as to the behavior of the alpha particles and its bearing on the disintegration products, is, I regret to state, a little too much for me. I am afraid that I can not quite grasp its possibilities or the extent to which you propose to apply it. I should, however, be much interested to hear more of it in its further development.

Personally, I am rather inclined to the view that the disintegration of uranium, or of one of its successors (before radium), is not a simple change, like the change Ra-A to Ra-B for example, but is a more complex change which results in the production of a number of different bodies (Ra, Th, Ac). Something analogous perhaps to the original creation of Adam, the formation of Eve from one of his ribs, and then the orderly succession of parent and offspring forever after. As to actinium, Bumstead has offered the suggestion that perhaps the succession of changes in the radium family is accompanied by the expulsion, at each change, of a considerable number of alpha particles, while in the actinium series perhaps only one alpha particle is given off at a time. Thus actinium may be an intermediate product between uranium and radium notwithstanding the fact that its proportionate part of the total activity is so small. I have not been able to find any conclusive argument against Bumstead's suggestion, but I presume that there is a good one of which I am ignorant.

Bumstead tells me that he has written you of the work which he carried out at the Cavendish and of the results which he obtained, so I wont be able to give you any news of that matter.

With regards and best wishes, Sincerely yours,

BERTRAM B. BOLTWOOD

1. BBB, review of Baskerville's *Radium and Radio-Active Substances*, in *J. Am. Chem. Soc.*, 27 (Dec. 1905), 1569–70. If Rutherford expected his friend to write a fiery denunciation of this book he must have been disappointed, for Boltwood's criticism was limited to pointing out mildly that the book was unorganized, unclear, and ambiguous in places. While this may have been a stronger review than this journal was accustomed to publishing, such was not generally the case in other periodicals.

2. J. C. McLennan, professor of physics at the University of Toronto, was a leader in the study of radioactivity of the air, soil, water, etc.

3. Ramsay, review of Duncan's *The New Knowledge*, in *Nature*, 72 (13 July 1905), 241–42.

4. After receiving his Ph.D. degree from Heidelberg in 1903, Leo F. Guttmann spent two years as a demonstrator at University College, London, and then four years at the City College of New York. At first, he was a Carnegie Research Assistant to Baskerville, and then he taught physical

chemistry, with the rank of instructor. In 1909, he moved to Canada, as assistant professor at Queen's University.

10 OCTOBER 1905

The Macdonald Physics Building
McGill University, Montreal

My dear Boltwood,

I am much obliged for your last letter & for the enclosed Ur-oxide. I am so fearfully busy at present that I have not time to devote to the experiments on the relative activity of Ur and Ra. Hahn has arrived and settled to work & seems a keen man—an organic chemist initially—with not much physical knowledge but the latter I hope to rectify. I think from what he has shown me there is no doubt that he has separated a very active fairly permanent constituent from Thorium. His specimens are possibly not quite so active as he thought but are certainly over 20,000—giving out α, β and γ rays & Th Eman. He thinks that he has separated a constituent between Th & ThX pointing to the conclusion that Th itself like Act is non-active.[1] Ramsay calls it radio-thorium for him and is apparently giving papers on Hahn's work to the Radiology Congress at Liege and to the French Academy. I wonder how much will be left to Hahn when these publications appear.

By the way, I am getting Hahn to repeat some of Hofmann's results on radiolead in order to see if my conclusion that it is radium D + E + F are correct—See my last paper among the number I forwarded you. I think uraninite is the best stuff to work with. Can you inform me where I could get a few hundred grams of a good sample to work with? I would be much obliged if you would do so. I want to get that matter of radiolead settled rapidly.

Tell me when your critique of Baskerville's work appears. My

90

opinion on it is unwritable and, under the present conditions, I had better keep mum since I have the honour of the dedication. I recognise you had a difficult task to fulfill in reviewing the book.

By the way, you may have seen that Becquerel has been up to his usual game of trying to dam me. See C. R. Sept 14.[2] He concludes my decrease of activity of the α rays after passing thro. matter is mythical. I need hardly tell you I am right & it will not be very long before I sail into friend B. in good style and reduce him to atomic fragments if not to electronic. His position that the α rays are homogeneous after Bragg's[3] work is very foolish. I think I can see clearly why he should not have got any difference at any rate on the outer edge of his image of the α ray beam. My opinion of B. does not increase with length of acquaintance. I think he feels it is about time I was discredited.

So much for the present. Yours ever,

E. RUTHERFORD

By the way Hahn tells me that Sackur[4] (a friend of his) wrote an abstract of our paper on the amt. of Ra in minerals in the Berichte.[5] Your letter to the Editor (which was sent to him) rather hurt Sackur, for Hahn says that it was an accident overlooked in the proof and that Sackur knows a good deal about radioactivity. I thought I would let you know this as an example of the smallness of the radioactive world & the way things are disseminated.

1. Actinium was believed to be inactive because of the difficulty in detecting its weak beta emission. This, and the problem of deciding whether thorium itself is active or merely contains an active constituent, are illustrative of the points that had to be settled in establishing the decay sequences.

2. H. Becquerel, "Sur quelques propriétés des rayons α du radium," *Comptes Rendus, 141* (11 Sept. 1905), 485–90. Henri Becquerel, the discoverer of radioactivity in 1896, was the most famous of four generations of eminent scientists. His grandfather, Antoine César Becquerel, for many years held the professorship of physics at the Museum of Natural History

in Paris, being succeeded by Henri's father, Alexandre Edmond Becquerel. In 1892, the chair passed to Henri who, in turn, was succeeded by his son, Jean Becquerel. Radiation, be it optical or invisible, seems to have been a family interest. Henri's early work was on phosphorescence and, indeed, it was his familiarity with this phenomenon and his possession of phosphorescing uranium crystals that led to his great discovery. Becquerel pursued his investigations of radioactivity in 1896 and early 1897, but then appears to have felt the subject exhausted, for he returned to earlier interests. It took the Curies' discovery of polonium and radium in 1898 to resurrect widespread enthusiasm in the "Becquerel rays," although one wonders whether Rutherford's use of these rays as an ionizing source (in a comparison with the effect of X rays) would have reopened the field anyway. Becquerel now resumed his study of radioactivity, but aside from the proof that beta rays have the same charge-to-mass ratio as J. J. Thomson's recently discovered electrons, he accomplished rather little. By this time the Curies were the acknowledged leaders of this science in France. The 1903 Nobel Prize in physics was shared by Becquerel and the Curies. For further information, see L. Badash, " 'Chance favors the prepared mind': Henri Becquerel and the discovery of radioactivity," *Arch. Intern. Hist. Sci.,* *18* (1965), 55–66; "Becquerel's 'unexposed' photographic plates," *Isis,* 57 (1966), 267–69; "Radioactivity before the Curies," *Am. J. Phys.,* *33* (1965), 128–35.

   3. William Henry Bragg was at this time professor of physics at the University of Adelaide. His measurements of the ranges of alpha rays soon made him an important figure in radioactivity and resulted in his removal to England. At Leeds, Bragg enjoyed frequent contact with Rutherford, who by then was at Manchester, but his interest shifted more and more to X rays. Basic work with his son, William Lawrence Bragg, on X ray diffraction brought the two the Nobel Prize in 1915, in which year the elder Bragg moved to the University of London. His distinguished career was capped with the directorship of the Royal Institution of London, a position which his son also held. It is of interest to note that prior to this post, W. L. Bragg had succeeded Rutherford first at Manchester and then at Cambridge.

   4. Otto Sackur was a talented physical chemist whose career ended suddenly, during wartime experiments on high explosives at the Kaiser Wilhelm Institute in Dahlem, near Berlin.

   5. Sackur's abstract of ER and BBB, "The relative proportion of radium and uranium in radio-active minerals," *Am. J. Sci., 20* (July 1905), 55–56, appeared in the *Chemisches Central-Blatt, 9:2* (16 Aug. 1905), 536–37. Boltwood's letter to the editor seems not to have been printed.

12 OCTOBER 1905

139 Orange Street
New Haven, Connecticut

My dear Rutherford,

I have just received your good letter of the 10th and I have been much interested in all that it contains. I am glad that you are going to put Hahn on that radio-lead matter, and I feel sure that you wont have any difficulty in settling any doubts still remaining in that direction. You should be able to get some Joachimsthal pitchblende from Eimer and Amend who had a considerable quantity on hand when I last called on them, and who were asking only one cent per gram for it. It is also possible that the Foote Mineral Co. (1317 Arch St. Philadelphia) may have some on hand now, although they didn't have any last winter. Then there is Williams, Brown and Earle (918 Chestnut St., Phila.), who were selling a fairly good grade of Colorado pitchblende for 35 cents an ounce. The best grade of uraninite on the market which I know of can be had from the Christiana Bergbureau (A. Guldberg), Universitetsgaden II B, Christiania, Norway. They list Broggerite (primary Norwegian uraninite) at 10 krone per 100 grams, which is a reasonable price for this material. I think that the best material for your purpose would probably be the Colorado uraninite, since it contains only about 0.7% of lead, and the active products would therefore be obtained initially in a more concentrated condition. I think that the chemical method of separating the inactive lead from the active constituents which promises best at the start is the electrolysis of a solution containing the lead as silicofluoride. This is used in technical work for the preparation of pure lead and is known as the Betts' process.

What you say about Hahn's new element is very interesting. I think that it is now up to him to separate it from the ordinary

93

thorium salts of commerce. I have been wondering myself as to where the credit due to Hahn was going to come in, since I saw Ramsay's article on "Le Radio-Thor" in the last number of the Jour. Chem. Phys.[1] The article is scarcely suggestive of collaboration.[2]

I noticed Becquerel's article on the alpha rays, etc., and was amused but not at all surprised at the subtle animus which pervaded it. I hope that when you go for him that you will give him such a shock that he will give out gamma pulses like an X-ray tube.

Speaking of going for people, I certainly did go for Sackur, when I read his stupid review of our joint paper. I am afraid that my letter to the editor of the Central-Blatt[3] sounded even worse than I had intended, but I followed the practice of the Germans themselves and when I got an opening I drove into it. The Germans have been so rotten at radio-activity themselves that I quite lost patience when they showed their inability to quote the work of others. The trouble with Sackur is that he is very careless. Gutmann told me that he prides himself on his ability to prepare a maximum number of reviews in a minimum time, and his work shows it. I think that when he has had time to think it over he won't feel so sore over my criticism.

I haven't been accomplishing very much recently. I have been feeling rather stale, the result I presume, of having plugged away all through the summer. I suppose that with decent success, I shall have a right to look forward to a vacation some time in the future. The fall weather is putting me on my feet and I expect to get real busy before long.

Thank you very much for the reprints which have afforded me an opportunity of going over your interesting papers at my leisure.

With kind regards, Sincerely yours,

BERTRAM B. BOLTWOOD

1. Ramsay, " Un nouvel élément, le radiothorium, dont l'émanation est identique à celle du thorium," *J. Chim. Phys.*, *3* (1905), 617–24. This is the

text of a report presented to the Congress of Radiology, Liège, in September 1905.

2. Boltwood exaggerates somewhat, for Ramsay gives credit to Hahn in the paper.

3. See note 5 to previous letter.

29 OCTOBER 1905

139 Orange Street
New Haven, Connecticut

My dear Rutherford,

I want to thank you most sincerely for the complimentary copy of the new edition of your book [1] which reached me last week. I am obtaining a great deal of pleasure in reading through it for it is certainly most valuable and satisfactory in every particular. I think that everyone interested in the subject is immensely indebted to you for having prepared such a splendid treatise.

It is perhaps unnecessary for me to tell you how proud it makes me to see my own humble contribution appear in such distinguished company. Very sincerely yours,

BERTRAM B. BOLTWOOD

1. ER, *Radio-Activity* (2d ed. Cambridge, University Press, 1905). Rutherford attempted to have this volume as much up to date as possible, including extensive discussions of work done in the past year. This edition, therefore, was almost 50 percent larger than the 1904 edition.

30 OCTOBER 1905

The Macdonald Physics Building
McGill University, Montreal

My dear Boltwood,

Just a line to ask you if you have received a copy of the second edition of my book, which I asked to be forwarded to you before

I left for New Zealand. In case you have not, I shall send you one of my own copies immediately. I am sorry that I omitted in the hurry of my departure to make mention of your name at the head of your article on Rad Minerals. You will find, however, a statement of the same in the preface.

I hope work is progressing satisfactorily. I am up to my neck in work of all kinds. Yours sincerely,

E. RUTHERFORD

6 NOVEMBER 1905

139 Orange Street
New Haven, Connecticut

My dear Rutherford,

I have just been trying to make some calculations and I have gotten myself into an awful muddle. Will you be so good as to help me out of it?

It is all the question as to the *most probable* value for the activity of pure elementary Radium in terms of Uranium. Now on page 14 of your book you state (line 21 from top) that the activity of "pure radium" is estimated by the Curies at about 1,000,000 times that of uranium. On page 458, in estimating the value of λ for uranium you take the activity of "pure radium" as two million times that of uranium. But the French dealers are advertising radium bromide of an activity 1,800,000 times uranium, and their price lists of preparations of a lower activity appear to be worked out on the assumption that the activity of pure radium bromide is about two million. If it is 1,800,000, then the activity of radium must be about 3,000,000. Please understand that the matter of the four alpha ray products is perfectly clear, but what is bothering me is the activity of the radium itself as distinct from the bromide.

Can you lead me out of darkness? Sincerely yours,

BERTRAM B. BOLTWOOD

12 NOVEMBER 1905

The Macdonald Physics Building
McGill University, Montreal

My dear Boltwood,

You are not the only one who is not certain of the activ[ity] of RaBr$_2$, for I have been doing a good deal of high thinking on the subject. I was intentionally vague in my book as to the value on account of the uncertainty attaching to it. The problem of relative activities viewed from the point of the experiments of Bragg is rather a difficult one. In a *thick* layer of RaBr$_2$ (a thin layer of powder is a thick layer from the point of view of the α rays) the α rays come from different depths. The actual activity (measured by the ionization) thus involves the density or rather weight per unit area of the matter being tested. Taking as the simplest (probably fairly accurate) assumption that the absorption of α rays is proportional to density, we see that the rays for example from radium C (which have a range of about 7 cms in air) just reach the surface from the bottom layer when the weight of RaBr$_2$ per unit area is $7 \times$ density of air $= 7 \times$ .0012 $=$ .0084 grams or 8.4 milligrams. The rays from the other products have ranges less than this but we may take the average range about 5 cms i e on an average the rays emerging from the bottom of a weight of RaBr$_2$ of 6 milligrams per sq c will just be able to ionize the gas at the surface. The actual ionization observed is thus due to rays of all ranges between o & 5 cms. as will be seen in curve.

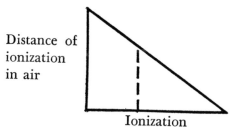

Distance of
ionization
in air

Ionization

The total ionization measured by an electroscope is proportional to the area of this triangle and this can be shown to be proportional to $\frac{1}{2}$ maximum range $\times$ total number of α particles which reach the surface. If therefore we replace RaBr$_2$ by pure Ra, the maximum range is the same but the total number of α particles which reach the surface comes from the same weight of Ra per unit area as of RaBr$_2$ & consequently the activity

$$\frac{\text{pure Ra}}{\text{RaBr}_2} = \frac{\text{At W. Ra}}{\text{Molec weight RaBr}_2} \cdot \frac{1}{}.$$

Taking the Curie's estimate of RaBr$_2$ as 1860000 the activity of pure Ra comes out about 3 million. I think this is the most probable value of the activity of Ra on existing data & fits in with our results of the quantity of Ra in Ur.

My reason, however, for entering into detail into this method of looking at the activity is that we require to determine whether one α particle comes from Ur for four α particles from Ra present with it. The ionization from a thick layer of Ur for the average α particle is proportional to (maxm. range in air).^{2} This you will readily see must be the case for the total number of α particles which escape with ionizing power into the gas is ::al. to depth from which they reach the surface which in turn is proportional to the range in air. We, therefore, see that in order to accurately compare theory with experiment, it is necessary to know the maximum range of the α particle from Ur & Ra. The latter is known but not the former; so that the range of Ur rays must be determined before we can compare theory & experiment. I hope to tackle that sometime but it is rather difficult on account of the weak ionization of Ur. There is also another result which follows from this point of view. The percentage of the activity of Ra at its minimum must depend on whether the Ra is in a *thin* or *thick* layer. It should be greater for a *thin* layer than for a *thick*. This point must be examined with great care as a 25 per cent minimum has always been assumed. One trouble will be that the Ra must always be cleared first of radium F the activity of which will amount to several per cent in radium a few years old.

I have been trying experiments on the relative activity of Ur & Ra by adding known quantities of Ra to uranium solutions, & testing in solution. The emanation is a source of trouble and the results are still incomplete but they appear to give an activity of Ra compared with Ur of about 6 millions—which I think is too high. The whole subject of comparison is a very difficult one and will take lots of work to clear it up thoroughly. Your experiment on solid mixture of Ur & Ra to reproduce uraninite should throw light on the question. Have you seen that Meyer and Schweidler [2] have got my products E & F out of radio-lead —so it fixes that point. The Lord has delivered Becquerel into my hands. My reply which I hope will appear in Jan Phil Mag [3] should make him tear his hair. Yours ever,

E. RUTHERFORD

Have you seen Nature on Baskerville's book. Rather uncomplimentary. The heading is very funny for a review of a book.[4]

1. The second half of this equation should be inverted. The atomic weight of bromine is 80 and that for radium is 226; the molecular weight of $RaBr_2$ is 386. If x is the activity of pure radium and 1,860,000 (times that of an equal quantity of uranium metal) is the activity of $RaBr_2$, then

$$\frac{x}{1{,}860{,}000} = \frac{386}{226}$$

or, x is slightly larger than 3 million.

2. Stefan Meyer and Egon von Schweidler were among the early, notable workers in radioactivity, jointly investigating the physical properties of the radiation. Both were *Privatdozenten* at the University of Vienna, Meyer in physics and Schweidler in physical chemistry, and both later became professors there. Meyer also was director of the famous Radium Institute in Vienna.

3. ER, "Some properties of the α rays from radium," *Phil. Mag.*, *11* (Jan. 1906), 166–76. In this paper Rutherford reinterpreted Becquerel's evidence, and added results from his own experiments, to show that the alpha rays are complex and not homogeneous as Becquerel had claimed.

4. The unsigned review appeared in *Nature*, *73* (2 Nov. 1905), 2, and the heading admired by Rutherford was "Induced radio-activity." The

criticism here is withering, for the book is called disappointing, the text little more than a collection of abstracts of papers, and Baskerville is faulted for presenting significant and insignificant material, and contradictory experiments, without indicating the importance or relative value of the work he cites.

18 November 1905

139 Orange Street
New Haven, Connecticut

My dear Rutherford,

I was very glad to get your interesting letter of the 12th, and I am greatly obliged to you for the detailed explanation of the relative activity of radium and uranium and related matters, which were in accord with, but much more conclusive than my own attempts to unravel the somewhat complicated tangle. As to the matter of the maximum range of the uranium particles, and the question as to whether any indications can be obtained by the method of Bragg and Kleeman [1] of more than one alpha ray change in uranium, I think that you will be glad to know that Wheeler and another man are just going at that problem and expect to have some results before very long.

The National Academy of Science held a meeting here last week and I was so fortunate as to be invited to deliver a paper at their meeting. The subject which I took was "the disintegration products of thorium as indicated by the proportions of lead and helium in minerals," and I feel sure that some of the data which I collected will be of interest to you.

Except where an exception is noted the values used are taken from Hillebrand's analyses. The Roman numerals refer to the specimens as numbered in my paper in the Oct. Am. Jour. Science. [2]

Assuming that Hillebrand's values for nitrogen when divided by 7 give a maximum value for helium,—and I am confident that in general for minerals containing considerable helium Hillebrand's numbers are more to be trusted than Ramsay's— and assuming that lead is a disintegration product of uranium and *not of thorium*—the latter assumption being borne out by the data which follows—it is possible to obtain a clew to the source of the helium. Thus for example in number V, where the indicated per cent of helium is 0.34%, if it is assumed that the helium was produced by the change Radium → Lead *only,* then the amount of helium present is in excess (really 126%) of the amount to be expected from this change only. If, however, the helium is produced by the change Uranium→Lead, then this sample of mineral really contained only 79% of the total helium formed in this manner, which is a reasonable number. It is to be expected that the proportion of the total helium formed which will be retained in the mineral will be dependent on the density of the mineral, and in the following table the minerals have been arranged in the order of their specific gravities and the percentages of their total helium (on the above assumption) which they contain are given in the second column.

No.	Sp. G.	% He	No.	Sp. G.	% He
V	9.62	79	XVI	8.93	11
VIII	9.35	63	XII	8.89	13
XIII	9.14	13	XIV	8.32	12
X	9.08	9	XIX	8.29	6
XV	8.96	11	IX	8.07	5 (Ramsay)

In the different samples the differences in initial composition must naturally have an effect on the density and the composition (proportion of rare earths, etc.) varies considerably. The above relations therefore seem to be in surprisingly good agreement with the assumption that helium is produced by the breaking down of uranium only. If the escape of helium is dependent on the porosity then with less helium in the mineral we should expect that more water will have obtained entrance

from without. The minerals are arranged in the following table
in the order of the helium content and the per cent of water
present is given in the second column.

No.	% He	% H_2O	No.	% He	% H_2O
V	79	0.43	XV	11	0.77
VIII	63	0.68	XVI	11	0.79
XII	13	0.74	X	9	1.21
XIII	13	0.73	XIX	6	1.48
XIV	12	0.74	IX	5	1.96

The value for the water in V, is not directly comparable with
the others since the water was determined by a different method
which would probably have allowed hydrogen to escape. The
three highest values for water are also uncertain since the mineral was superficially somewhat altered, probably into gummite
which contains much water. I think that these tables indicate,
however, that a slight increase in the density would probably result in the retention of *all of the helium* formed, but that the
impervious mineral would still contain hydrogen (water)! Also
that helium is not formed by the thorium which is present in
No. V to the extent of 10% ThO_2 and in No. XIX to the
amount of 6.7% ThO_2. The most convincing proof is, however,
furnished by thorianite, which according to Dunstan and Blake
contains 0.39% of helium. This number of theirs is incorrect, as
an inspection of their paper shows, for the amount of helium
given by 1 gram of the mineral is distinctly stated to be 10.1 cc.
They have apparently taken the density of helium as compared
with hydrogen as 4 and not as 2 (the correct value), which
makes their result just twice as great as it should be. The
amount of helium present is therefore only 0.19% when properly calculated. This is equal to only 50% of the helium formed
by the change Uranium→Lead as calculated from their analyses, so that this mineral (density not given) has really lost about
half of the helium which was produced within it. There is
therefore no indication whatever that the large proportion of

thorium in this mineral has in any way contributed to the production of the helium found in it, notwithstanding Ramsay's positive statements to the contrary.

If now, using your method of calculating the age of a mineral from the relative proportions of lead and uranium contained in it,[3] using the rate of disintegration of radium as determined by you as the basis of the calculation, the ages of the different minerals are calculated, we find that they are as follows:

Number	Locality	Age in millions of years.	
V	Glastonbury, Conn.	92	
III	" "	94	
I	" "	94	
II	" "	98	
IV	" "	98	
XX	Marietta, S.C.	107	
X	Flat Rock, N.C.	119	
VII	Branchville, Conn.	122	
VI	" "	126	
VIII	" "	126	
XIa	Flat Rock, N.C.	127	
XVI	Norway	296	
XII	"	300	
XV	"	314	
XIV	"	319	
Thorite from nearby		330	48% ThO$_2$ (analysis
XIII	Norway	337	by Lindstrom)
XXI	Canada	374	
XVIII	Arendal, Norway	383	
Thorite from	" " 50% ThO$_2$	320	Analysis by
XIX	Llano Co., Texas	390	Nordenskiold
Mackintoshite from	" " " 45% ThO$_2$	405	Analysis by
XVII	Arendal, Norway	402	Hillebrand
Thorianite, Ceylon		438	Analyses by
	" "	487	Dunstan
	" "	570	and Blake.

I think that these numbers afford a surprisingly good confirmation of the assumption that lead and helium are the disintegration products of uranium only. There is considerable difference in the calculated ages of the three samples of thorianite, but I am not surprised at this, for in my opinion these analyses of Dunstan and Blake are of a rather low order of excellence. Another point in support of the relative values of the ages of the different minerals is the fact that they are (according to my geological friends) not contradicted by the geological data available on the relative ages of the different deposits.

Now taking the average age of thorianite as 500 million years, it is evident that since thorium predominates so largely in this mineral we ought to be able to determine from its composition what elements have been formed by the disintegration of the thorium. If the analyses of Dunstan and Blake are to be relied on at all, it would appear from them that, if the rate of decay of thorium as estimated by you is of at all the right order of magnitude, the only constituents of the mineral which are present in sufficient amount to be disintegration products of thorium are the rare earths, cerium predominating. Now, the composition of thorianite itself does not exclude the suggestion of Strutt that uranium is a disintegration product of thorium, but a thorite containing 66% of ThO_2 which is found with the thorianite contains only 0.46% of UO_2, so that uranium is here excluded. This thorite according to theory should contain about 0.08% of lead, and this amount might easily have been present and have escaped notice. It is an impressive fact that cerium is the predominating rare earth in this thorite, as it is in a number of others of which analyses are given in "Dana."[4] If thorium breaks down into cerium, however, there is such a large difference in their atomic weights (92 units) that it would be expected that there would be some other substance formed also in considerable quantity. The difference (92) comes pretty close to the atomic weight of zirconium (90), and most of the analyses of Hillebrand indicate the presence of zirconium in the uraninites containing high proportions of thorium. It must be kept in mind that the analytical separation of thorium and zirconium offers very great difficulties, so that it is impossible to be sure from the published analyses that zirconium is not present in the theoretical proportions in the different minerals. The point is at all events well worth looking into, and I am going to make some analyses myself with this point in view, beginning with thorianite of which I now have a considerable quantity. It is also interesting that if it is assumed that thorium disintegrates according to the equation: $Th(232.5) = Ce(140) + Zr(90) + ?$ (2.5), that the amount of water shown by the analyses of the least hydrated minerals (V to XV in table on p. 2) is of about the right order of magnitude to warrant the assumption that the expelled alpha particle from the thorium family consists of hydrogen. You will see that a really good and reliable analysis of thorianite will throw some interesting light on this question also. I don't know how you will look on these speculations, but I feel sure that there is something at the bottom of them all, and they in any event are of great assistance to me in indicating *what* to look for and *where* to look for it.

You will probably be interested to hear that I have obtained some good indications of a separation of "radio-thorium" from ordinary thorium salts. My friend, Walden,[5] of the Scientific School is going to repeat my work with a larger quantity of material and we hope to have something definite before very long.

I am looking forward with much interest to the appearance of your paper in reply to Becquerel and I sincerely hope that you will clip his talons permanently. I think that his last paper in the Physikalische Zeitschrift [6] was not only in very bad taste but was quite uncalled for.

That review of Baskerville's book was certainly a "daisy." The title was certainly a little unusual but was very expressive.

With best regards, Sincerely yours,

BERTRAM B. BOLTWOOD

1. An Australian physicist who worked on alpha particle ranges with Bragg, Richard D. Kleeman, then spent the years 1905 to 1913 in Cambridge. After this he taught at Union College and worked at the General

Electric Company's research laboratory, both in Schenectady, New York.

2. BBB, "On the ultimate disintegration products of the radio-active elements," *Am. J. Sci., 20* (Oct. 1905), 253–67.

3. Rutherford and Boltwood were the pioneers in devising a means of radioactive dating. The idea apparently was Rutherford's, while Boltwood worked out the details and made the measurements. For information on this subject, see L. Badash, "Rutherford, Boltwood and the age of the earth: The origin of radioactive dating techniques," *Proc. Am. Phil. Soc., 112* (June 1968), 157–69.

4. The reference is to either James Dwight Dana's *System of Mineralogy* (1837) or his *Manual of Mineralogy* (1848), both of which have been revised many times and are still available. Dana, who became son-in-law to Benjamin Silliman, Yale's famous professor of chemistry in the first half of the nineteenth century, was himself professor of geology at Yale for many decades. Silliman had founded the *American Journal of Science,* which Dana later edited with Silliman's son. During the nineteenth century this was the most influential scientific periodical in America, though by the end of the century *Silliman's Journal,* as it was also called, was very largely restricted to papers in geology. While the journal was privately owned (it was given to Yale in this century), it nevertheless was something of an outlet for Yale science. Boltwood and others published in the *American Journal of Science* because it was convenient, their papers were more readily accepted by editors who knew them, and from a feeling of obligation to support the local product.

5. Percy T. Walden was typical of many American chemists of this period in that he spent a year in German universities absorbing scientific techniques and attitudes. His entire teaching career was devoted to the Sheffield Scientific School at Yale.

6. Becquerel, "Über einige Eigenschaften der α-Strahlen des Radiums," *Physik. Z., 6* (15 Oct. 1905), 666–69.

5 DECEMBER 1905

The Macdonald Physics Building
McGill University, Montreal

My dear Boltwood,
    I have been so busy over my Silliman Lectures that I have had little liberty for private correspondence. I find I have so

much to do of all kinds that I have cut research for the past fortnight.

You appear to have been diving deeply into the mysteries of
matter and certainly manage to obtain very plausible results.
The way the ages of the radioactive minerals work out is certainly striking and I am glad to find that a professional chemist
when properly infected is quite as rash in theorizing as a
physicist. I have been much amused at various articles the last
six months, notably in Engineering Journals, who hold up their
hands at the audacity of the imaginations of the workers in
radioactivity and sagely reflect how Newton would have sat
down and worked out the whole subject and then given a theory. It never occurs to them that it would have wanted half a
dozen Newtons to accomplish the experimental work in a lifetime and even these could not have put forward any more
plausible theory than we work on to-day. These dam'd fools—
whom I think must once have been chemists—(excuse me—no
personal reference) have'nt the faintest notion that the disintegration theory has as much evidence in support of it as the
Kinetic Theory of Gases and a jolly sight more than the electromagnetic theory which they all swallow as the eternal verities.
Apart from this miniature outburst, I quite agree with you that
the only way to get any idea of what are the products of the
radioelements is to examine carefully every available mineral. If
we don't find it that way, I think it is extremely improbable we
shall get any further at all. I feel *sure* helium is the α particle of
Ra & its products but it is going to be a terrible thing to prove
definitely the truth of this statement for I feel confident e/m
will come out to be 5×10^3 instead of 2.5×10^3. It may con-
ceivably be a hydrogen molecule—a half atom of helium or a
helium atom with two charges and nothing but a fine scientific
nose can say with certainty that one is more probable than the
others. My nose (which may be prejudiced) leads me to avoid
the H molecule like the devil. It is too plebeian in character to
be sired by such blue-blooded stock like radium whose ancestors

certainly existed before the flood. However for plebeian thorium, hydrogen seems to be very well fitted. I really see no valid reason why *all* the active bodies should emit Helium—actinium & radium certainly do—but H is the next most likely material to be thrown off. However, it will be mighty difficult to prove. Until you fix me with more evidence, I shall still cleave to Helium if only for Galileo's doctrine of simplicity.[1]

You remind me of Japhet in search of a father for you seem bent on finding a mother at any rate for the two waifs cerium and zirconium. Your proofs seem to me too convincing to be true but all things are possible if Thorium B busts up into two fragments of about equal weights. I have long thought such an effect must occur among some of the products and I feel confident actinium owes its origin to some product which has two distinct forms of equilibrium—the smaller percentage part yielding actinium. I thought I had a fair amount of scientific nerve but I am left far behind in your last essay. This search for a father is becoming positively indecent. Why not accept the Chemists' view of separate creation and rest happy.

I wish you luck in your research into thorianite. Now that the Silliman Lectures are on my mind & helium obstructs my vision, can you send me some lead-helium results for different minerals—half a dozen will do, so that I can discuss the question of lead-helium with some plausibility. I would be much obliged as I have'nt much time for sorting out a series of papers to get some unreliable data. The beauty about my Silliman Lectures will be the comparative age of the data at the time of its appearance. I find it a hard business rewriting after my second edition. I will be at the Physical Soc in New York on Dec 28. Will you & Bumstead be there. Yours ever,

E. RUTHERFORD

1. This doctrine of simplicity, often called Occam's razor, means merely that of two competing hypotheses the less complicated is preferable. This is extended to deny the likelihood that both hypotheses are valid.

10 DECEMBER 1905

139 Orange Street
New Haven, Connecticut

My dear Rutherford,

Your very interesting and amusing letter of the 5th afforded me much pleasure and entertainment, but really, you know, I do think that you are a bit hard on the chemists, whose chief fault is a defect in early education, and whose attitude toward recent advances in science has been vastly more liberal than anybody could have expected from their past behavior. And then too, there are some physicists who seem to be quite down to the chemical standard and I don't see any excuses to be offered in their case. Apropos to this, have you seen the review of Duncan's "New Knowledge" by your friend and colleague, the Hon. R.J., in a recent number of the "Speaker." [1] Well, I thought that Ramsay laid it on pretty thick, but Strutt has quite outdone him in praising that literary and scientific abomination. And Strutt is certainly no chemist!!

As to my attempts to trace the lineal decendents of thorium, my efforts may be misdirected but they are none the less earnest. I am beginning to believe that thorium may be the mother of that most abominable family of rare-earth elements, and if I can lay the crime at her door I shall make efforts to have her apprehended as an immoral person guilty of lascivious carriage. In point of respectability your radium family will be a Sunday school compared with the thorium children, whose (chemical) behavior is simply outrageous. It is absolutely demoralizing to have anything to do with them.

My work on the composition of thorianite has gone far enough to indicate that in a carefully selected sample containing 78.8% of ThO_2, the proportion of other rare earths is not much over 1%, thus confirming Dunstan and Blake's analysis No. III in this particular, which is hardly what I expected. These rare earths appear to consist almost wholly of Cerium (At. Wt. 140.2), Lanthanum (138.9), and Didymium (143.6 and 140.5), relative proportions as yet undetermined. I haven't as yet found any Zirconium. The significant fact about these figures is that they indicate that your calculated rate of disintegration for thorium is too high!! I am sure that some, if not all, of these substances are the thorium disintegration products, because they are the *only* constantly present constituents of thorium minerals. This same mineral contains approximately 0.9% of water, which supports the assumption that the thorium alpha particle is hydrogen. In order to make this fit with Hillebrand's analysis of Connecticut uraninites it is, however, necessary to assume that hydrogen is also produced in the uranium-lead series. My calculations, which are too complex to repeat here, suggest that in the uranium-lead series one H atom is produced for every 4 or 5 helium atoms. This, of course, on the assumption that the part played by actinium is insignificant.

I am mighty sorry that the value of e/m for the alpha particle from radium is going to come out improperly. I don't suppose that it will be possible for some time, at least, to determine this constant for the thorium alpha particle, but it would be mighty significant if this could be found to give 5×10^3 on the assumption that it was hydrogen. However I am sure that you will get it all straightened out before very long.

I have recently reopened the campaign on the radium-uranium ratio. One interesting point has been definitely cleared up. My original evaporated solutions of uraninite and uranium nitrate have been standing undisturbed in desiccators over sulphuric acid all summer, and I took advantage of some of the recent dry weather to compare their relative activities. I was surprised to find that while at the time of their preparation they

had not agreed among themselves they now agreed very respectably. For example, two solutions of 0.01 gram of uraninite each
when first evaporated gave 0.95 and 0.77 div. per min. respectively. They now give 1.51 and 1.54 div. per. min. (the sensitiveness of the electroscope when the first readings were made
and now is slightly different, but I have not bothered to reduce
them to the same scale, since the initial readings are obviously
of no absolute significance). A third sample of equal amount
prepared at the same time now gives 1.5 div. per min. Two similar samples from which the polonium (hydrogen sulphide
group, including radium-D and -E) had been removed, gave
originally 0.90 and 0.85, they now give 1.20 and 1.20. (The
filter paper with the separated precipitates (with H_2S) gave
0.91 and 1.26 originally). Two films of uranium nitrate equal
in quantity to the uranium in the above gave when first prepared, and for several weeks after, gave 0.33 and 0.38, they are
now equal to 0.37 and 0.37. I give these numbers in order to
show that the same sort of diffusion in the solids seems to take
place in these mixtures as was observed by Godlewski[2] in the
case of uranium salts and uranium-X. Also that the relative absorption of the rays is, as would be expected, very high in the
case of the polonium in the solid residue. I don't think that it
will be possible to make any headway with residues obtained by
evaporation.

I am going to tackle the question in a new way. I am going to
heat the mineral to a low red heat to drive off most of the
emanation, make films of this de-emanated material and measure them, and simultaneously determine the proportion of
emanation which is present. When the films have stood for 30
days, and during this interval, I shall measure their recovery of
activity, and at the end I shall determine the proportion of
emanation in a duplicate sample of material reserved for this
purpose. This ought to give a reliable basis for calculations.

I give below some lead-helium numbers:

Mineral.	Locality	Sp. G.	U%	Pb%	He%	
Uraninite	Glastonbury, Ct.	9.62	72	2.86	0.34	
"	" "	9.12	70	2.92	?	
"	Branchville, Ct.	9.35	74	4.04	0.38	
"	" "	9.73	74	4.04	?	
"	Elvestad, Nor.	9.14	66	9.35	0.18	
Thorite	Hitterö, Nor.	?	8.2	1.17	?	Lindström, Dana p. 488.
Uraninite	Arendal, Nor.	?	61	10.18	0.18	
Thorite	" "	4.38	8.9	1.55	?	Nordenskïold, Dana p. 488.
Uraninite	Llano Co. Tex.	8.29	55	9.37	0.08	
Mackintoshite	" " "	5.43	19.7	3.48	?	Dunstan and Blake average of 3.
Thorianite	Ceylon	?	11.2	2.38	0.19	
Thorianite	"	9.0	11.2	2.66	?	My own analysis.

Other than exceptions noted the analyses are by Hillebrand.

I presume that the above is what you want. If not let me know and I will do what I can for you.

In regard to the relative proportion of radium and uranium in minerals I want to tell you that I have discovered an error in my previous determination of this ratio. This error was due to the fact that in the determination of the percentage of uranium in the minerals, the uranium was separated and weighed as the phosphate. According to all the text-books this phosphate contains 68.55% of uranium. My own experiments have shown, however, that only 62.6% of uranium is present in this phosphate. The composition of the minerals given in my paper in the Phil. Mag.[3] is therefore uniformly too high with respect to uranium, and the uraninite which I sent you, which is the same as I used in the calculation of the uranium-radium ratio and the same as No. 1 in the table in Phil. Mag., contains 68.2% of uranium instead of 74.6%. This gives the relative proportion of uranium and radium in minerals as 1 uranium to 8.1×10^{-7} radium, which is essentially the same as the value which you gave in your last edition of "Radio-activity." This illustrates, if further illustration is necessary, the rotten uncertainty of much chemical analytical data.

Bumstead and I are both planning to attend the meeting of the Physical Society in New York and we are both delighted to hear that you are going to be there. Can't you arrange to spend Sunday and Monday following with me here in New Haven? Nichols [4] of Columbia and Mackenzie [5] are both going to be here stopping with the Bumsteads at that time, so we ought to be able to get up quite a jolly party. We should be awfully glad to see you.

With best regards, Sincerely yours,

BERTRAM B. BOLTWOOD

1. Strutt, review of Duncan's *The New Knowledge*, in *The Speaker, 13* (18 Nov. 1905), 162–63.

2. Tadeusz Godlewski, a Polish physicist, studied with Rutherford in 1904–05, then returned to Lemberg, where he eventually became professor in the Technische Hochschule.

3. BBB, "The origin of radium," *Phil. Mag., 9* (Apr. 1905), 599–613.

4. Ernest Fox Nichols, then at Columbia, had earlier been professor of physics at Colgate and Dartmouth. In 1909 he returned to Dartmouth as president of the college, but left in 1916 for a professorship at Yale. Still highly mobile, he soon accepted an industrial position, as head of the Nela Research Laboratories, and not long thereafter was appointed president of the Massachusetts Institute of Technology. Ill health, however, prevented his assuming his duties at M.I.T. and he remained at Nela.

5. Arthur S. Mackenzie, a Canadian, was professor of physics at Bryn Mawr until 1905, when he moved to Dalhousie. After five years, however, he returned to the United States for a professorship at Stevens Institute of Technology. Both Mackenzie and Nichols were with Bumstead at the Cavendish Laboratory.

UNDATED, BETWEEN 1905 AND 1907

The Macdonald Physics Building
McGill University, Montreal

Just a line to mention that the new standard was twice heated nearly to redness in a glass tube to get a supply of emanation.

How far does this affect your chemical conclusions from solubility[?]

I trust you have not too much difficulty in deciphering my writing. I am sorry for you.

ER

15 DECEMBER 1905

The Macdonald Physics Building
McGill University, Montreal

My dear Boltwood,

Just a line to thank you for the information you forwarded me. I shall be in New York Friday & Saturday and feel very tempted to accept your kind offer to visit Yale on Sunday & Monday.

As far as I know at present I shall be able to go, so I trust you will allow your invitation to remain a little unsettled till I write again. Yours sincerely,

E. RUTHERFORD

P.S. I think I will have an interesting pronouncement on e/m at the Meeting.

27 DECEMBER [1905]

The Macdonald Physics Building
McGill University, Montreal

My dear Boltwood,

I find I shall be able take advantage of your kind invitation to go down with you to Yale. I presume we shall get there Saturday evening and I shall leave Monday afternoon to connect with night train for Montreal. Bjerknes,[1] who is an old acquaintance of mine, is coming back with me to Montreal.

I am giving 2 papers at the Physic Society—one a petard for Becquerel [2] and the other e/m for RaC.

I am looking forward to seeing you all again. Yours ever,

E. RUTHERFORD

1. Wilhelm Bjerknes was professor at the University of Christiana (now University of Oslo), then director of the Geophysical Institute in Leipzig.

2. This paper, bearing the same title, was no doubt similar to Rutherford's reply to Becquerel in the *Phil. Mag., 11* (Jan. 1906), 66–76. For an abstract of this paper, presented at the American Physical Society meeting, see ER, "Some properties of the α rays from radium," *Phys. Rev., 22* (Feb. 1906), 123–25.

28 JANUARY 1906

The Macdonald Physics Building
McGill University, Montreal

My dear Boltwood,

I have been intending to write you for some time but have been very busy. I had a very good time at Yale and must thank you again for your kindness in looking after me. I expect you know that I have definitely refused the Yale offer. I hope Bumstead will be successful in pulling it off.

I am enclosing a letter from Eve [1] in regard to radium standards. There is undoubtedly something wrong somewhere and it appears to me likely your radium standard solution is playing up like mine. There is no doubt the radium precipitates in the glass in the course of time. Your value of the amount of emanation in Eve's sample appears to me too high by comparison of α ray activities. Let me know whether your emanation standard is at fault. If there is any doubt about it, we will have to make up a new one to send you to see if the *value* found with the bottle I sent you for the amount of Ra in Uranium is correct. The bottle was alright originally but did any precipitation occur in the short time before you got it from me? This behaviour of radium is a nuisance and complicates matters considerably.

I am hard at work on e/m in my spare time. I have practically finished radium A, C and F and thorium B, all about e/m = 5×10^3. I am convinced the α particle is a helium atom with *two* charges. It is interesting that the α particle from thorium is the same as from radium. Between *ourselves,* Hahn has found by Bragg's method [2] another product in thorium B, very well marked but has not yet had time to separate it. The consecutive nature of radium A and B is now fixed. B, as Schmidt [3] recently showed, gives out some easily absorbed β rays which has previously thrown out the comparison of theory with experiment. You will have seen my Phil Mag paper—very mild but I think crushing.[4] Bragg's communication, soon to appear in the Phys Zeit, is another indictment.[5] You will have seen McCoy's paper in the Phil Mag [6]—pretty good of its kind.

The Silliman Lectures keep me very busy. By the way, can you send me 10 to 20 cc (or more) of decently pure helium. I want to try an experiment or two with it. With remembrances to Mrs. Boltwood.[7] Yours ever,

E. RUTHERFORD

1. When asked what was his greatest scientific discovery at McGill, Rutherford is reported to have said "Arthur S. Eve." This high compliment was directed at a man who was Rutherford's elder by almost ten years, but his student in radioactivity. Eve had been graduated from Cambridge University with distinction in mathematics and physics, and then taught for a number of years in a secondary school, before beginning his work in experimental physics at the age of 42. He soon established a reputation for the accuracy of his radiation investigations, particularly in connection with atmospheric electricity. His later work in geophysics was equally distinctive and well known. After Rutherford's transfer to Manchester and the retirement of McGill's other physics professor (and department chairman John Cox), Eve was named professor. In the reorganization that seemed to affect every university after World War I, Eve

became director of the laboratory. A reserve army officer, he was the only Highland colonel in the British navy during that war. (The Senior Service wanted his scientific abilities in submarine detection research, but would offer him only a lieutenancy, a rank whose pay was insufficient to support his family.) A few years before his retirement in 1935, Eve was considered for the part of Theodore Roosevelt, whom he strongly resembled, in a Hollywood movie. However, writing, not acting, was to occupy his later years, for he was the author of the biography Lady Rutherford asked him to prepare after her husband's death.

2. The method of Bragg and Kleeman was to measure the ionization of a sample as a function of distance from the sample. Since each alpha ray has a definite range and is most intensely ionizing near the end of that range, the ray from each emitter in the sample will plot as a distinctive peak.

3. Heinrich Willy Schmidt received his Ph.D. degree in 1901 from Göttingen, taught there briefly, and then spent the remainder of his career at Giessen. He visited Rutherford's Manchester laboratory for a few months, as is mentioned in these letters. Schmidt's paper, referred to by Rutherford, is "Über den Zerfall von Radium A, B und C," *Physik. Z, 6* (15 Dec. 1905), 897–903.

4. This remark refers to Rutherford's attack on Becquerel.

5. Bragg, "Die α-Strahlen des Radiums," *Physik. Z.,* 7 (1 Mar. 1906), 143–46.

6. H. N. McCoy, "The relation between the radioactivity and the composition of uranium compounds," *Phil. Mag., 11* (Jan. 1906), 176–86.

7. Boltwood was a lifelong bachelor and the reference is to his mother who lived with him. Rutherford met her on his recent visit to New Haven, when he was Boltwood's guest.

1 FEBRUARY 1906

139 Orange Street
New Haven, Connecticut

My dear Rutherford,

I have been hoping to write you "tomorrow" for the last three weeks, that is, I have been waiting to write until I had some final results, and it has looked every day as if the next day would bring them. As it is there are still some points to be looked into before reaching final conclusions, but the receipt of your letter of the 28th with the enclosed letter from Eve has encouraged me to at least give you some idea of how things are going.

First as to Eve's difficulty. The bottle of radium bromide solution which you brought down to me appeared to be all right at the time that I removed the sample from it. The solution was clear and there was no indication of any sediment in the bottom. I took out a weighed portion, diluted this with distilled water, *added a little hydrochloric acid,* and sealed it up after having first boiled off all emanation. The emanation was boiled out after a couple of days and tested, and the maximum value calculated. The bulb was then sealed up and allowed to stand for two months, when the emanation was then again removed and tested. The maximum value thus directly determined was a trifle larger than the one first calculated, but agreed with it well within the limits of error. It is therefore evident that the solution did not alter appreciably in two months. After having once been compared accurately with the natural mineral (N.C. Uraninite), the mineral and not the solution was afterwards used for purposes of standardization. Eve's uraninite was therefore not compared with the standard solution but with the standard mineral, so that any alteration which the solution has undergone has no effect on the present results. I believe that the whole trouble with your solutions could have been avoided if the solutions had been made slightly acid at the start. They probably were not, and so the water has attacked the glass, the solution has become alkaline, and the silica and other things have precipitated the radium.

Now as to his (Eve's) alpha-ray measurements. In the first place, the N.C. Uraninite which I sent you does not contain 74% of Uranium but only 68.2% Uranium. I wrote you this fact in a letter of Dec. 10th, but you have probably overlooked it. Now my chemical nose would tell me in two minutes that

Eve's uraninite contained over 40% of uranium from just smell-
ing of it, so that I am perfectly positive that 27% is quite out of
the question. If I thought that there was the slightest doubt
about it I would gladly make a chemical analysis of the material, but there isn't. I have been working with a 56% uranium
pitchblende from the same locality (Joachimsthal), identical in
its general appearance, and *its* alpha-ray activity corresponds exactly to its content of uranium as determined by the emanation
method. So there is something wrong at the Montreal end of the
telephone. I shall be very glad, however, to do anything in my
power to clear up the trouble, wherever it lies. If Eve cares to
send on any further samples I shall be pleased to test them.

Now a word as to my own troubles. I think that I have got
the matter of the relative proportions of the different radioactive constituents in minerals pretty nearly cleared up. It isn't
quite finished yet, there are a number of sharp corners still to
be rounded off. But I can see the end and it doesn't look to be
very far away. It is about like this. In the first place the activity
of old radium (Ra + Ra Em + Ra A + Ra C), is just what
it should be according to Bragg and Kleeman's numbers, namely
5.6 times that of radium (Ra) itself. This has been proved by
direct experiments with radium salts. A very thin film of radium chloride kept in a desiccating atmosphere over sulphuric
acid retains only about 70% of its emanation. In the second
place the activity of a uranium mineral free from thorium (the
maximum activity) is equal to about 5.5 times that of the uranium contained within it. In the third place the ratio U +
Ra + Ra · Em + Ra · A + Ra · C + Ra · F + x : U + Ra +
Ra · F + x is just about 1.73. The value of the separate factors
determined in the above is Ra = 0.52 U; (Ra · Em + Ra · A +
Ra · C) = 2.42 U; Ra · F = 0.42 U; and X (4% ThO_2 + Ac) =
1.18 U (by difference). I find that the range of the alpha particles from polonium is sufficiently less than those from radium
(Ra) to account for the difference between 0.52 and 0.42, while
the relative ranges of radium (Ra) and uranium suggest two

changes in uranium rather than three. As to the question of the changes and ranges in uranium, let me say that Wheeler is still piddling along on that research and is (except in complexity of apparatus) no further along than he was when you last saw him. I am afraid that his uranium will all disintegrate before he gets his measurements completed.

What I now want to clear up is the question as to actinium. This value for x, *i.e.* 1.18 is too near to about 3 times 0.40 to be convincing. Deducting the 4% of thorium leaves it 1.16 U, and if actinium were a weaker ionizer than polonium it might still be in the uranium-radium series. As a matter of fact my measurements indicate that actinium is a more efficient ionizer, has alpha particles of longer range than polonium or uranium. But I am going to separate the stuff from a known weight of mineral and determine by direct measurement just what proportion it contributes to the total alpha-ray effect. This is what I have to still do before I can feel that I am ready for publication.

A very interesting point has come up in the course of this investigation. I find that in minerals containing thorium, the activity increases by a certain constant amount for each per cent of thorium present. That is, the activity of the thorium in the different minerals is constant and depends only on the amount present. But the activity of thorium from certain commercial thorium salts is sometimes as much as one-half less than the activity of the thorium in the minerals. I have some thorium salts however which I have prepared myself and which are of a high degree of chemical purity, the thorium in which is just as active as the thorium in the minerals. I am absolutely certain of all this because Dadourian [1] working with the emanation and excited activity from solutions of these salts and minerals comes to exactly similar conclusions. There is a lot to be done on this yet, but I am leaving it for the present until I can finish up the other matter. It is evident that certain chemical treatment separates at least half of the radio-thorium, but it is also clear that the radio-thorium is a product of ordinary chemical thorium.

The activity of the thorium in the minerals is about the same as that of the uranium.

I am much interested in what you tell me about the value of e/m for the alpha-particle from Th-B. I am absolutely convinced from the mineralogical data, however, that thorium certainly doesn't produce helium. There is something mysterious about that half-helium business; perhaps we have some sort of new matter to deal with, primordial matter with a predisposition to form hydrogen or helium. It is all getting terribly complicated in its very simplicity.

I can't say that I was disappointed to learn that you had refused the Yale offer. I didn't feel that there was any chance of their being able to get you, so that I expected that you would decline the proposition. I am, however, mighty sorry that you are not going to be here. Bumstead will get the position without any doubt, and owing to your own good offices in the matter I have learned unofficially that they are going to find a small position for me in the department. It will be a big relief to me to get my boat tied up to a wharf somewhere. I am immensely indebted to you.

I should like to make this letter longer and to go into details somewhat, but it is almost midnight and I must take the last car or foot it. With regards and best wishes, Very sincerely yours,

BERTRAM B. BOLTWOOD

P.S. Will send the helium just as soon as I have a chance to separate it.

1. Haroutune M. Dadourian entered the Sheffield Scientific School in 1900, immediately upon his arrival in the United States. Within three years he received a bachelor's degree in electrical engineering, and in another three a Ph.D. in physics. Between 1906 and 1917 he taught physics at Yale. World War I and the Turkish massacre of his Armenian people changed his intention of returning to his homeland. He therefore accepted a professorship at Trinity College, Hartford, Connecticut, where he remained the rest of his career.

16 FEBRUARY 1906

McGill University, Montreal

My dear Boltwood,

Just a line to congratulate you on being fixed up to a good anchorage and I trust you will continue to unload as many good things as in the past. I think both Bumstead and you owe a debt of gratitude to Dana [1]—who is a very sensible man. I have the surest evidence of it as he agrees with me in all particulars except one and that is now comfortably buried!

I have'nt time to discuss your last long letter but am glad you are pushing it to a conclusion. You are quite right about actinium rays being far more penetrating than uranium rays. If you ask Bumstead, he will tell you of an extraordinary effect I have got hold of. I have'nt [time] to describe it to you just now as I am too rushed for time. Let me hear from you soon. Yours ever,

E. RUTHERFORD

1. Not James Dwight Dana, who died in 1895, but his son, Edward S. Dana, who was professor of physics at Yale from 1890, as well as editor of the *American Journal of Science*.

28 FEBRUARY 1906

The Macdonald Physics Building
McGill University, Montreal

My dear Boltwood,

You will remember that I told you I thought I had got hold of a tangential expulsion of α rays but I find this is not so in reality although the results appear to indicate it. I got onto this effect as follows. If I take a photograph with the α rays (mag deflex. apptus) with a *narrow* slit, each band has a white line down the centre thus:═══very well defined & beautifully clear. This is shown with or without a magnetic field. This appears to indicate that the edges of the active wire supply most of the α particles. As a matter of fact, the ordinary light effect is exactly opposite. The line is darkest in centre & penumbra at the sides. This effect can, however, be explained on the natural supposition that the α particles are expelled equally in all directions. In light, there is the cosine or Lamberts' law of distribution in which the intensity varies as the cosine of angle with normal. An *active* plate coated with radium C gives a strong intensity of rays ‖ to its surface while the corresponding light disc does not. I will illustrate this with a photograph or two I have taken. Suppose one takes a square rod whose surface is equally coated with radium C on all four sides. Place a photog plate just above one of the sides ‖ to it. On developing the plate shows as below.

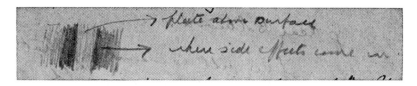

The centre weak effect is of exactly width of rectangle. The effect is illustrated still better below where the square rod 2 cms high is placed vertically, sitting on the plate thus. [*See next page.*] You see the white square centre marking size of square. The dark cross exactly opposite the sides is the place of weakest photog effect. Where the sides supply radiation effects are stronger. This is exactly opposite to light. I enclose also photog of hexagonal rod got in same way. You will see natural size of hexagon well defined & the six armed cross and six little equilateral triangles. All these can be qualitatively & quantit[a-

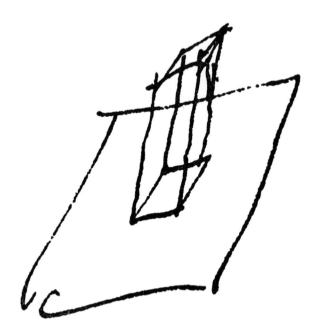

tively] explained on the assumption α particles are thrown out equally in all directions. It looks as if the tangent planes provide most but this is not so. This fooled me at first.

Please show these to Bumstead. He will appreciate what they mean at once.

By the way, if you can let me have that *helium,* I would be much obliged—the sooner the better when you can find time. Yours ever,

E. RUTHERFORD

Eve is going to send you down a new radium standard directly. He *considers* your standard is *wrong.* The matter must be cleared up at once or it may cause trouble.

7 MARCH 1906

139 Orange Street
New Haven, Connecticut

My dear Rutherford,

Thank you ever so much for your very kind letter of congratulation and good wishes and also for the very interesting letter with the photographs of the curious effects obtained with the radiation from the active deposit from radium.

I hope that you have not given up all hope of ever receiving the helium that you wanted, but I have been very busy indeed for the last few weeks, and the days have slipped by in spite of my best efforts to hold on to them. As I told you last vacation, I had expected to carry out some experiments involving the separation of helium from thorianite, but other things have kept me so busy that I have not got round to it yet. So as I knew that you must be in some hurry, I have specially worked up 20 grams of the mineral for the helium and am sending you by this mail a package containing two tubes of gas, one marked "pure" containing about 100 cu. cm. of the gas from the mineral, under slightly *less* than atmospheric pressure, and one marked "impure" containing about 100 cc mixed with some air and sealed up at about atmospheric pressure. Both of the samples of gas contain acid fumes and moisture, and even the "pure" one probably contains slight traces of air. Since you have liquid air on tap you can entirely purify the helium by Dewar's charcoal method, if you need absolutely pure material.

I shall be interested to hear whether the tubes reach you in good condition. Very sincerely yours,

BERTRAM B. BOLTWOOD

11 MARCH 1906

The Macdonald Physics Building
McGill University, Montreal

My dear Boltwood,

Just a line to let you know I received the helium safely. I am much obliged for your kindness over the matter and hope I did not give you too much trouble. I am intending trying a number of experiments with it preliminary to going in for some gas work. Things are going on fairly satisfactorily here—nothing particularly novel. Hahn & Levin are both indefatigable workers. The former has worked out the Bragg curves for thorium and actinium and incidentally has found some interesting points. I have not a great deal of time for research myself just now. I go down to Philadelphia to speak [?] on Franklin on the occasion of his bicentennial.

Please remember me to Mrs. Boltwood. Yours ever,

E. RUTHERFORD

I hope your work is coming out alright.

1 APRIL 1906

139 Orange Street
New Haven, Connecticut

My dear Rutherford,

Eve's letter of March 21 reached me on Friday the 23rd and the sample of radium bromide arrived here on the 26th. Preparations were immediately begun for making up the standard solutions of radium. In the first place I took a very small beaker containing about 5 cc of distilled water, placed this on a piece of black paper, and dropped the fragment of radium bromide into it. The bromide began to dissolve immediately with the copious evolution of minute gas bubbles. This action ceased shortly, leaving a considerable portion of the original material, which might easily have been one-third of the original amount, *which refused to enter into solution* even when the liquid was heated almost to the point of boiling. On adding a small amount (one or two cc) of strong hydrochloric acid, this insoluble residue immediately passed into solution with the evolution of further gas bubbles. After further heating the liquid was examined with a glass and no trace of undissolved solids could be detected even after the most careful scrutiny. The little vial in which the radium had been sent was washed out with concentrated hydrochloric acid and with water, and these washings were added to the original solution. The radium solution was then introduced into a graduated flask and diluted with freshly distilled water to exactly 1000 cubic centimeters, after which the solution was mixed very thoroughly. Of this first solution, exactly 10 cc were transferred by a standard pipette to a second graduated flask, a couple of cc of hydrochloric acid were added, and the whole was diluted to 1000 cc and mixed thoroughly.

Of the second and more dilute solution exactly 10 cc were transferred to a small glass bulb, diluted somewhat with distilled water, and boiled for about 20 minutes to remove the emanation present. The solution was then sealed up, the bulb was allowed to stand for exactly four days, and the emanation which had accumulated was then boiled out, introduced into the electroscope and its activity measured. The leak observed at the end of three hours was 4.27 div. per min., corresponding to a leak of 8.44 div. per min. for the equilibrium quantity of emanation from the radium present. The leak corresponding to the equilibrium quantity of emanation from the radium associated [with] one gram of uranium in a mineral is 206 divisions per minute. Assuming that the original salt was pure radium bromide (0.27 mg), the amount of radium bromide in the solution from which the emanation was measured should have been 2.7×10^{-5} mg, and the amount of radium 1.57×10^{-5} mg. These data indicate that the weight of radium in equilibrium with one gram of Uranium is 3.83×10^{-7} gram of Radium.[1]

Now as to the significance of the above. In the first place it is obvious that the original material could not have been pure bromide, since it was not soluble in water. Giesel (Berlin Berichte, 3608, 1902) and others have called attention to the fact that radium bromide on standing gives off bromine, becomes alkaline and absorbs carbon dioxide from the air to form carbonate. The fact that that portion of the salt which was not dissolved by water went into solution with the evolution of gas on adding acid is strong evidence that the original material contained notable quantities of carbonate. Moreover, solutions prepared as Eve's were made up, without the addition of acid, would be sure to give fictitious values for the strength of any portion of them in radium, aside from the further precipitation of radium from them on standing which Eve has already noted.

It is interesting that the factor obtained by the use of this new standard gives a very good agreement for the amount of radium in Eve's uraninite as determined by him by the gamma ray method. He finds 0.32 mg of radium per kilo, while the present standard gives 0.31 mg.

The present standard throws out all my calculations as to the ages of minerals, since the ages as originally calculated are over 100% out. The oldest mineral, thorianite, will now have an estimated age of over 1000 million years. It also gives a very astonishing activity for radium bromide, namely about 4,400,000 times uranium. It really mixes up a lot of things in an entirely unexpected manner.

I hope that I may hear from you soon as to your opinions in the matter.

With kind regards, Sincerely yours,

BERTRAM B. BOLTWOOD

1. Boltwood and Rutherford had earlier given a value of 7.4×10^{-7} gram of radium in equilibrium with one gram of uranium: *Am. J. Sci., 20* (July 1905), 55–56.

3 APRIL 1906

The Macdonald Physics Building
McGill University, Montreal

My dear Boltwood,

I am glad to hear the "war of the standards" is now over but I am sorry that I have been indirectly at fault in the mistake that has arisen. There is no doubt that the time I found out your solution, half of the radium was calmly sticking like a brother to the glass. However, the only way to do is to make the correction required as promptly as possible. The best method I think is for Eve to publish an account of his experiments on γ rays and the standards in the Amer Journal and for ourselves to supply another in the same number putting things right. This allows Eve a free hand to record his experiments & we can at the same time refer to his paper for further details of how the error was unmasked. Eve has prepared a rough draft of his proposed paper, which I forward you to give an idea of its scope. It has, however, still to be knocked into shape as you will see.

I feel very grateful to Eve for clearing up this error as promptly as possible. I do not think that the actual change of the number will have much effect, as in the case of your ages of minerals, they depend also on the life of radium which is a devilishly uncertain question. By the way, you have probably recognized that Eve is a true John Bull in regard to the tenacity with which he hangs on to his ideas. He is really a fine fellow & I know none better. I think your amusing remark that you could tell by the smell of the pitchblende that more uranium was present than he calculated stirred him up to assert himself and I have not been lacking in amusing jeers at the quandary of the standards.

All's well that ends well. I have hastily written out a sort of draft of the type of paper we should write. I should be glad of your views of the question & would also be glad if you would take the paper in hand & put it into shape. My draft is rather long & can be cut up I think with advantage. Let me hear your views as promptly as possible. Yours ever,

E. RUTHERFORD

I am worked to death as exam papers and the Franklin paper hang over my devoted head. Send back Eve's paper as soon as you are through with it.

8 APRIL 1906

139 Orange Street
New Haven, Connecticut

My dear Rutherford,

Your letter of the 3d reached me in due time, but the drafts of the two papers suffered the usual delay of third class matter and did not arrive until yesterday morning.

I heartily approve of the plan for publishing a joint paper to correct our earlier inaccuracies, and also of Eve's paper, which I now enclose herewith. In the latter I have taken the liberty of crossing out a reference to the calculation of the ages of minerals since no data on this has as yet been published.

I have recently received some samples of uraninites from

Hillebrand which have been analyzed by him. I am comparing these with my own standards in order to detect any lack of agreement resulting from our different methods of analysis. I want to have that ratio of radium to uranium as near right as it is possible to get it before publishing any more numbers.

By the way of a suggestion, I would advise you to add a little hydrobromic acid to all solutions of radium bromide that you make up in the future. I refer particularly to such cases as those where you want to get the radium bromide back by evaporating the solution. Also in the cases of those solutions which you mentioned, where the radium has become stuck in the bottle, I think that by the addition of a little hydrobromic acid and by allowing the solution to stand some time you will be able to get most of the radium to dissolve again.

I will get our joint paper into shape as soon as possible and send it on to you for approval.

With best wishes, Sincerely yours,

BERTRAM B. BOLTWOOD

16 APRIL 1906

The Macdonald Physics Building
McGill University, Montreal

My dear Boltwood,

Just a line to let you know that my two Germans Hahn and Levin are anxious to meet you all in the flesh (I have warned them there are six feet five of you) and are intending to pay a flying visit to New Haven on Friday of this week. They leave here at night, change at Springfield, and are scheduled to arrive at 10 am Friday morning at N.H.

You will find them both good fellows and any thing you can do to give them a good time is the same as if you had done it for me. Hahn, poor fellow, is not quite himself as he only heard a week or so ago of the sudden death of his mother. For my sake, avoid the topic of Ramsay as if he were the devil himself—not to mention Hahn's friend Sackur. Hahn is naturally a Ramsay-ite though possibly not à la Jones.[1]

I am off to Philadelphia tonight to pile homage on the great Benjamin and in passing to pass through the ordeal of a lecture and an LLD thrown in for my trouble.[2]

I have given Hahn the address of Bumstead at the Sheff—but if you were not too busy I thought you might be on hand when they turn up.

With kind regards to Mrs. Boltwood. Yours ever,

E. RUTHERFORD

P.S. They want to meet Dadourian & Wheeler and would like to have a look over the Univ a little. Also show them Marsh's horses' toes! [3]

1. Harry C. Jones was professor of physical chemistry at Johns Hopkins University. His book, *The Electrical Nature of Matter and Radioactivity* (New York, Van Nostrand, 1906), was generally favorable to Ramsay.

2. In Philadelphia Rutherford spoke at the Franklin Institute's bicentennial celebration of Franklin's birth. His talk was entitled "Modern theories of electricity and their relation to the Franklinian theory." The honorary LL.D. degree, awarded by the University of Pennsylvania, was his first, though it was soon followed by a similar presentation from the University of Wisconsin, and later by several others. While Rutherford always was conscious of his worth, he seems to have been rather amused that universities would wish to honor a young man in such fashion. To him, honorary degrees were the perquisites of the aged.

3. Othniel C. Marsh, professor of paleontology at Yale in the mid-nineteenth century, had found fossil ancestors of the modern horse with three and four toes, proving that the horse was indigenous to America. These fossils are on exhibit in Yale's Peabody Museum of Natural History.

21 APRIL 1906

139 Orange Street
New Haven, Connecticut

My dear Rutherford,

Your letter of the 16th was duly received and I was somewhat surprised, not to say astonished, at your warning about mentioning Ramsay to your Dr. Hahn. I had supposed that Hahn had come over to you for information and enlightenment, and from what you said I feared that you had neglected your first duty and had left him groping in darkness. But I took the advice in good grace and prepared to make you reap the whirlwind of your iniquity and to heap coals of fire on your head by taking advantage of any opportunity offered to laud and praise "the first chemist of Great Britain" until even Jones himself would have his belly full of it. But all my well laid plans went astray and the best I could do was to feebly defend Ramsay against Hahn's frequent criticisms. "Great oaks from little acorns grow" and you must have dropped some of those little seeds quite unconsciously into Hahn's gardenpatch. At all events he is not the Ramsayite that you appear to believe and in all our conversation touching on the great master I was the only champion who spoke up for him. I hope that I did my duty.

We all enjoyed the visit of Hahn and Levin very much and found them every bit as attractive as you have described them. We gave them as good a time as we could in the short time at our disposal and would have liked to have had them stay longer. I was sorry not to meet them on their arrival, but your statement that they would get here at 10 o'clock while of the right order of magnitude was just enough out to make me miss them at the station.

I am enclosing the draft of our proposed paper on uranium-radium. When you have fixed it up to your satisfaction you can send it back to me and I will turn it over to Dana.

I hope that you had a pleasant time at Philadelphia.

With best regards, Sincerely yours,

BERTRAM B. BOLTWOOD

28 APRIL 1906

The Macdonald Physics Building
McGill University, Montreal

My dear Boltwood,

I am sending today Eve's paper [1] and your own [2] for publication in the Amer Journ. I shall be glad if you can arrange with Dana for them to appear together in the same number. I got Eve to alter his paper a little so as to bring out the new point in his paper and not to unduly emphasise the standard's part.

Hahn & Levin are obviously very pleased at the way you all looked after them in New Haven. You really surprise me about Hahn. I gathered his belief in Ramsay was of largely "bread & butter" origin but I always avoided the subject of Ramsay's greatness. It must have been amusing to hear you defending Ramsay—I am sorry I was'nt there.

I had a thundering good time in Philadelphia but am now reaping the aftermath—a bad cold & general upset of my system. I am off tomorrow for a week in the Univ. of Illinois which apart from a few lectures will be rather a holiday for me.[3] I am rather interested to see these places & see what they are doing.

I was down at Washington to the Phys. Soc. but was dead tired all day. The dinner in the evening to Lorentz passed off very well but the physicists were largely from the Bureau of Standards.

I am feeling off work for a bit as I have to spend such a time in putting papers in order & writing books.

I have come to the conclusion that I ought to be allowed to

do nothing I don't like for a few months but I find I have a number of papers to write up before long. When are you publishing your account of the Ur Ra Act paper & the results of your analysis?[4] With kind regards to all the happy family. Yours ever,

E. RUTHERFORD

1. A. S. Eve, "The measurement of radium in minerals by the γ-radiation," *Am. J. Sci.*, 22 (July 1906), 4–7.

2. ER and BBB, "The relative proportion of radium and uranium in radio-active minerals," *Am. J. Sci.*, 22 (July 1906), 1–3.

3. Though not an especially polished lecturer, Rutherford's complete command of his subject and great enthusiasm left his listeners well satisfied. He was in great demand as a speaker and accepted so many invitations that Sir Oliver Lodge was prompted to write: "I trust you will not waste your time in lecturing but will go on with your experiments and leave lecturing to others" (4 Jan. 1904, RCC).

4. Rutherford probably was referring to a paper Boltwood read on 24 Feb. 1906, at the American Physical Society meeting at Columbia University. Only an abstract appeared: "On the relative proportion of the total α-ray activity of radioactive minerals due to the separate radioactive constituents," *Phys. Rev.*, 22 (May 1906), 320. Note that Boltwood, a chemist, may properly also be considered a physicist. Since radioactivity was a hybrid science, having connections to both disciplines, Boltwood was a member of the A.P.S., and served in a physics department, first as an assistant professor and then as professor of radiochemistry.

9 MAY 1906

The Macdonald Physics Building
McGill University, Montreal

My dear Boltwood,

I return herewith proof of our paper which seems alright. Please forward to publishers. I asked Eve to forward his proof at once to save time.

I recd. a paper from Bragg who has been mathematically investigating effect of screens in cutting down total ionization of thick & thin layers of active material. He find that the rays from Ur, Th & Ra have *nearly* the same penetrating power i e they have a range about 3.5 cms. Hahn finds 3.9 cms for radiothorium which shows he is not far out. He calculates that Th breaks up .19 rate of Ur. This work of Bragg does not quite fall in with Wheeler's for I think he could not have failed to observe the effect of a product of Ur of range as great as 4.5 cms. Let Wheeler know of Braggs' result. Bragg of course does not apply his first method to the problem, and Wheeler's arrangement ought to give the best result.

By the way, what is your final ratio of the ionization in a thick or thin layer of Ur to Ra (by itself).

I feel confident Ur emits 3 α particles but it seems devilish difficult to prove it. I saw the abstract of your paper in the Phys Rev. When are you going to publish it? Let me know how your final results stand.

I had a pleasant week at Univ of Illinois and have returned to find a batch of papers for the Phil Mag to be passed in judgment.[1] Hahn gets through a lot of work. Bronson has finally finished up RaA, B & C. They are successive, periods 3, 28 and 21 mins respectively. Theory & experiment agree very closely, but B gives out easily absorbed β rays. This fact fooled us for a long time. Soddy writes me that his nose is kept to the grindstone with routine work & that he has practically no time for research.

I heard from Bumstead that your heat engine was out of order but hope all is patched up again.[2] Yours ever,

E. RUTHERFORD

1. Rutherford served as a referee for the *Philosophical Magazine* and for *Nature,* advising the editors whether or not to accept a manuscript that had been submitted for publication. As a Fellow of the Royal Society he effectively performed the same function when he "communicated" a paper from a nonmember to the Society.

2. Bumstead had written to Rutherford that "Bolty had an upset tummy the other day and the progress of science was some what delayed" (29 Apr. 1906, RCC).

17 MAY 1906

139 Orange Street
New Haven, Connecticut

My dear Rutherford,

Your good letter of the ninth was duly received and I was much interested in its contents. I read Wheeler the part about Bragg's results. He did not have anything particular to say in the matter. I am very much afraid that before Wheeler gets his experiments finished his uranium will have all disintegrated, so that his final results will hold for lead only. As bearing on Bragg's calculated rate of disintegration for thorium as compared to uranium, I find that one gram of thorium, containing its equilibrium quantity of radiothorium and disintegration products, has the same activity as 1.32 gram of uranium.

As to my final ratios for the relative activities of uranium and radium (itself), I find that the radium in a mineral has an activity equal to 0.52 that of the uranium present, and this value taken in conjunction with the latest value for the quantity of radium in equilibrium with one gram of uranium, gives the activity of one gram of radium (itself) as equal to the activity of 1.35×10^6 grams of uranium. 1 gram of 30-day old radium retaining all of its emanation would therefore have the same activity as 7.6×10^6 grams of uranium, and one gram of radium bromide retaining all of its emanation would have activity equal to 4.4×10^6 grs of uranium. This last comes out pretty high, but in the first place it is stated in the German edition of Mme Curie's book,[1] page 32, beginning of last paragraph, that the activity of the pure radium chloride is about 10^6 times greater than that of the *minerals* from which it is obtained; and in the second place I am confident that very thin films of *pure radium salts* do not retain as much as 50% of the total emanation formed within them.[2]

I am going to publish two papers in the June number of the American Journal[3] and I am enclosing proofs of them with this letter, thinking that you will perhaps be interested to look them over. The work on the other matters is practically completed, but I am going to hold up the rest of the papers until after I am in the Sloane Laboratory, which will be early in the summer. I think that it will be just as well to bring my ship up to the wharf with a small cargo ready for unloading. Moreover, I am in correspondence with McCoy and am helping him to get his own results on the activity of uranium minerals straightened out somewhat. He has sent me a couple of his minerals, one of them, his uraninite No. 1, loses no less than 13% of its emanation; and his carnotite loses *33.6%* of its emanation. As you will perhaps remember, he found that minerals (per gram of uranium) were 4.1 times as active as uranium, while I find the ratio to be about 5.3 when all emanation is retained. I think that I can convince him of his errors and can get him to publish an explanatory paper with my own, so that people will not have to puzzle over the disagreement of our results and say: "McCoy found 4.1, but Boltwood says 5.3. Which is right?"

Thank Eve for the reprint of the paper which he sent me, and tell him that I am afraid that his γ-ray standard of thorium oxide will not be very satisfactory.

I sent you by express today a box containing 500 cc of each of the new Radium Bromide standard solutions and also the sample of uraninite which Eve sent to me. I hope that they will reach you in good condition. The disarrangement of my machinery which Bumstead wrote you about was not at all serious. Sincerely yours,

BERTRAM B. BOLTWOOD

1. Boltwood did not read French well, if at all, though he was fluent in German, having studied and traveled extensively in that country. Marie Curie's book was her doctoral thesis presented to the Faculty of Sciences of Paris: *Recherches Sur Les Substances Radioactives* (Paris, Gauthier-Villars, 1903).

2. Boltwood's letter has the following marginal notation bracketing the first two paragraphs: "for thin films in all cases."

3. BBB, "The radio-activity of the salts of radium," *Am. J. Sci., 21* (June 1906), 409–14; "The radio-activity of thorium minerals and salts," *Am. J. Sci., 21* (June 1906), 415–26. These papers contain the details of the work whose results Boltwood presented to the American Physical Society the previous February. That this subject was of particular interest at this time may be seen from the fact that McCoy and Dadourian also had papers on relative activities in this same issue of the *American Journal of Science*.

14 OCTOBER 1906

The Macdonald Physics Building
McGill University, Montreal

My dear Boltwood,

I have not heard from you for an age but presume you are still alive and kicking. I heard from Bronson that Bumstead & yourself were busy knocking the laboratory into shape all the summer, so you no doubt have been enjoying a varied existence. I spent two months in California and had a first class time.[1] I returned via the Grand Canyon of Arizona and it impressed me as few things have done for I am blasé of the wonders of this world. I am feeling pretty vigorous this year as I have no book to worry me & hope to accomplish something in consequence. I have got lots of thing to tackle about which more anon when I get going. I have done a few expts. recently which show that the emanations are completely absorbed in cocoanut charcoal at ordinary temperatures.[2] I think this will prove useful for some experiments. You will see an account in Nature of the same in a week or so.[3]

I have a couple of papers which should have appeared in the Phil Mag of this month [4] and another on the way [5] —all to do with e/m of the α particle & such like problems. I gather you must have a number of papers ready to be launched, when are you going to publish your paper on analysis of radiations of uranium-radium minerals? I want to know when I can make use of the results you communicated to me long ago. Has Wheeler yet got down on the products of Ur? If he has'nt it done, I intend to do it myself soon. Hahn & Levin as you know are away but a Dr. Rummelin [6] of Göttingen—Levin's Brother in-law—comes out directly. He is a physicist by training. Levin is married & I expect is now at the Cavendish. Bronson since his return has shown *definitely* (to a 1 per cent accuracy) that the activity of Ra is not altered up to 1600°C. Exit [?] Makower [7] to the land inhabited by sloppy experimenters.[8] Soddy, you will have seen is booming, with the big drum going pretty steadily. He writes me that he is engaged to a Miss Beilby of Glasgow. I won't believe that he has got the α particle *uncharged* until I see it with my own eyes. He may, however, have reduced the charge from 2 to 1. Remember me to Bumstead, Wheeler & Dadourian & give my remembrances to Mrs. Boltwood. I hope you are well & flourishing. Yours ever,

E. RUTHERFORD

1. These two months were spent at the University of California, Berkeley, where Rutherford conducted a summer session course in radioactivity and was introduced to the beauties of California by, among others, Jacques Loeb the eminent marine biologist.

2. Only a few years earlier James Dewar had shown the value of coconut charcoal for absorbing gases in his cryogenic apparatus.

3. ER, "Absorption of the radio-active emanations by charcoal," *Nature*, *74* (25 Oct. 1906), 634.

4. ER, "The mass and velocity of the α particles expelled from radium and actinium," *Phil. Mag.*, *12* (Oct. 1906), 348–71; "Mass of the α particles from thorium," *Phil. Mag.*, *12* (Oct. 1906), 371–78.

5. ER, "The velocity and energy of the α particles from radioactive substances," *Phil. Mag.*, *13* (Jan. 1907), 110–17.

6. Gustave Rümelin, a Göttingen Ph.D., later worked at Freiburg, Göttingen and Aachen. He was at his last post only a few months before his death in the war.

7. When Rutherford went to Manchester he found that Walter Makower was a better physicist than he originally thought. Makower, in

fact, stayed on about ten years, becoming assistant director of the laboratory. During this time he published a book on radioactivity and collaborated with Hans Geiger on a laboratory text for students of radioactivity.
Makower later worked in industry and then was appointed professor of
science at the Royal Military Academy, London.

8. Makower, "On the effect of high temperatures on radium emanation," *Proc. Roy. Soc.*, *77A* (Mar. 1906), 241–47.

7 NOVEMBER 1906

Sloane Laboratory, Yale University
New Haven, Connecticut

My dear Rutherford,

I certainly was mighty glad to get your good letter of October
14th and I have been intending to write to you ever since the
beginning of the summer, but everything was so upset and I was
so infernally busy all of the time that I never found an opportunity. In the first place I had to get packed up to move my
laboratory belongings, and packing began about the middle of
June. I moved up here about the first of July and from that
time on I did not have one minute that I could call my own.
Owing to illness in his family Bumstead had to go out to Illinois
before the vacation and could not get back until the first of
August. He left me in charge of the renovation of Sloane Lab.
in the mean time and I had all I could attend to even after he
got back. I can not begin to describe the state of things that we
found here. I shall reserve this until I see you again, but it has
taken an awful lot of work to get things in running order. It was
certainly a wierd sort of place. We had masons, painters, carpen-
ters, plumbers and electricians, and we had to boss them about
from morning until night. We had to move things from the cellar to the attic and from the attic to the cellar, and we went to
bed early at night in order to begin early in the morning.

And then just as we began to get sort of settled we had to put on our good clothes and our company manners and listen to the postponed Silliman lectures which broke in on our time and brought a lot of guests and visitors who had to be looked out for.

The lectures viewed from a popular standpoint were not a great success. Nernst [1] himself proved to be most agreeable and we enjoyed him greatly. He struggled with the language most heroically and did his best to be interesting, but I am afraid that most of his audience came from a sense of duty rather than from any interest in the subject presented.

I have been gradually getting things into shape for the last three weeks, fixing up apparatus and sorting out my materials, and just as soon as Nernst left us, last Friday, I really settled down to my own experiments. I was really keen at getting back again into harness but I must acknowledge that I am more than encouraged by the way things have started off this time. I have found the long-sought intermediate product between uranium and radium. It is actinium. You will remember that I have suspected for a long time that actinium was the father of that radium infant, and, as I wrote you last winter I was planning, I just put the suspected gentleman under observation. I separated the actinium from a kilogram of carnotite containing approximately 200 grams of uranium and sealed the solution of it up in a glass bulb. About two months later, on April 25th, I boiled off the emanation and tested it (the radium emanation only). There was at that time 5.7×10^{-9} gram of radium present. On Monday last, 193 days later, I again repeated the test. There was then 14.2×10^{-9} gram of radium in the solution. The radium had increased by 8.5×10^{-9} gram, a very respectable amount, and since the quantity of Ra in equilibrium with 200 grams of uranium is 7600×10^{-8} gram, the indicated value for λ is $2.2 \times 10^{-4}(\text{year})^{-1}$ and for the half-value period is 3100 years.[2] This ought to be near enough to your own latest value, i.e. 2600, to remove any theoretical objections to Papa Actinium on your part. And so I have sent off a brief communication to the Editor of Nature [3] and a note for the December number of the Am. Jour.[4] exposing the old man's duplicity.

It seems to me that this new family complication will make it necessary to modify the reasoning which you used to argue against the intermediate formation of actinium on the basis of its activity as compared to uranium and radium (in equilibrium mixtures) , and may require the assumption that the atoms in the radium series give off two alpha particles on disintegration. I haven't really had a chance to think out all the possibilities which suggest themselves, but I have written knowing that I would be sure to find you interested. I am going to repeat the whole operation from the start with special precautions, so as to get a close value for λ. I am also going to test my uranium solutions again, for they certainly ought to be showing a little radium by this time.

Hoping to hear from you soon, with best regards, Sincerely yours,

BERTRAM B. BOLTWOOD

P.S.—If you want to know about the uranium changes you had better tackle the job yourself. Wheeler hasn't really made any progress since you saw him here last winter.

1. Walther Nernst, low temperature expert at the University of Berlin, received the 1920 Nobel Prize in chemistry for his work in chemical thermodynamics.

2. The decay constant, or radioactive constant, λ, represents the fraction of the total number of atoms present which decay each time unit. Boltwood's growth figure of 8.5×10^{-9} gram radium in 193 days is equal approximately to 1.7×10^{-8} gram per year. Since the equilibrium amount is 7.6×10^{-5} gram, $\lambda = 1.7 \times 10^{-8}/7.6 \times 10^{-5} = 2.2 \times 10^{-4}$ per year. The basic decay equation is $N = N_0 e^{-\lambda t}$, where N is the number of atoms at time t, N_0 is the number of atoms at time zero, and e is the base of the natural logarithms. After one half-period, the ratio $N/N_0 = \frac{1}{2}$. Taking the logarithm of both sides of the original equation we get for the half-life $t = .693/\lambda$. For the case at hand, the half-life of radium, Boltwood obtained $t = .693/2.2 \times 10^{-4} = 3100$ years.

3. BBB, "The production of radium from actinium," *Nature*, 75 (15 Nov. 1906), 54.

4. BBB, "Note on the production of radium by actinium," *Am. J. Sci.*, 22 (Dec. 1906), 537–38.

10 NOVEMBER 1906

The Macdonald Physics Building
McGill University, Montreal

My dear Boltwood,

I got your letter yesterday and you can imagine my interest. Japhet in search of a father is nothing to the search for the elusive parent of Ra. Congratulations on your success which you deserve thoroughly in the face of such damnable evidence against actinium being the parent of Ra.

You may remember that I instituted some experiments to see if actinium grew Ra (see Bakerian Lecture) about two-and-a-half years ago. I took 2 grams of actinium of activity 200 and dissolved it in nitric acid & found that the RaEm present (by the method of bubbling—about 3 litres of air passed through into a big electroscope—corresponded to about 2×10^{-8} gr RaBr$_2$. This was compared with my earliest standard which I think was pretty accurate. I then precipitated successively with Ba & reduced the amount of Ra to $\frac{1}{40}$ of this amount. Observation over two months showed little change or not enough to be sure of. Fearing radioactive contamination, I corked the bottle and it has remained undisturbed for two years and 4 months. In the meantime a little of the solution had evaporated through the cork & some of the stuff had ppd. Immediately after your letter, I dissolved this & tested for emanation by boiling. The actinium is now full of emanation—a damd. sight more than there ought to be according to rough calculations from your data. I will soon have the amounts accurately. I can fortunately test for any accidental contamination by determining the Ra content of some of the same sample of actinium which has been kept in the solid state. I will let you know how things work out later—but at present I see no chance of any contamination amounting to a fraction of the amount observed. The question is why did not the amount of Ra increase a great deal in the first few months of observations? I have about six separate determinations—all agreeing within moderate limits. There is the possibility that the Ra formed continued to precipitate & consequently I did not get the true amount of Eman or that there is some intermediate material removed with the Ba. I will be in a position in a day or two to say whether these results are reliable or not.

As you say, actinium as a parent of Ra does'nt seem to fit in with the home of her ancestors—pitchblende. Is there not a fair chance that actinium is not the real parent but only the foster parent? the *true* parent always appearing with actinium. This is a parent which your observations so far will not throw very definite light upon. I am quite prepared to accept actinium as parent if you will show me where her immediate children were hidden in pitchblende. They make a mighty poor show in the activity of the Ur-Act-Ra family or your own observations are in some way at fault. You have examined this question pretty thoroughly. What do you think of actinium—can it be squeezed in without too much pressing?

I am quite prepared to believe you are right about the relationship but it makes thing rather difficult to fit in on our present knowledge or rather ignorance. The main point, however, is that you have grown a reasonable quantity of Ra in a reasonable time and these other points must be attacked later.

I am much worried how to account for the devil of a quantity of Ra in my actinium after lying by for 2 years or more but of this more anon. I live in dread of contaminating things but don't see how it was possible in this case. This brings me to a note of warning. Keep all radium in quantity out of the Sloane Lab as if it were the plague. You may keep a closed tube of Ba for the benefit of visitors, containing a gram of the precious metal. My laboratory is in a perilous state for fine experiments and I see no hope of improvement.

I am delighted to hear of your success. It does not worry me that I might have done it myself by examining my bottle of actinium for, if I had found a big growth, I would have been so alarmed of the possibility of contamination that I would have had to wait another long period to make sure of it. By the way how does the activity of your actinium preparation in a thin film compare with Ra? Is it any where near what it ought to be? Give my best wishes to Bumstead. With remembrances to Mrs. Boltwood. Yours ever,

E. RUTHERFORD

19 NOVEMBER 1906

The Macdonald Physics Building
McGill University, Montreal

My dear Boltwood,

Just a line to tell you things are now progressing quite satisfactorily in the direction of your views. I found the dam'd stopcock I used in my first expts. was contaminated. I thought it was a new one but was let in badly. In consequence of this, I have discarded the results of the solution, although I find the solution itself cannot have been itself much infected. When I discovered this, I refused to use anything in the Physics Bdg but retired to the Chemistry Bdg & tested the solid actinium which I had put aside more than $2\frac{1}{2}$ years ago. I find (I am speaking only from memory, as I have not my numbers with me) that the amt. of radium has increased nearly 7 times in that period. The growth per year per gram is about 1.6×10^{-8} gr Ra. As the activity of this actinium is between 200 and 300, this result appears to be of the same order as you have found. I feel quite confident of these results, but have not yet detd. my old standard in terms of the new but I am sure this will not make much of a correction in the results.

I felt so mad with my contaminated actinium solution, that I spent two whole days in subjecting it to a chemical cure & find I have practically got rid of the whole of the radium in it.[1] If I have'nt separated the radioactinium in the process, I expect to be sure of the growth in a fortnights' time. By the way, I wonder what our friend S-y's feelings will be when he reads your letter in Nature. He must feel rather down and moreover his earlier observations will want some manoeuvering to stand.[2] By the way, you of course see that when you get a measurable growth in your Ur solution, you can also determine the period of actinium. It is bully to have a method of getting both experimentally. Yours ever,

E. RUTHERFORD

1. Note that Rutherford had become reasonably adept in the chemical manipulations required to separate various radioactive materials, and when he had no "resident chemist," such as Soddy or Hahn, he performed necessary work himself. Rutherford, however, regarded his chemical investigations as a means to an end, the end being in the realm of physics. This attitude was in contrast to that of Marie Curie who, although trained as a physicist also, found her greatest successes in the area of radiochemistry.

2. Soddy had been interested in the growth of radium in uranium solutions, as discussed in the note to Rutherford's letter of 16 Sept. 1905. He did not believe that actinium was the parent of radium.

9 DECEMBER 1906

Sloane Laboratory, Yale University
New Haven, Connecticut

My dear Rutherford,

I received both of your letters in due order and was highly interested in all the news which they contained. I had well remembered that you had announced the planting of your actinium tubers in your Bakerian lecture and I also well remembered the promise you made me last January that you would examine the garden when you got back to Montreal and see whether any radium blossoms had appeared. But you didn't keep your promise and so I got the bouquet out of my own yard. Well I will forgive you, only I don't deserve much credit for it, it was too easy.

Now as to the question of the activity of the equilibrium quantities of actinium and radium with their respective families. I am quite *sure* from my experiments that the activity of the actinium group in a uranium mineral is *not greater* than the activity of the uranium present; and further that the activity of the radium itself is at least half that of the uranium. In other words—Ac + Radio Ac + Ac · X + Em + Ac · A +Ac · B = U; and Ra = 0.5 U. The activity of the actinium group is certainly not very much greater than the uranium; it may be even less however since my accurate experiments have all been of such a nature as to give the maximum value (assuming that no unidentified radioactive body is present in the minerals). Just now I am conducting some experiments to determine what its minimum activity must be, and from some rough preliminary experiments undertaken last winter I believe that it will come out not far from the maximum.

I am very much afraid that the theory of successive products will have to be modified to fit the case, for I haven't the least suspicion that actinium is not the true father. You may doubt the sharpness of my chemical nose, but I can assure you that I felt perfectly confident that I should find radium growing from actinium because *there is no final disintegration product of* actinium in the uranium minerals.[1] So I am unwilling to believe that the intermediate product between uranium and radium is merely entrained with the actinium. Besides the latter is altogether too plebeian an idea and wholly discreditable to the parent.[2]

I am awaiting with interest some further news of your own actinium nursery.

Please let me know whether you are planning to come down to New York this Xmas vacation.

With best regards, Sincerely yours,

BERTRAM B. BOLTWOOD

1. The end product of the actinium series is lead. Since an understanding of isotopes did not come until 1913, Boltwood could not know that the lead in his uranium minerals was a mixture of the products of the actinium and uranium series, plus original lead, plus the product of the thorium series also, if that element were present in the mineral.

2. While Boltwood wrote this with tongue-in-cheek, and while a discourse on the philosophy of scientific method is out of place in this work, it may suffice to point out that Boltwood, like many other scientists, was guided to a certain extent in his scientific research by esthetic feelings and ideas of propriety. These influences, sometimes beneficial, sometimes otherwise, have been felt in rational science since the time of the earliest Greek philosophers.

11 DECEMBER 1906

The Macdonald Physics Building
McGill University, Montreal

My dear Boltwood,

Just a line to ask you if you could come back with me from the Physical Society in N.Y. & stay with me a few days in Montreal. My wife & I would be delighted to have you with us. We cannot give you a particularly lively time but will allow you to smoke as much as you like. I am sure you are in want of a good bracing up after your work at Yale—especially after your attention to the "confinement" of actinium.

There [is] another reason why you should come also. Between ourselves, I think it extremely likely that this is the last Xmas I shall spend in the Americas for some time to come—verb sap.[1] Do come & liven us up.

Another word re Physical Society. I am encroaching on your ground & am giving a paper (short) on the "Production of Ra by actinium." I think I can not only corroborate your results in several directions but also fix the parentage with dead certainty —with far more certainty anyway than falls to the lot of most us mortals.[2]

I think you should give your paper also at the Physical Society and not bury it in your local journal. (Save me from Dana!) If you decide to do so, write to Merritt[3] that you would like your paper to appear on the list before mine.

Remember me to Bumstead, Wheeler, Hastings, Dana and my other friends—some of whom I hope to see in New York. I think I shall leave for N.Y. the night of Dec. 26 & possibly come back by day on the 28th—or something of that kind to be arranged later. Give my remembrances to Mrs. Boltwood & tell her that she will have to spare you for a few days. Yours ever,

E. RUTHERFORD

1. *Verbum sat sapienti:* a word to the wise is sufficient.

2. ER, "Production of radium from actinium," *Nature,* 75 (17 Jan. 1907), 270–71. Rutherford was far less certain in this paper than he indicated in his letter. He felt that Boltwood's findings pointed to actinium, but did not entirely exclude the possibility that the parent of radium was merely entrained with the actinium.

3. Ernest George Merritt was professor of physics at Cornell University, where he later became head of the department and dean of the graduate school. In 1914–15 he was president of the American Physical Society.

17 DECEMBER 1906

The Macdonald Physics Building
McGill University, Montreal

Dear Boltwood,

Just a line to add to my previous letter. I assumed that the Physics Soc meeting was on the 27th. Merritt informs me it will be held on Friday & Saturday. If such be the case, I will descend on New York Friday morning & come back Saturday evening, I trust in company with you.

Merritt tells me you have your paper down & he has placed mine after it. Yours ever,

E. RUTHERFORD

18 DECEMBER 1906

Sloane Laboratory, Yale University
New Haven, Connecticut

My dear Rutherford,

I shall be greatly pleased to accept your very kind invitation to spend a couple of days with you in Montreal after the Physical Society meeting. I must only stipulate two things, however, one of which is that you must let me have a *real quiet time* with plenty of smoke, which I note you already concede, and the other is that you let me get away so as to be back here for the first of January. The paragraph of suggestion as to possible changes in the future causes feelings of both pleasure and regret, if I read between the lines rightly, the former because you are going to have what you desire and the latter that we on this side are going to lose you from among us.

As to the matter of the papers before the Society, I had already written Merritt announcing a paper when your letter came, and I have since heard from him that the order of the two on the program will be made according to your suggestion. I am mighty glad that you are also going to have something to say on the matter of actinium.

You will be interested to hear that the amount of radium in my solution of 48 grams of uranium is now (2 years and 7 mos. from the time of its preparation) less than 10^{-11} gram. Long live actinium! Very sincerely yours,

BERTRAM B. BOLTWOOD

24 DECEMBER [1906]

The Macdonald Physics Building
McGill University, Montreal

My dear Boltwood,

I am delighted to hear you will come along. I shall be careful to obey your behests & not worry you with social duties. There are a few men about here like Eve, Cooke [1] &c who would like to have the opportunity of walking round you to have a good look at you but they are not obnoxious.

I think I shall leave for New York Thursday night & arrive early Friday. Will probably put up for the night at the Manhattan. I am not sure whether we will be able to leave Saturday morning but if not Saturday evening. This will allow us to reach Montreal Sunday in time for breakfast. If you must return by New Year, you could leave by Monday nights' train but I hope you will not make your stay so short.

I shall travel by the Grand Trunk Ry which, as you know, leaves Union Station in the early morning & evening.

I shall see you at the meeting. I have settled a couple of points about actinium. One, however, is not so satisfactory as I had hoped. Yours ever,

E. RUTHERFORD

1. H. L. Cooke, a graduate of McGill who was a demonstrator in physics there, in 1903 received an 1851 Exhibition Scholarship for three years' study in Cambridge, England. This was the same award that enabled Rutherford to leave New Zealand for the Cavendish Laboratory in 1895. The scholarship was funded from the profits of the famous Exhibition held in mid-century. Cooke later went to Princeton University where he rose to professor of physics.

6 JANUARY 1907

The Macdonald Physics Building
McGill University, Montreal

My dear Boltwood,

I was very glad to hear you got back O.K. The fire in the Chemistry Bdg turned out to be a small affair & only one small room in the back part partly burnt & scorched. The fire was due to crossing of a time circuit wire with high potential power lead of the city.

My appointment is now announced here and in England, so my time of worry is over.[1]

Just a word or two about your determination that amt. of Ra in 49 grs of Ur is now less than $1/10^{11}$ gr after 2.5 years. 49 grs of Ur has $49 \times 3.8/10^7 = 1.9/10^5$ gr Ra contained [?] with it. Taking λ for Ra $= 1/4000$ $\therefore$ wt. of atoms of Ur breaking up per year $= 4.8/10^9$. $\therefore$ Wt. of atoms of actin per year produced $= 4.8/10^9$. Initially after 2.5 years $1.2/10^8$ gr. $\therefore$ mean value $= 6/10^9$ gr. If λ_a (year) $^{-1} =$ value for actinium

$$\frac{6}{10^9} \; \lambda_a \; \alpha \; \frac{1}{10^{11}}$$

$$\lambda_a \; \alpha \; \frac{1}{600}$$

$\therefore$ half period greater than *420 years*. This is a point, I think, worth bringing out pretty soon. It shows that actinium has a life comparable with Ra.

I have sent a letter to Nature re actinium in which I counsel an attitude of "go easy" on speculation till we get right down on some of the peculiarities of Ur-Act-Ra.[2]

My wife sends her kind regards. Yours in haste,

E. RUTHERFORD

1. Rutherford was appointed Langworthy Professor of Physics at the Victoria University of Manchester, succeeding Sir Arthur Schuster who had

retired early on the condition that Rutherford would receive the chair. Schuster, a former student of James Clerk Maxwell and one of Britain's leading physicists, had improved the laboratory in Manchester such that it was one of the country's finest. Rutherford, while a full professor at Mc-Gill, was junior to Cox. He showed his ability in Montreal to run a large research group, but was as yet untried in the management of the entire laboratory. His years in Manchester (1907–19) as director of the laboratory proved his considerable skill in this area.

2. ER, "Production of radium from actinium," *Nature,* 75 (17 Jan. 1907), 270–71.

1 MARCH 1907

The Macdonald Physics Building
McGill University, Montreal

My dear Boltwood,

You appear to get lazier with increasing age for if I remember aright, you owe me a letter. I have been working away at various things in a quiet way as I don't intend to bust myself before I get over to the other side. I have not the slightest difficulty in growing radium in actinium but it is very difficult to get any evidence of where it comes from. I hope, however, in another two months' time to have some definite light on the problem. I am sure that actinium B does not go bang into Ra anyway.[1] I have become quite expert in separating Ra, radioactinium &c from Actinium & have got some new methods but these are by the way. My mineral "Rutherfordite"[2] is an excellent thing to work with as it all dissolves in HCl. I intend to repeat your original expt. of separating actinium some time for my own education.

I derive much edification & amusement from our friend J. Joly[3] in Nature.[4] His letter explaining the rain of Ra on the earth, I thought was fine & an excellent example of inability to appreciate the order of evidence. Have you read Soddy's paper

154

on the absorption of gases by heated calcium (R.S. Proc)? [5] It is the best piece of work he has done [6] but like Soddy the results are carefully all exposed in the front window.

Eve has come to the bottom of some of his troubles. The effect from Carbon was a mixture of radium emanation combined with an electroscope whose natural leak grew with time. He gets a small effect in passing outside air through the carbon but other experiments show that carbon only absorbs a small fraction of the emanation unless velocity of air current is very small. He has examined the amount of Ra in various rocks round Montreal & finds values of the same order as Strutt. You may have heard that Barnes [7] is appointed in my stead. He is the natural man to fill the post and I am sure will do very well.

I leave here about the second week in May. Au revoir,

E. RUTHERFORD

1. One of the difficulties in selecting actinium as the parent of radium was arranging the decay sequence. It was known that actinium decayed into actinium X, actinium emanation, and actinium A and B, in that order. Since radium also decayed into emanation and lettered products, it was no easy matter to merge the two series into one.

2. This uranium ore from German East Africa was named after Rutherford by Willy Marckwald, chemistry professor at Berlin, who did much work in radioactivity. See Marckwald, "Ueber Uranerze aus Deutsch-Ostafrika," *Centr. Mineral. Geol.* (1906), 761–63.

3. John Joly, professor of geology at Dublin, had a lively interest in radioactivity, particularly its application in geological dating.

4. Joly, "Radium and geology," *Nature*, 75 (7 Feb. 1907), 341–42.

5. Soddy, "Calcium as an absorbent of gases for the production of high vacua and spectroscopic research," *Proc. Roy. Soc., 78A* (2 Feb. 1907), 429–58.

6. It is curious that Rutherford should not consider the disintegration theory as Soddy's (and his) best piece of work. In later years Soddy was bitter that credit for this theory often was given to Rutherford alone. This resulted from the "convenience" of citing only the senior author and not from a "plot" on the part of numerous scientists, as Soddy seems to have believed, or from any action of Rutherford. Most likely, by best piece of work, Rutherford simply meant an independent investigation by Soddy.

7. Howard T. Barnes was an expert on heat measurements (having

been trained by Rutherford's predecessor at McGill, Hugh L. Callendar) who collaborated with Rutherford in determining the heat output of several radioactive substances. He succeeded Rutherford as Macdonald Professor, and then became director of the laboratory upon Cox's retirement in 1909.

15 MAY 1907

Sloane Laboratory, Yale University
New Haven, Connecticut

My dear Rutherford,

I am writing this letter in the hope that it will reach you before you sail for England. The intervening months have certainly passed very quickly and it is very difficult to realize that you will so soon belong to another continent. I hope that even though an ocean separates us that you will not quickly forget your friends here in America and that it will be my own good fortune at least to see you again at some time not far distant in the future. But old Father Time plays sad pranks even on those who confide in him and I am rapidly losing confidence in his promises for the future.

I have been very much interested in Hahn's last paper [1] on "a new intermediate product in thorium" and his conclusions are not only certainly correct but I should have reached the same views myself in a week or so if his paper had not arrived just at the critical moment. I was just remeasuring my old thorium oxide films prepared from 12 to 18 months before and was finding a marked falling off in the activity of all of them which amounts to from 15 to 30 per cent. and is highest in those which were originally found to have the normal specific activity. The films included a number which were not mentioned in my published paper and with the data given by these and additional data obtained from freshly prepared material it did not take very long to determine where and how the mesothorium was separated.

With the knowledge thus obtained it was an easy matter to pick out from among my various products a number which contain no thorium at all, which a couple of years ago had been tested and found essentially inactive, but which are now very active indeed and contain radiothorium equivalent to several grams of normal thorium oxide. Confidentially I will tell you that the easiest way to get mesothorium is from the ordinary thorium-X residues prepared in the usual manner by precipitating the thorium as hydroxide from the solution of the nitrate. I have also worked out a process by which I expect to be able to separate the equilibrium amount of mesothorium from thorianite. Many interesting possibilities have suggested themselves if I can get considerable amounts of mesothorium in this manner.

I see that Bronson's paper [2] has not yet convinced Makower that his ideas about the effect of high temperatures on the radium products are without foundation.[3] You have something to look forward to when you reach Manchester!

With best wishes to you and Mrs. Rutherford. Sincerely yours,

BERTRAM B. BOLTWOOD

1. Hahn, "Ein neues Zwischenprodukt im Thorium," *Ber. Deut. Chem. Ges., 40* (1907), 1462–69.

2. Bronson, "The effect of temperature on the activity of radium and its transformation products," *Chem. News, 95* (25 Jan. 1907), 39–42.

3. Makower and Sidney Russ, "On the effect of high temperatures on radium emanation and its products," *Nature, 76* (2 May 1907), 21.

28 JULY 1907

Mullion, Cornwall

My dear Boltwood,

After my arrival in England, I spent five weeks or so in Manchester doing some work and getting the lie of things generally.

The laboratory is good but there was not much in the radioactive line. The latter, however, I will have in good shape by October. I have been occasionally to London, attended the Soirée of the R.S., the Bakerian Lecture on the at[omic] w[eight] of Ra, a meeting of Chem Soc where Ramsay held forth, not to mention other scientific amusements. The Bakerian Lecture by Thorpe [1] was a fizzle. He had been given the radium preparation from about a ton of residues from Joachimstahl given to the R.S. He adopted Mme Curie's methods in intirety and after 3993 successive fractionations of the chloride had got down to 2/3 Barium & 1/3 Ra about !! Nothing about the atomic weight except the gratuitous statement that Mme Curie was wrong. I gently suggested that the bromide method was preferable. I don't think he used a single electroscope determination.

By the way, I have got the polonium & actinium residues from the R.S. to see what I can do with them. The latter is in form of hydroxide 40 kilos in weight. On drying it reduces to 6 kilos, activity about 40, so I hope to get some active material out of it. Can you give me the benefit of your advice as to the best method of rapidly concentrating the actinium. Do you recommend the oxalate method? I have several methods in view which I shall try. I am not going to worry much about Giesel's or Debierne's [2] methods as nothing seems to have come out of them. I am at the same time going to try to separate "paradium" [3] from the actinium if I can. I am sure it must be there in fair quantity. I shall probably have a chemist or two to turn onto it, keeping a close tag on things by radioactive & growing radium tests.

By the way, you will have seen Ramsays letter in Nature [4] giving the various gases &c he gets out of the emanation by different methods. He is very anxious to convert me & showed me all his methods. He is quite sure about it but he always is. I shall not be sure of them until I try it myself but at present, I intend to take a negative position. You will have seen he wants to reduce the life of Ra to 240 years or thereabouts. I addressed the Chem Soc on the subject to their great gratification telling them how obstinate the physicists were in believing that they were right. Ramsay has a host of enemies who don't believe a word of what he says. At the same time, the weakness of Ramsay's results lies in the fact that the neon result has only been got once; the argon is frisky, while the lithium I must confess is rather more than I can momentarily swallow. Unfortunately, no one has any Ra to test his results. I *hope* to be able to raise a good deal before the end of the year. This is one of the advantages of being on the fighting ground instead of at a lonely outpost. If R. is right, the subject of radioactivity enters a new phase but I want to know why neon &c are not always found in radioactive minerals. Also why he got a *brilliant spectrum of helium* out of a radium bromide solution a year or two ago & why it turns to neon now. Little things like this trouble a reflective mind. Verb. sap—don't give me away. Now for work. As soon as I got to Manchester, I found they were full of high pressure bombs & apparatus—all due to Petavel [5]—a physical engineer who just got his F.R.S. He had a bomb handy for exploding cordite. The maxm. temperature reached inside the bomb is 3000°C or thereabouts. So we put emanation in, measured by the γ rays outside & explode. A decrease of 9% of γ rays every time; why, I don't know. I hope it is a distribution effect but the bomb is exactly spherical & experiments so far have not supported that view. I also found by running the electroscope during an explosion that there was no *burst* of γ ray activity; so there is one point of interest settled anyway.

I give an account of this [6] & of the production of Ra [7] at the B.A. this week.

By the way, *between ourselves,* your letter to Nature [8] re Soddy's attack [9] was forwarded to me to report *whether it was not too personal for publication.* I replied that Soddy's letter was extremely personal & provocative and that your language was far more restrained!! than Soddy's; otherwise your letter would have been returned with thanks. Soddy is an awful fool to exhibit his sores before a critical world; your letter distinctly rubbed it in but not more than was to be expected after his outburst. I have'nt seen Soddy yet but when I do I shall see if I can give him a word or two of advice.

Now for my holidays; I have spent a fortnight by the seaside in Cornwall and had a lazy but pleasant time. I go tomorrow to the B.A. at Leicester. My only worry is that I have to introduce a discussion on the "Constitution of the Atom." After the B.A., I return for 2 weeks to Martinhoe [?], Devon, & then back to start work. I think Manchester will suit me admirably. They are prepared to help me as far as possible and I think the social atmosphere is distinctly attractive. The climate is the drawback according to reports.

I forget whether I thanked you for your trouble in helping Barnes to get the photograph album. I appreciate it very much and it will serve as a constant reminder of my pleasant times in America. Remember me to Bumstead, Wheeler, Dadourian, Dana & Schwill [10] & any others who value such a remembrance. Let me hear from you how things are progressing in this weary world. I am in good form—certainly not lighter. I will have quite a collection of researchers next year to keep in order. Yours ever,

E. RUTHERFORD

1. T. E. Thorpe, for many years a government chemist, became professor of chemistry at the Royal College of Science, South Kensington, London, in 1909.

2. André Debierne began working with Pierre and Marie Curie in 1899, and in that year discovered actinium in the pitchblende residues from which the Curies earlier had extracted polonium and radium. Following Pierre's death in 1906, he became Marie's chief assistant in running the laboratory.

3. Rutherford's choice for the name of the immediate parent of radium. By this time he was convinced that the parent was not actinium, but merely entrained with it.

4. Ramsay, "Radium emanation," *Nature*, 76 (18 July 1907), 269. Ram-

say had been fascinated with the transmutational changes of radioactivity since he and Soddy found the spectral lines of helium in radium emanation. Rutherford considered that the helium resulted from the emanation's disintegration, in which alpha particles are emitted, but Ramsay's views are unclear. Now Ramsay claimed further changes: if the emanation is alone or in contact with hydrogen or oxygen, helium is produced; in contact with water, neon is produced; in contact with copper sulphate, argon is produced. Since Ramsay was the discoverer of these inert gasses it was difficult to question his work in this field. However, Rutherford had long since cast a jaundiced eye at anything Ramsey did in radioactivity and now was inclined to be doubtful.

5. Joseph E. Petavel was both an engineer and physicist, known for his work in measuring pressures in exploding gaseous mixtures. In 1908, he was appointed professor of engineering and director of the laboratory at Manchester, and in 1919 became director of the National Physical Laboratory.

6. ER and Petavel, "The effect of high temperature on the activity of the products of radium," *Brit. Assoc. Advance. Sci. Rept., 1907,* abstract on pp. 456–57.

7. ER, "The production and origin of radium," *Brit. Assoc. Advance. Sci. Rept., 1907,* abstract on p. 456.

8. BBB, "The origin of radium," *Nature, 76* (25 July 1907), 293.

9. Soddy, "The origin of radium," *Nature, 76* (13 June 1907), 150. The controversy dates to 1905, when Boltwood criticized Soddy's results claiming the growth of a measurable quantity of radium in a uranium solution.

10. Possibly Rudolph Schwill, an assistant professor of Spanish, who later changed his name to Schevill.

2 AUGUST 1907

Sloane Laboratory, Yale University
New Haven, Connecticut

My dear Rutherford,

It is such a long time since I have heard anything from you that it seems as if you had been gone for a year. I had hoped to get a line telling how you found things in England, but I suppose that you have been so busy and so occupied ever since you have been there that you haven't been able to find the time.

What do you think of Ramsay's latest announcement concerning "Radium Emanation" which appeared in Nature? [1] Can what he claims be right or is the man crazy? I was more astounded when I read his communication than I have ever been by anything that has appeared in scientific literature. And so far as I can discover there is not the slightest support for his claims to be found anywhere, the composition of uranium–radium minerals containing copper, the activity of copper-uranium minerals (torbernite for example), or anything else. The whole thing is most disturbing.

Ramsay's statement that he has observed the production of helium by thorium nitrate solutions certainly must be wrong. I have been working on the activity of thorium recently and have reached the conclusion that the change thorium-mesothorium is an alpha-ray change but that the activity of one gram of thorium is only about 7 to 8 per cent of the activity of one gram of uranium. This means, it would seem, that thorium is disintegrating so slowly that it would be quite impossible for helium to be detected even if it were formed. [2]

I have also been following up the mesothorium matter and have found where the mesothorium is separated in the working up of monazite. I have also got a method for securing the mesothorium. The process is being applied for me by the Wellsbach Co. to considerable quantities of monazite and I hope before very long to have generous quantities of both mesothorium and radiothorium for experimental purposes.

What have you been doing to Soddy and what under heaven made him write such an asinine letter to Nature? [3] Has he been bitten by Ramsay? Or did the mere fact that he had you on his side of the water give him courage which was previously lacking? I spent over a week trying to compose a decently polite reply to his communication. I don't mind a fair fight in the open, but when a man gets behind some other person's wall and then slings mud over it I draw the line. Please smooth him down for me, for if I ever get over to England I would rather have him for a friend than otherwise. But why he was willing to dig up that stinking corpse of his is more than I can understand!

Everything is going on as usual here. I am planning to work all summer with perhaps a week off before the beginning of the college year. With kindest remembrances to Mrs. Rutherford and regards and best wishes to yourself. Sincerely yours,

BERTRAM B. BOLTWOOD

1. Ramsay, "Radium emanation," *Nature, 76* (18 July 1907), 269.

2. Thorium's half-life is about three times longer than that of uranium: 1.39×10^{10} years vs. 4.51×10^9 years. Note that Boltwood is not now so adamant that the alpha particle of the thorium series cannot be helium.

3. Soddy, "The origin of radium," *Nature, 76* (13 June 1907), 150. This is Soddy's reply to Boltwood's criticism of almost two years ago. See notes to Rutherford's letter of 16 Sept. 1905. In this issue of *Nature* Soddy defends himself against Boltwood's charge that he unknowingly introduced radium into his experiments on the growth of radium, and attributes the discrepancy to their different methods of purification. Rutherford, he feels, inclines towards this view in his *Radioactive Transformations* (London, Frowde, 1906), the published Silliman Lectures. History, Soddy feels, has repeated itself, for Boltwood's recent belief that radium comes from actinium and Rutherford's denial may be explained by differences in their methods of purifying their materials.

23 SEPTEMBER 1907

Sloane Laboratory, Yale University
New Haven, Connecticut

My dear Rutherford,

Your good long letter of the 28th of July was received with joy and was greatly appreciated, especially as it found me hard at work in the laboratory with a strong yearning for news from the outer world. It contained just the news that I wanted, about Ramsay and Thorpe and especially about the Soddy letter. I am not surprised that Thorpe's lecture was a fizzle, your English chemists are such a sorry lot with Ramsay in the lime light. And that address of Smithells' at the B.A. meeting, could anything be more hopeless? [1]

The more I read about Ramsay the more I am inclined to believe that the man has gone clean daffy. If this last outburst of his proves to be wrong I hope that he may be buried so deeply in the mire that even his name may be forgotten. If he is right then it is one of those unaccountable pieces of luck which pass all understanding. For my own part I am willing to plug along over the old road until somebody shows him up for fair. He has already made enough breaks to kill any ordinary ass.

As to the Soddy letter, I suspected that it had been held up somewhere because of the delay in its publication. By your approval of it you not only did me a good turn but you saved for me my high opinion of the fairness of Nature which would certainly have gone by the board if they had been unwilling to let me defend myself. It wasn't that I cared a bit about Soddy, but I did about the other people who having heard the lion roar so loudly unchecked would have naturally assumed that he had devoured the lamb. Now that I have read Soddy's paper in the Phil. Mag.[2] I am sure that he is really the best friend and supporter that I have, for no one could have paid me a greater compliment than he did. But what is the matter with the man, who, so far as I can figure it out, must have written at about the same time those two papers, the one so bitter and the other so appreciative!!

What you write me about your own work is highly interesting and exciting. I can't see any explanation of the results that you got with the bomb unless there is a reversal of the change and you get radium formed from helium and emanation. The first thing I should want to try would be to see whether there was any radium present after the explosion, and if not radium then uranium. But you have undoubtedly tried that long ago, only as you didn't say anything about it occured to me as a possibility.

As to my own work, I certainly have been having plenty of it for I have been hard at it all summer, seven days a week and nine hours a day with only one holiday when I took off a Saturday to go down to the shore to see Bumstead. Things have turned out pretty well and I am feeling as fine as a fiddle. You will probably have seen my letter in Nature about the radium parent before this reaches you.[3] It is a thoroughbred radioactive element all right with all the essential attachments. It gives out nice slow α particles with a range of less than 3 centimeters in air and a very "soft" β radiation which is readily stopped by about 0.5 mm of lead but a good deal of which will pass through 0.5 mm of aluminium. The activity of this new element in a mineral is about 0.8 that of the radium (itself) with which it is associated. I have sent off a second communication to Nature [4] giving the above facts and proposing the name "Ionium" from "ions", etc. It is a curious and interesting fact that ionium was the chief, if not the only, radioactive constituent of the radioactive substance that I separated from pitchblende in 1899 and which I had always supposed was actinium owing to Debierne's perfectly rotten statements in the matter.[5] I think that Debierne has probably had the stuff in his hands for years and has not had the sense to identify it. In my own case I feel that with the insignificantly small amounts of material that I have been able to get to work with that there is some excuse for my having overlooked it.

With the data that I now have, or will have shortly, I think that I shall be able to show that the life (half-value period) of radium is not far from 2000 years. It will probably come out a little under this, say about 1900, but I shan't know definitely for about two weeks more. Also I shall be able to show that ionium is the last of the radioactive substances present in uranium minerals.[6] I have also got a lot of data about mesothorium, which as a matter of fact has the same chemical properties as radium and can be separated from minerals in the same manner.[7] But I shall hold up this for some time yet in order to give Hahn a chance, for I feel that his priority in the matter should be recognized; even though he wrote me last spring that he was going to keep his information for "commercial" purposes. And the German chemists still look down on the American because they are so commercial! I am hoping that Hahn may see the light before long.

The best way that I can suggest for you to treat your "actinium" residues is the following:—Get the stuff into solution as chloride and if much silica is present get rid of this by evaporating to dryness. In all events have *very little* free acid in the solution which should be fairly dilute and add about 10 grams of oxalic acid (in solution) per liter of liquid. The solution should be boiling hot when the oxalic acid is added or you are likely to have the devil of a time in filtering out the precipitate. Let the mixture cool and stand for at least 24 hours. Then filter off the precipitate. The precipitate can then be decomposed by heating with dilute (1:1) sulphuric acid. Evaporate to drive off water and heat gently to destroy oxalic acid and remove excess of sulphuric acid. The residue must not be strongly heated or the sulphates will be decomposed and the insoluble oxides will be formed. The residue should be ground to a powder and added slowly to *cold* water with constant stirring. It should finally dissolve completely unless, as is quite possible, the oxalate precipitate contains calcium. If calcium is present insoluble calcium sulphate will be formed and will not dissolve. It can be filtered off. Add an excess of ammonia to the cold solution of the sulphates, heat to boiling and boil a short time, filter off the precipitated hydroxides. If the hydroxide precipitate is large enough to handle conveniently I would advise dissolving it in a slight excess of hydrochloric acid and repeating the precipitation with oxalic acid and the other operations. Dissolve the precipitate (of hydroxides) in hydrochloric acid, have only a slight excess of hydrochloric acid present, heat the solution to boiling and add an excess of sodium thiosulphate. Boil the mixture until the odor of sulphurous acid can no longer be noticed in the steam and while the solution is hot filter off the precipitate. This precipitate, if your chemical assistants know their business, should contain the ionium with any thorium present in the original residues. By treating it with hot, dilute hydrochloric acid the ionium and thorium will be dissolved and a residue of sulphur (containing radioactinium) will remain. The actinium should be contained in the filtrate from the sodium thiosulphate precipitate. It may be a good plan to add some rare earths to the first solution of the residues and rework them for actinium for there are some indications that the actinium separation is not a complete one. To get the actinium from the other rare earths separate the lanthanum (this is according to Giesel, I have never carried matters that far). If you insisted on it I would not reject the offer of the loan of about 100 grams of your dried residue. I might be able to get some information which would help you in working up the main quantity. I wish you much joy in the process which is bound to be somewhat tedious.

Let me hear from you again when you have a chance. With best regards to you and to Mrs. Rutherford, Yours sincerely,

BERTRAM B. BOLTWOOD

1. Arthur Smithells, professor at the University of Leeds, was president of section B (chemistry) at the British Association's annual meeting. In his address, printed in *Nature*, 76 (8 Aug. 1907), 352–57, he expressed admiration for the radioactivity workers, but voiced the old-school chemists' fear that developments of profound importance were being made through experiments on inconceivably minute quantities of matter. The traditionalists, he added, were also disturbed at the invasion of chemistry by mathematics and by the "speculative philosophy" accompanying radioactivity. The unwillingness to accept certain conclusions of radioactivity because the measurements had been made on imponderable quantities was real and widespread. Marie Curie, for example, had to prepare sufficient quantities of radium to determine its atomic weight before it would be accepted as a new element; spectroscopic and chemical proof were not enough.

2. Soddy and Thomas D. Mackenzie, "The relation between uranium and radium," *Phil. Mag., 14* (Aug. 1907), 272–95.

3. BBB, "The origin of radium," *Nature, 76* (26 Sept. 1907), 544–45.

4. BBB, "The origin of radium," *Nature, 76* (10 Oct. 1907), 589.

5. In announcing his discovery of actinium in 1899, Debierne said that his new radioelement had chemical properties similar to thorium. Now Boltwood is claiming that the preparation that he and his student, Langley, obtained eight years earlier was really ionium (which is an isotope of thorium). Debierne, says Boltwood, had a mixture of actinium and ionium, but believed he had a single element. This confusion accounted not only for Boltwood's initial belief that actinium was the parent of radium, but for the controversy whether actinium and Giesel's emanium were identical, despite their dissimilar chemical properties.

6. By determining the relative activities: the sum of the relative activities of all radioelements in the series, taken individually, must equal the activity of the uranium mineral at equilibrium.

7. Here is another example of observed chemical similarity between radioelements with different half-lives. In the next half dozen years such examples accumulated until, in 1913, Kasimir Fajans and Frederick Soddy showed that these radioelements were chemically identical, not just similar; they were isotopes.

27 SEPTEMBER 1907

University, Manchester

My dear Boltwood,

Your letter re the "Origin of Radium" in Nature to-day prompts me to write you a letter. Our last letters crossed & I trust a similar fate will befall this one. First of all, I find myself in very general agreement with your remarks in Nature. I have not got so far as to find the parent of radium gives out α rays; in fact, I have done but very little since I left Montreal. Your explanation of my separation of pa-radium by ammon[ium] sulphide is incorrect. I did not use it in solution at all but added ammonia & then passed H_2S into it. I noticed sometimes fine particles in the solution which I put down to sulphur. I expect the separation is due to that as I believe sulphur separates out with sodium thiosulphate. I laid no confidence that Am_2S would always work out but from my point of view (physical) I did'nt care a dam whether it worked a second time or not. It did the trick I wanted first time so I did not pry too closely into the mechanism. You will observe how far I am still from the correct chemical frame of mind. I acknowledge I have sometimes the most devilish luck considering my general ignorance of chemical methods. I am just starting into an examination of my residues contg actinium from the R.S.[1] It is too early yet to make any definite statements but I think some interesting points probably in confirmation of your own will come out of it.

I start lectures next week & the preliminaries are now in progress. I am expecting 4 Germans to work here, one a physicist, one a physical chemist, one a chemist & the other H. W. Schmidt of Giessen. The latter can only get away 3 months. You will know him by his papers on Rad A, B, C. What with the local product, I shall be pretty busy I expect. I may mention in confidence I hope to get *half a gram* of radium by Xmas for use. I wonder whether the chance of working with this to confirm (?) Ramsay's discoveries of the past year may bring you over to assist. I wish you could. I want a chemical expert & I think we could settle some important things pretty definitely. I should be delighted to have you over to remind me of old times & to look after me and my morals. The weather here has been extraordinarily fine & sunny for the past month—quite a record. The lab is in good shape for work. Give my kindest regards to Bumstead & to my other friends. Mrs. R & Eileen send best wishes. Yours ever,

E. RUTHERFORD

I am glad to see you stick by your guns & make Ra have a period of 1900 years. I told Ramsay in the Chem Soc that physicists were a difficult people to convince and although I was open to conviction, *nothing* would convince me the period of Ra was 250 years. He must have got some personal emanation! in with the Ra.

1. The Royal Society obtained a large quantity of radioactive materials from Austria and placed them at the disposal of Rutherford, Ramsay, and possibly others.

20 OCTOBER 1907

17 Wilmslow Road
Withington, Manchester

My dear Boltwood,

I was very much interested in your letter and congratulate you on your success in getting one element to your credit. I feel a sort of paternal feeling with regard to it, having taken part in its inception. I don't care much for the name "ionium" but can't suggest a better. I would have liked a name to show its place somehow in the radioactive family. I have some experiments going with the R.S. residues, treating them after your methods but will have to wait to see how the curves go for a week or two more. You deserve to get the last of the radioactive family. I never felt that Debierne deserved much credit for actinium—he could'nt miss it. As a matter of fact, if there had been a dozen elements with actinium, he had not enough radioactive sense to find it out.

I am sending you 100 grams or so of the residues for you to look at. The activity as wet paste is six times UrOx & when dry about 70 times. I have been delaying to get the formal sanction of the R.S. for the transfer. I shall be glad to know what you make of it. What you say about Hahn & "commercial work" is I think a little unfair. Hahn had to give a promise to Knöffler & Co. not to describe his methods of separation until he obtained

1. Henri Becquerel, in his laboratory at the Museum of Natural History, Paris. The large electromagnet in front of him is the one with which he studied the deflection of beta rays in late 1899.

2. Marie Curie, in her laboratory at the Sorbonne, Paris. On the table in the foreground is the piezo-electrometer, designed by her husband Pierre and his brother Jacques, with which she measured the radioactivity of her sources. Courtesy of the New York Academy of Medicine.

3. Frederick Soddy. Courtesy of the *British Journal of Radiology*.

4. William Ramsay. Courtesy of Mrs. Muriel Howorth.

5. The McGill University Physics Department staff, 1907, in front of the laboratory building. L to R: front row: J. Cox, E. Rutherford, R. K. McClung, A. S. Eve; row 2: H. T. Barnes, G. Rümelin, H. Bronson; row 3: R. W. Boyle, L. LeGrow, S. Podville, R. Lawrence, G. Dunn. Courtesy of McGill University.

6. Some staff, research students, and vistors to Rutherford's Manchester laboratory in 1910, in front of a shed used to accommodate the laboratory's "overflow." L to R: H. Geiger, A. F. Kovarik, B. B. Boltwood, W. Kay, W. C. Lantsberry, W. Wilson, J. A. Gray, R. W. Boyle (seated). Courtesy of Lansing V. Hammond.

7. Otto Hahn, Bertram Boltwood, Ernest Rutherford, and Otto von Baeyer in Munich, 1910, after the completion of Boltwood's year in Manchester. Courtesy of Otto Hahn.

8. Hans Geiger, while on army reserve training during the summer of 1910. Courtesy of Yale University.

9. The Manchester University Physical and Electro-Technical Laboratories staff and research students, 1912. L to R: front row: R. Rossi, H. G. J. Moseley, J. N. Pring, H. Gerrard, E. Marsden; row 2: H. Geiger, W. Makower, A. Schuster, E. Rutherford, R. Beattie, H. Stansfield, E. J. Evans; row 3: C. G. Darwin, J. A. Gray, D. C. H. Florance, Margaret White, May Leslie, H. R. Robinson, A. S. Russell, H. Schrader, Y. Tuomikoski; row 4: J. M. Nuttall, W. Kay, H. P. Walmsley, J. Chadwick. Courtesy of Kasimir Fajans.

their permission. This was the condition of allowing him to examine all their residues. If you get more radio- or meso-thorium than you want, you might send me over some to play with. I want samples of every thing radioactive.

I am now in full swing of work. Classes are all going. I lecture to one of 150. I have started a course of lectures on Radioactivity especially for the chemists & have a roll up of 70. This is a pretty active place and but for its climate has a number of advantages—a good set of colleagues, a hospitable & kindly people and no side any where. However, I ought not to complain of the climate so far, for the weather has been first class.

I go to a dinner to a Statistical Society here this week. J.J.T.[1] comes up as guest of honour & on me falls the duty of proposing his health. He lectures here again on Nov 4 & I will probably see something of him then. I have had a bad cold but am in good form again. I find the students here regard a full professor as little short of Lord God Almighty. It is quite refreshing after the critical attitude of Canadian students. It is always a good thing to feel you are appreciated. We are all well & flourishing. Tell Bumstead to drop me a line when the spirit moves him.

Best regards to Dana. Yours ever,

E. RUTHERFORD

1. Joseph John Thomson. He was widely known by his initials, so much so, in fact, that when he was knighted he was commonly referred to as "Sir J.J." instead of "Sir Joseph."

30 OCTOBER 1907

Sloane Laboratory, Yale University
New Haven, Connecticut

My dear Rutherford,

I was very glad to get your letter of the 27th of September and to hear how things were going at Manchester. I do not think that there is the slightest doubt as to the individuality of ionium. I have been able to separate preparations of it from carnotite (which is essentially free from thorium) having an activity of about 2000 times uranium. It is not entirely free from other radioactive products when thus prepared and contains small proportions of other things emitting alpha-particles of longer range, but Wheeler has examined it in his modified Bragg apparatus and finds that the preponderance of alpha-particles have a range of about 2.8 cm in air and my measurements by the scintillation method give a similar value. The beta-radiation which I attributed to ionium does not belong to it but is due to uranium X which is present in the freshly prepared material. This is evident from the fact that the β radiation is falling off at a rate corresponding to half-value in about 22 days and is absent from my older and weaker preparations. The value for the coefficient of absorption which I find for these β rays is 17.0 $(cm)^{-1}$, which does not agree very well with Levin's value of 27 and is different from yours of 14. Still I think that it is not far from right and mean to check it up later by a direct measurement of uranium-X.

If I could only get about a hundred pounds of a good grade of carnotite ore to work up I think that there would be no great difficulty in obtaining preparations with an activity of several hundred-thousand times uranium. I have written to one of my miner friends in Colorado, the one who supplied me with the carnotite I have been using, asking him to send me some more mineral, but as I have heard nothing from him I am afraid that he has moved away.

Your treatment of your actinium preparation was not really a treatment with ammonium sulphide at all, but should properly be called a treatment with hydrogen sulphide in ammoniacal solution. The separation which you got was probably due to the ammonia alone, which appears to precipitate the ionium immediately and the actinium only after some time. You will remember that both Levin and Hahn found that actinium was not readily precipitated by ammonia, but that they had to let the mixture stand in order to get an actinium-free filtrate. The hydrogen sulphide probably played no part in the separation. You want to look out for this same phenomenon in working up your actinium residues or you may miss a good deal of the actinium.

Your suggestion about my going over to Manchester to work is certainly an attractive one. I know of nothing that appeals to me more strongly just at present. What I would like above everything else is to be with someone who was energetic and enthusiastic, for now I sometimes feel doubts as to whether it is really worth while working nights and Sundays. One does get so lonesome all by oneself at such times. But it really isn't feasible for me to think of going over at present. In the first place I could not afford it financially and in the second place I could not get away from here this year as I have taken a part of the elementary laboratory instruction in order to get an additional $500 which I really needed.

It certainly looks as if you were going to have a good group of men working with you and I am glad to see the chemists among them for that means hope for the future. H. Willy Schmidt is certainly promising, it seems to me that considering his opportunities his work has been of a very creditable character.

My own work is progressing regularly. I am engaged in getting the loose ends pulled together for formal publication on the three topics of the relative activities of the different constituents of uranium minerals, the radium parent and the life of radium. As they are all closely related it will be rather difficult to arrange my data properly in the three papers. There is too much for a single article. If it is not asking you too much would you be willing to give me an opinion (confidential of course) as to whether McCoy is justified in assuming a simple absorption law in calculating his activities of uranium minerals. He finds (Phil. Mag., Jan., 1906) [1] the ratio as 4.15 while I find 5.4. I know of some reasons for the discrepancy but it seems to me that his main assumption is not justified. Just at the moment I am attempting to separate ionium from my pure uranium nitrate (three years old). It looks as if I was going to find it in about the right amount.

With regards and best wishes, and kindest remembrances to Mrs. Rutherford and Eileen, Yours sincerely,

BERTRAM B. BOLTWOOD

1. McCoy, "The relation between the radioactivity and the composition of uranium compounds," *Phil. Mag., 11* (Jan. 1906), 176–86. In this paper, McCoy reported that if the activity of a given amount of uranium be taken as one, the activity of this uranium, plus the radium and radium products found with it at equilibrium, will be 4.15.

24 NOVEMBER 1907

Physical Laboratories
The University, Manchester

My dear Boltwood,

I should have written to you before but I have been very much occupied alround. You will have seen the letters in Nature; [1] by the way "picradium" was a misprint for "preradium." As a matter of fact, I care very little what it is called "what's in a name" anyway, provided it does'nt take the suggestive character of "Soddy." By the way you will have seen another letter in Nature by F.S., again rubbing it in to some unoffending persons about electrons & high vacua.[2] Apropos of Nature what an amusing critique in Nature of friend Duncan's "Commercial Chemistry."[3] Really, I think the Englishman sometimes does good in his quiet way. The only objection I have is that it is an indirect gibe at American Technical science. Hahn's letter is good & suggestive.[4] I hope you can fix the period of Ra with certainty, so as to knockout Ramsay straight off. I believe he got nitrous oxide with his emanation & did'nt know it. Soddy says he has a man with him who finds the radium rays produce quite a considerable amt. of nitrous oxide out of air.

This brings me to the Radium question. I think I told you the Austrian people [5] promised me about half a gram of Ra. Apparently they changed their mind at the end & decided to try Ramsay's expts &c themselves. I believe they have nearly 3 grams in all and I don't blame them. Apparently Ramsay had been promised some too, so they finally gave us 250 mg $RaCl_2$ *in common*. Of course this is very awkward but I am making arrangements with Ramsay. He of course begs me to let him have it first because he knows the Austrian people are on his trail. We have finally compromised. He is to provide me with Emanation when I want it from his own & the Austrian fraction & the Radium is to come into my possession in a year or so's time. This is of course quite private. I am not anxious to change with Ramsay under the conditions as it would mean I would have to get down to work on the emanation & nothing else & I hate to be tied down.

By the way, I hope you recd. the actinium sample. We have been making preliminary expts. with it but have not settled yet how to tackle it. I want a good man to go at it continuously. Let me know if you can suggest a method of attack after you have tried the sample. There is a lot of Ra in it. I calculate 6 mgrs in the whole cask. I want of course to get the "ionium" & "actinium" separated as simply & inexpensively as possible.

I have now got 5 Germans in the Lab. & one Jap not to mention the local article.[6] They all seem pretty good fellows who have had plenty of experience at research before. Schmidt has to leave at Xmas to take up his lectures again. He has nearly done one small piece of work here on the question of recombination of the active deposit of Ra. As I expected the + charged carriers behave like ions. I go to London on Saturday to attend the annual R.S. dinner. Michelson & Morley [7] are to be over. I am running down to Cambridge on Dec. 10 to a Trinity dinner. I am getting through a number of lectures to various societies—a duty for a new-comer. I think I am converting the chemists here to proper views but don't expect any result from it. Nearly all the chem students in the second & third year attend lectures I am giving on Radioactivity.

You asked a question re the absorption of α rays. I forgot to look up McCoys paper. I shall do so at once & let you know my opinion. Personally, however, I would not lay much stress on results that involve absorption factors which are not accurately determined. You know Bragg showed the curve of absorption of α rays from a layer while not exponential looked dam'd like it over a considerable range.

I have a popular lecture on tomorrow evening & have to think what I am going to say.

With kind regards. Yours ever,

E. RUTHERFORD

1. N. R. Campbell, "The nomenclature of radio-activity," *Nature, 76* (24 Oct. 1907), 638. ER, "Origin of radium," *Nature, 76* (31 Oct. 1907), 661.

2. Soddy, "The Wehnelt Kathode in a high vacuum," *Nature, 77* (21 Nov. 1907), 53–54. In this letter to the editor Soddy criticizes O. W. Richardson and Wehnelt.

3. Anonymous review of R. K. Duncan's *The Chemistry of Commerce. A Simple Interpretation of Some New Chemistry in Its Relation to Modern Industry* (London and New York, Harper, 1907), in *Nature, 77* (21 Nov. 1907), 49–50. The reviewer faults the book for being no more than "detached fragments," published earlier in journals. Duncan, he feels, has little sympathy for theory and gets "effectually lost." Most disturbing is the journalistic style, for the author has a "passion for strong words, and his vocabulary is simply amazing."

4. Hahn, "The origin of radium," *Nature, 77* (14 Nov. 1907), 30–31.

5. The Austrian Academy of Sciences.

6. Rutherford's laboratory was always something of an international gathering place. He also had, at various times, several women working on radioactivity; this in an age when few women pursued scientific careers.

7. Albert Michelson and Edward Morley, the American team famous for the "ether drift" experiment, which showed there was no difference in the velocity of light, whatever the direction of the observer's motion.

28 NOVEMBER 1907

Sloane Laboratory, Yale University
New Haven, Connecticut

My dear Rutherford,[1]

I want to thank you ever so much for your kindness in sending me the 184 grams of the R.S. "Actinium" residues. The material was duly received about two weeks after the time that you sent it off and I have completed a preliminary examination of it. It requires quite a stretch of the imagination to designate it as "Actinium" though, for as you have probably found out ere this, it contains a good many other things radioactive and otherwise. The scheme which I suggested for working it up was an altogether too simple one under the circumstances, and it really has to be treated quite in the manner of a crude mineral. The following process has worked fairly satisfactorily. The material as received was transferred into a porcelain dish and about 200 cc. of dilute hydrochloric acid added. The mixture was heated and thoroughly stirred, and evaporated to complete dryness on a water bath. The residue was moistened with dilute hydrochloric acid and treated with about 400 cc. of hot water; the mixture was heated to boiling and filtered hot; the residue remaining on the filter was washed with boiling water. On cooling, a considerable quantity of lead chloride crystallized out and was removed. The solution was concentrated by evaporation, again cooled and more lead chloride removed. The solution was diluted to about one liter with water and an excess of hydrogen sulphide run in. The precipitated sulphides (lead, antimony, tin, bismuth, Ra D and Ra F), were filtered off and washed with H_2S water. The filtrate was boiled to remove hydrogen sulphide and again filtered. This filtrate was heated to boiling and about 25 grams of oxalic acid in hot aqueous solution

177

added. After standing 24 hours the precipitated oxalates were filtered off and washed repeatedly with boiling water (a large portion of the precipitated oxalates consisting possibly of zinc oxalate were removed in this manner). The remaining oxalates were ignited to oxides, dissolved in dilute hydrochloric acid, the solution evaporated to dryness. A small quantity of hydrochloric acid was added to the residue which was then dissolved in hot water and the solution filtered. The solution was heated to boiling and a solution of 10 grams of oxalic acid in hot water added (total volume of mixture about 100 cc). The mixture was allowed to stand for 24 hours, the oxalates filtered off, ignited to oxides, dissolved in hydrochloric acid * and then treated three times with sodium thiosulphate under the conditions described in my last letter. At the point marked above with a star, the solution was diluted to about 200 cc. and the rare earths present precipitated from the boiling solution with an excess of ammonia hydroxide, the mixture was allowed to stand for 24 hours and the hydroxides were filtered off. They were dissolved in the least possible quantity of hydrochloric acid and the treatment with sodium thiosulphate conducted with this solution.

After the third precipitation with sodium thiosulphate the solution was filtered and the material remaining on the filter was digested with hot dilute hydrochloric acid. The sulphur and paper fibre was filtered off and the solution (about 50 cc) was made strongly alkaline with ammonia. On heating to boiling a very slight precipitate appeared. This was filtered off and together with the paper was ignited in a platinum crucible. The residue remaining weighted only a fraction of a milligram and had an activity equal to about that of one gram of uranium. The activity of this preparation appears to be due entirely to ionium, although I have not had it under observation long enough to be sure that there is no actinium or other similar product present. It looks very much, therefore, as if but a small proportion of the ionium present in the original mineral was retained in these residues, which is not at all surprising if its properties are similar to those of thorium. If this is so then it explains in part why the element which I call ionium has not been previously identified.

And this last statement reminds me of the interesting communications by Campbell [2] and yourself [3] re "ionium" which have appeared in the columns of Nature. I can not help recalling the conversation of the White Knight with Alice in the last part of "Through the Looking-glass" which refers to a song which he is going to sing to her. In this case the name of the thing is "ionium"; the thing is called "paradium," and the name of the thing is called "uranium A"! If later we can succeed in getting the lady (Hahn calls it "die Muttersubstanz," so *it* must be a *she*) respectably tied up to uranium, then I will not have the least objection to her changing her name. But for the present my motto is "fest sitzen."

What you say of Hahn is undoubtedly true and I would not for the world do him the least injustice. He is a fine fellow and I really think most highly of him.

With regards and best wishes to you all, I remain, Yours sincerely,

BERTRAM B. BOLTWOOD

1. Only page 3 of the original letter is preserved in Cambridge. The entire letter exists, however, in a typed copy, also in Cambridge.

2. N. R. Campbell, "The nomenclature of radio-activity," *Nature,* 76 (24 Oct. 1907), 638.

3. ER, "Origin of radium," *Nature,* 76 (31 Oct. 1907), 661.

15 FEBRUARY 1908

University, Manchester

My dear Boltwood,

I have'nt written to you for an age or at any rate I feel correspondingly guilty. I shall be writing up in a week or two an account in the Jahrbuch der Radio-akt &c[1] of the work on the origin of Ra. Send us along as many of your papers as you have for reference. I may mention that they don't take in the Amer Jour Sci in our Library but I have to go a special pilgrimage to the Lit & Phil Society[2] here to get it. I have not been doing any more on the problem but I presume you have got things pretty well cleared up by this time. Let me hear how things stand. I have been at work on my method of detecting a single α particle[3] & hope in a few months to get a good few of the magnitudes of radioactive quantities straightened out. It involves a good deal of rather tricky work but I think I see my way to the end alright.

To day is Sunday & I feel considerably picked [?] up as the Austrian Acad have kindly sent me some 7% Ra preparation containing about 500 mg $RaBr_2$. I am now quite independent of Ramsay & have got more than he has—so should selfishness (not of my self) be always rewarded. I understand that the Austrian Acad were not altogether pleased with the mode of distribution proposed by Ramsay for the joint use of the first sample with myself—hence the result. All's well that ends well. I shall probably get off the emanation by heating. Ramsay uses solution and *assumes* that all the emanation comes off. I should not be surprised if he measured the amount of Ra Eman in his measuring tube by γ rays instead of assuming it, he would find the life of Ra 50 years instead of 150. I speak with some authority as he has sent me up a number of draws of emanation from his main quantity of Ra. I am going first of all to have a look at the volume of the emanation. If I don't reduce it to 1/10 of his, my theoretical predictions are not worth a dam. I expect it will take me some little time to get things going in good shape. I have fortunately an A_1 glass blower[4] alongside who can do anything that is possible & what is more can do it well.

I have heard nothing more of the lithium, neon & argon production. I heard a fairly reliable rumour that he had repeated some of the old expts. with the large quantity of Ra Eman &

now considers the subject is *not worth working at!* However, we shall know in time.

As for myself, I am in pretty good form with plenty to do & very little time to do it. I visited Dublin the other day to give a lecture & had a good time & fine weather. I get a little golf & manage to keep in good spirits notwithstanding the proverbial effect of an English winter. I think the place will suit me first class.

Tell Dana I am much obliged for the pretty card he sent me & for his good wishes. I shall try & write to him before long. Give my kind regards to Bumstead & Wheeler & Dadourian whom I hope are still alive & kicking.

Drop me a line when the spirit moves you. Any gossip of American science is quite acceptable to my frivolous temperament. Yours ever,

E. RUTHERFORD

1. The *Jahrbuch der Radioaktivität und Elektronik* (Leipzig) and *Le Radium* (Paris), both founded in 1904, were the earliest journals devoted to radioactivity and related studies. Both barely survived World War I, merging then with stronger periodicals.

2. Founded in 1785, the Literary and Philosophical Society of Manchester was the most important provincial scientific society in England.

3. Rutherford may here be referring either to electrical counting or counting the flashes of light produced when an alpha particle strikes a scintillation screen. Both these methods were developed about this time, with the important help of Hans Geiger.

4. Otto Baumbach, about whom more later.

3 MAY 1908

Sloane Laboratory, Yale University
New Haven, Connecticut

My dear Rutherford,

It does not seem possible that so many weeks can have passed since I received your last letter of the eighteenth [1] of February, but the time has gone very rapidly and it does not seem as if I had accomplished much in the interval. I have been hard at work at a number of problems and have not yet been able to find anything very exciting in any of them. One of the things that I have been trying to do is to split up uranium into two or more separate radio-elements; I have found some indications of such a possibility but nothing conclusive.

I note with regret what you say about the American Journal not being taken in your library, and I don't think that you show a proper sort of friendship for Dana in not insisting that it be subscribed for. You surely ought to be able to convince the librarian that it is absolutely essential that you have that periodical immediately at hand so as to keep posted on the recent advances in geology, paleontology and bugology. However I have attempted to make up the deficiency by sending you a proof of my paper in the May number [2] along with my reprints, and I am now enclosing herewith a proof of the paper which is to appear in the June issue.[3] Please do not forget to send me a reprint of your paper in the December Phil. Mag.,[4] which up to the present I have not received, and also a copy of that Adamson Lecture of J.J., if there any spare copies available.

I certainly felt half-a-head taller when I read your discourse at the Royal Institution as it appeared in Nature [5] and I had to buy a larger hat the very next day. "You certainly were good to me," as the saying goes, and I fully appreciate it.

I shall be very much interested to learn of the outcome of your experiments with the radium emanation and to hear how Ramsay's epoch making work is progressing. That last communication of his in Nature [6] bore some of the ear marks of an early crawl, but still it seems almost time for another outbreak. I wonder why it hasn't occured to him that radium emanation and kerosine form lobster salad!!

Speaking of radium emanation reminds me that Perkins,[7] one of our graduate students, has completed a comparison of the rates of diffusion of the emanation and mercury vapour, both monatomic and having molecular weights of the same order of magnitude. The experiments were conducted at 200° C and over, and show that the molecular weight of the emanation is greater than that of mercury vapour, indicating a value of about 230. I nearly split my head in attempts to devise apparatus which was approximately fool-proof, for he is not a very good experimenter and the problem was not a simple one. His paper will appear in the June number of the Am. Journ.[8]

I suppose that Bronson has written you about the results of his experiments on the relative activity of the emanations and active deposits of thorium and actinium. What do you think of the matter as it stands, and how does it fit in with your fundamental objection to the expulsion of unequal numbers of α particles by members of a radioactive family?

Let me hear from you when you get a chance for life is always more worth the living after the receipt of a letter from you. With regards, best wishes and remembrances to all, Sincerely yours,

BERTRAM B. BOLTWOOD

1. Rutherford's letter was dated 15, not 18 February.

2. BBB, "On ionium, a new radio-active element," *Am. J. Sci.*, 25 (May 1908), 365–81.

3. BBB, "On the life of radium," *Am. J. Sci.*, 25 (June 1908), 493–506.

4. ER, "The production and origin of radium," *Phil. Mag.*, 14 (Dec. 1907), 733–49.

5. ER, "Recent advances in radio-activity," *Nature*, 77 (5 Mar. 1908), 422–26.

6. Ramsay, "Lithium in radio-active minerals," *Nature*, 77 (5 Mar. 1908), 412.

7. Perry B. Perkins received his Ph.D. from Yale in 1908, then held a succession of positions at Trinity College (Hartford), Howard, Brown, and finally Mt. Allison University (New Brunswick). He spent the year 1913–14 in Rutherford's Manchester laboratory.

8. Perkins, "A determination of the molecular weight of radium emanation by the comparison of its rate of diffusion with mercury vapor," *Am. J. Sci.*, 25 (June 1908), 461–73.

23 AUGUST 1908

Llanrwst, N. Wales

My dear Boltwood,

I am writing this in the country free from all distractions and where there is nothing to do but eat, sleep, & be lazy. Under these conditions, I feel exceedingly fit to start another year's work. You will have seen my [illegible] to Bumstead with an account of what I have been doing to set the radioactive house in order. This at once brings me to consideration of Ramsay, who has done so much to put it into disorder. You will have seen that Mme Curie has blown his lithium production.[1] I may mention *in confidence* that we have also found his neon production to be derived from the external air. I can easily detect the neon yellow in 1/15 cc of air & can get the whole spectrum out of less than 2/10 cc. All his work of the last few years appears to be disintegrating at a very rapid rate. The more I go into it, the more I perceive his inability to do anything decently. I am quite sure his motto is "Better to have boomed and bust than not have boomed at all." His spectrum of the emanations has not yet seen the light; I hope it will not prove to be still-born. You will [have] gathered from my letter to Bumstead how nimble our friend is.[2]

I am going over to Dublin to the B.A. in a week or so but am going to look on as far as possible. They are always pestering for papers, and then find that not more than five minutes can be allowed to give an account of them. I was much interested in Bronson's paper on the number of α particles from the emanations &c.[3] I find on reading some of my old papers, that I had done experiments on the relative activity of the ThEm & active deposit long ago & recognized that they would'nt fit in. I find I have now reached the stage of forgetting what I have worked at in the olden days. We are going on with the number of α particles business. Could you spare a sample of your *purest* uranium oxide & of a good sample of uraninite (with percentage of Ur) so we can compare the relative number of α particles emitted compared with Ra. Any details of the best way of getting a really thin film would be very acceptable. I have a number of researches I want to tackle as soon as I get back to finish up the helium business and other problems. It is a great pity we can't get a lead [?] on the actinium business to know where & how it comes in. If this were done, the whole show would be in line. Hahn writes me he has got two more products in the active deposit of actinium. They, however, are subsidiary & don't affect things much. He seems to have a sense of smell for such products. You will have seen that Hale [4] is doing good things on the sunspots & that Onnes [5] has got liquid helium at last. He deserves it after the trouble he has taken. The quest of the absolute zero will now be at end for some time to come until they try & find the liquefaction point of a collection of electrons.

I have thoroughly enjoyed my transference to England & find myself very much at home. I worked rather hard at the research end & shall ease up a bit next year. We have had an ideal summer fine weather, not too hot & not too cold. My wife & Eileen are both well & flourishing. The former sends her best wishes & we hope you will drop in to stay with us before long. I hope to see you all at Winnipeg [6] next year. Yours ever,

E. RUTHERFORD

1. Marie Curie and Ellen Gleditsch, "Action de l'émanation du radium sur les solutions des sels de cuivre," *Comptes Rendus, 147* (10 Aug. 1908), 345–49.

2. In his letter to Bumstead, of 11 July 1908 (a copy is preserved in RCC), Rutherford tells how he was able to photograph the spectrum of emanation, whereas Ramsay had long been unable to do this. As a courtesy to Ramsay, before publication, Rutherford mentioned his success and told him the general scheme followed. Ramsay immediately got to work and sent to the Royal Society a photograph of the spectrum, then told Rutherford he had gotten it by accident. However, Rutherford had

neglected to inform Ramsay how to separate the emanation spectrum from that of hydrogen, and Ramsay's claim of priority thus rested on inexact measurements of few lines. Rutherford was annoyed at first, but then settled down to enjoy Ramsay's dilemma.

3. Bronson, "On the relative activity of the emanation and the active deposit from thorium and from actinium," *Phil. Mag., 16* (Aug. 1908), 291–99.

4. George Ellery Hale, American astronomer who figured prominently in the organization of several observatories early in this century.

5. Heike Kamerlingh-Onnes, founder of the cryogenic laboratory at the University of Leyden.

6. The British Association for the Advancement of Science, which traditionally held its meetings in a different city each year, occasionally moved the location beyond the British Isles.

20 SEPTEMBER 1908

Physical Laboratories
The University, Manchester

My dear Boltwood,

You appear like myself to have a constitutional aversion to letter writing but for the moment the spirit moves me to give you an account of the Dublin Meeting of the B.A. and of the troubles of that greatest of chemists whose name is sung through all parts of the earth. There seemed to be a general idea that a scrap was likely to take place, so there was always a full turn up at the point of supposed danger. The ball opened with a paper by Ramsay on the atomic weights of the emanations based on holes in the periodic classification. 262 was assigned to the ThEm and lord knows what for actinium. I got up & poked fun at his arguments & gave my method of deduction. Just as the paper was over, Ramsay jumps over & says in an airy manner that the deduction of at weights by the α particle method was all very well but had been completely upset by his discovery that the emanations changed into neon. I was up & in three sentences told him I did'nt believe the latter. The chairman jumped in & Ramsay left. Shortly after Dewar got up & gave his paper on the rate of production of He—since appeared in Proc Roy Soc. He looked 10 years younger for he felt he could dance freely on R. at last. He gave utterance to a dozen or more sentences of a type only to be manufactured by Dewar which looked very sugary to the uninitiated but were really filled with gall. The audience sniggered audibly at the hits & Dewar swelled visibly. Altogether he gave our friend some nasty jars & by the way patted me on the back as a corrective.

In another day in the Chem. Section, Ramsay gave an account of the history of his discoveries of the inactive gases—all ancient & innocuous. Then Hartley gave his experiments on the distribution of lithium & danced on R. a bit & showed that he did'nt have much faith in the Cu-Li transformation—which you know has been riddled by Mme Curie. Ramsay got up & said that the neon expt. was quite sure but the proof Cu into Li was more difficult. I was called on & gave a brief account of my experiments on the changes of Eman into neon over water or rather on the absence of neon & that the neon he got was due to the air let in his apparatus.

I don't think I told you that one can detect the neon line easily from 1/15 cc of air & get a good spectrum with 2/15 while R. in his published expt. had an amt. of N of nearly .3 cc which leaked in. As a matter of fact if you exclude air you get He but devil a trace of Ne. His experiments are quite valueless. He took it fairly well & made a few airy remarks. I send you an account of the day written by one who knows in a Dublin paper.[1] I will have a tale to tell you later about his spectrum of the emanation but I must'nt blow it just yet.

So much for scientific gossip. How are you getting along? I presume you are still kicking. I am very fit & intend to get right down to work in a day or two.

Have you got any light yet on the position of actinium? I have left that phase of the subject & it is up to you to clear it up. We are all well.

With kind regards. Yours ever,

E. RUTHERFORD

PS Soddy is now married but have'nt seen him for a year.

The general impression at the B.A. was that R. was suffering from megalomania & that it was about time he was brought up with a sound turn. I am expecting shortly some further discoveries of his of the change of gold into silver or vice-versa for he has been whispering of some great discoveries in that direction.

The neon paper of ours will appear in a month or two.[2] I think it closes that phase of the subject.

1. Rutherford sent the newspaper clipping which is here reproduced in its entirety.

Among The Sections: Notes and Notabilities
By E. E. Fournier D'Albe, B.Sc., M.R.I.A.

It was a strenuous day. All the sections were working at high pressure. For yesterday was the high-water day of the British Association. Members were supposed to be back from their brief holiday, and ready for any amount of speaking and listening. And so the hour of ten a.m. saw most of the sections well filled. Presidents in their chairs, and speakers ready to ascend the platform or descend into the lecturing well, according to the architectural design of the place of meeting. And whether it is that truth is supposed to abide at the bottom of a well, as the Arabs have it, or for some other occult reason, it seemed somehow more appropriate and convincing to take your teaching from below upwards, than to look up to a man who adorned the platform and looked more like a political orator than a learned expounder of science.

Lecture Theatre Or War

Witness the stately opening of the Chemistry Section in its appropriate theatre. The well swarmed with celebrities, who filled it "from stem to stern," if I may use that aqueous expression. Was it the magic word "helium," or the expectation of another lively exchange, that drew together so great an audience? If it was the latter, the listeners

188

were not disappointed. For Sir William Ramsay, most brilliant of speakers, and most courteous of antagonists, was again exposed to a raking fusilade. Not only did Professor Rutherford roundly accuse him of having let air into his apparatus, and so obtained the false appearance of the spontaneous production of that strangely inert gas Neon from radium, but Professor Hartley, of the Royal College of Science for Ireland, following in the footsteps of Madame Curie, scouted all expectations of converting copper into lithium, as Sir Wm. Ramsay thought he had done, much to the detriment of the copper.

Ubiquitous Lithium

Ramsay was greatly struck with the appearance of the red ray of lithium shortly after a solution of a pure copper compound had been exposed to the emanation of radium. He was greatly struck, because lithium is comparatively rare, and less to be expected than sodium or potassium. But Mr. Hartley dispelled that fond illusion. He pointed out that lithium was anything but rare. He and Mr. Ramage had found it practically everywhere. "I found it," he went on to say, "where you would least expect it."

> "I found it in water, I found it in soot,
> I found it in marble and dust,
> I found it in mud from the heel of my boot,
> I found it in smoke and in rust."

Those were not Professor Hartley's exact words, but they convey somewhat of the substance of his speech and the rhythm of his delivery. Sir William Ramsay was called upon, somewhat maliciously I thought, to reply to each attack as it was delivered. He parried them with an easy air of superiority, expressing his hope that "out of so much heat some light might come." It was a drawn battle.

2. ER and T. Royds, "The action of the radium emanation upon water," *Phil. Mag., 16* (Nov. 1908), 812–18.

11 OCTOBER 1908

Sloane Laboratory, Yale University
New Haven, Connecticut

My dear Rutherford,
   You can have no idea of the pleasure and entertainment that your letters afforded me during the past summer or how greatly

I appreciated your goodness in writing them. As a correspondent I am simply abominable and I am getting worse as time goes on instead of better. I have only one excuse to offer and that is that I am living such a commonplace sort of existence that I really haven't anything worth writing about, while you, as you wrote me before leaving this country, are "now on the firing line." What a perfectly bully time you have been having and how interesting it is to hear all about it! And again, how good you are to let me know all the details! If I had only known in advance what a fine bull-baiting exhibition there was to be at the B.A. meeting at Dublin, I think that I would have made a strong effort to be present. Why even to hear about it has done me more good than a six months vacation.

I do hope, now that Ramsay has been treed, that you wont call off the dogs, but that you will keep on hammering at him until you have brought him down. He should be absolutely discredited in all matters radioactive, for he entered the field under false colors and has been playing to the grand stand ever since. During the last four years he has been guilty of bad faith, bad judgement and the rottenest scientific spirit. A lesser light would have been condemned to the inferno long ago but the Anglo-Saxon spirit of hero worship carries him along and I have no doubt that many a scientist today has only pity for those less "brilliant experimenters" who are unable to "confirm" the epoch making discoveries of the "greatest scientist since Faraday." And why will such men as Dewar, who feels so strongly about Ramsay, insist upon mixing their vinegar with so much oil and sugar that they only pour a sort of mild salad dressing over him which makes him all the more attractive to the popular palate. I am thinking especially of that last paper of Dewar's on the "Volume of Helium, etc" in which he takes an almost apologetic attitude. Why doesn't he come out and say what he thinks instead of leaving it more or less to the average reader to decide whether he or Ramsay has the better of it?

I write with some feeling on this matter because I had a devil of a time trying to persuade some of my chemical friends last summer that Ramsay was not the whole show in radioactivity. We had a general meeting of the American Chemical Society here in New Haven at the end of June and practically every mothers son that I met was firmly convinced that Ramsay was the biggest thing that could be seen on the horizon. Practically not a single one was willing to concede that he even "might be wrong." I did not try to persuade them that he *was* wrong, but only attempted to prepare their minds for the denials of his conclusions which I felt sure would be soon forthcoming. I think that most of them felt the same sort of pity for me that a good catholic feels for one who is not a true believer. For the Pope can do no wrong.

I had an interesting talk with Ames [1] last winter at the time of the Physical Society meeting. He got me to one side and asked me very cautiously what I thought about the "lithium, argon, neon" business. I asked him whether he had read the "Cameron and Ramsay" paper in the Journal of the Chem. Soc. He said that he had, and then I asked him whether he found anything to show that the lithium had not come from the glass or the reagents. He said "that was just what bothered him" and I told him that I thought the paper was all rot and rubbish. He replied "Th-th-that was just what I t-t-told Remsen [2] and he didn't like it." It was through Remsen that the first news reached the American press, he having been informed of the "great discovery" in a private letter from Ramsay.

It is unnecessary for me to tell you how much I have been interested in your (and Geiger's) four papers.[3] They are quite up to the top notch of your own standard and I think the best since the Bakerian Lecture period, which in my opinion can never be beaten. That Bakerian Lecture [4] is going down through history as *the classic*, and every time that I turn to it I am comforted with the thought that I possess a copy. The paper in which you determine the charge on the alpha particle (I have forgotten the title and by the way you must not forget to send me a reprint of each of them) is the one which interests me the most. I am not so sure that your estimate of the life of radium is better than mine, however, and for the following reason. Although in my paper I stated that the accuracy of the estimate depended "chiefly on the matter of the complete separation of the ionium," I purposely used the word "chiefly" because it does not *wholly* depend on this separation. Now I am confident that the range of the alpha particles from ionium is very close to 2.8 cm, not more than 0.1 cm out at most, and I am equally confident that the range of the particles from radium is not very different from 3.5 cm. That is, the ratio of the activity of the ionium to the activity of the radium with which it is in equilibrium is (or rather should be) very nearly 0.80. Now in calculating the disintegration constant of radium from the results obtained with the first four solutions I relied wholly on this ratio which has, I think, a sound theoretical basis, and which was *moreover* essentially confirmed by experiment. It was this *confirmation* which particularly depended (in this case) on the complete separation of the ionium. The separation of the ionium *was* incomplete in the first four solutions, but that should not have made any difference in the estimate of the life of radium since complete separation was *not* assumed in any instance. If the separation of ionium from the solution in which the radium had been grown had been incomplete when the solution was precipitated with ammonia in obtaining the material (oxides) from which the films were prepared, then the estimate of the amount of ionium in these solutions would have been too *low* and the rate of disintegration of radium would have come out *higher* and not lower than the true value. And so you see that I am inclined to believe that the half value period may be nearer 2000 years than 1760 years.

I spent a large part of last summer in attempting to split up uranium into two radioactive constituents but without success. After prolonged and elaborate chemical treatment I could not get a change of as much as one per cent. in the activity, and if there are really two substances present they are more intimately related (chemically) than are any two of the rare earths which have been separated from one another. Incidently I obtained about a kilogram of what I think is probably the purest uranium salt (nitrate) that has ever been prepared. Your reference to the problem as to the position of actinium reminds me of this material, which I have carefully preserved in a sealed bottle free from all radioactive contamination. I am considering the possibility of excavating a sepulchre and publicly entombing this uranium with the hope that some scientist of future generation may examine it and solve the mystery of the birth of actinium. I do not see any direct method of tackling this problem, but I should like to get my hands on a moderate amount of a good, strong preparation of actinium and see if I can't get it to grow radium or something. I hate that notion of an illegitimate branch of the uranium family like the very devil. I don't suppose that you could use your good offices for me with the Austrians and get them to loan me a little, the report of the Radium Commission (Haitinger) in the Monatshefte made my mouth water.

As a matter of fact I am getting a little down in the mouth on the radioactivity matter for I am afraid that the time is rapidly passing when one can hope to accomplish very much with homeopathic doses. I see that some one has given a lot of money for a Radioactive Institute at Vienna and I am afraid that the wholesale business will drive the small dealer like me to the wall.

Things are going well in the laboratory. We have five new graduate students but none of them far enough advanced to begin research. We have three more advanced men, making a total of eight which is promising. Bumstead had a misfortune in the loss of his father who died just before college opened, making it necessary for him to be away for the first ten days of the term. I had my hands rather full trying to get things in shape although it was not a really difficult proposition. Max Abraham [5] is in town, he arrived last Thursday. Perhaps you heard that they offered him a position at the Univ. of Illinois and he came over this fall to go there, but the final negotiations fell through and he did not take the position. He says that the trouble was that they wanted him to make a two years contract, that he did not like the place and would have practically no students, and so he refused. I heard an indirect rumor that there were also financial complications, that he wanted more than they were prepared to give him. He seems to be a very decent fellow, not very exciting or interesting on lines other than his own specialty, but much more agreeable than I was prepared to find him. I do not know how long he plans to stay, but he is to give us a talk at the Physical Club on Tuesday evening.

I am enclosing with this letter a sample of *purest* uranosouranic oxide (U_3O_8) made from uranium nitrate which was first purified chemically and then submitted to no less than 30 fractional crystallizations. The material from which this oxide was prepared was a part of the least soluble fraction. The oxide was ignited to a high heat in a current of oxygen and is A No. 1 material. I also enclose a small sample of my No. 2 Branchville uraninite (Am. Jour. Sci., xxv, p. 281), all of this material that I have left. It has been fine-ground in chloroform and loses in its present state of division approximately 2.2% of its total radium emanation. You will notice that it contains 6.1% of ThO_2. I also send a sample of No. 5 Uraninite from Joachimsthal, essentially a duplicate of the material that I used but not particularly finely ground. When fine-ground it loses, as you will see from my paper, about 6.2% of its Ra emanation. I am sending this because it is essentially free from thorium in contrast to the Branchville mineral.

In preparing your films I can suggest no better plan than a modification of the method described by McCoy in one of his recent papers. McCoy fine-ground the mineral in alcohol or chloroform and then suspended the solid in the liquid by stirring. This mixture he poured over his plates, allowed the solid to settle out and the liquid to evaporate. This gives the most uniform films but has the serious objection that with heterogeneous material like the mineral powder, a sorting due to difference in density is bound to occur and the material in the film has a different composition from the original powder. I think that this could be avoided if the plate were placed in a shallow dish and covered with chloroform, and a little of the powder added. The whole could be then mixed thoroughly with a *cleaned* camels-hair brush and then allowed to settle. Perhaps the best way would be to make a shallow tray by bending up thin aluminium foil, prepare a film on the bottom of this by the above method, cut out sections of this bottom of convenient size, and finally determine the weight of mineral in the film (after all radioactive measurements had been made) by weighing the film and foil, and then weighing the foil alone after the film had been removed by wiping with a soft cloth moistened with chloroform.

I don't think that I told you that last year just before Duane [6] left this country for Paris I gave him a measured portion of the standard solution of radium bromide which I had prepared from the material which you sent me. I wanted him to compare this solution with Madame Curie's standard and he was very willing and anxious to do so, thought there would be no difficulty whatever. I heard from him last winter and by what I could gather from his letter the Madame was not at all desirous of having any such a comparison carried out, the reason, I suspect, being her constitutional unwillingness to do anything that might directly or indirectly assist any worker in radioactivity out side her own laboratory. I feel sure that now there is no chance whatever, for Duane wrote Bumstead in the late spring that the Madame was very *sore* over the way I had gotten into Debierne on the actinium matter in my paper. It is a great pity that some people are so darn sensitive about criticism and the

Madame apparently has the idea that anyone associated with her laboratory is a sort of holy person. I must acknowledge, however, that I liked the way she summed up the situation in her "copper-lithium" paper. She certainly left no doubt in the mind of the reader as to where *she* stood in the matter.

Everything here is just about as it was when you last visited New Haven; Dana is well and drops in at the laboratory occasionally, but altogether too infrequently to satisfy me, for I enjoy talking things over with him immensely. Hastings has just married off his daughter and has been so occupied with the preparations that I have seen very little of him. Wheeler is the same old Wheeler, and so far as I know has made no progress at all on his measurements of the ranges of the alpha particles from uranium.

We are going to have a meeting of the Physical Society in New York on the 24th, but these meetings no longer have the same interest since you have left us. I certainly hope that Bumstead and I can manage to get out to Winnipeg next summer but I am afraid that it is very doubtful. It is bound to be a rather expensive trip and I am saving up in the hope of being able to get across the Atlantic. I certainly do hope that if you come over you will manage to get down to New Haven, that is in case I am unable to go to Winnipeg.

Mrs. Rutherford is awfully good to think of me and I am sure that nothing would give me greater pleasure than to drop in on you at Manchester. I constantly recall that very happy new year that I spent at Montreal. Please give my very best wishes to Mrs. R. and my love to Eileen, and believe me, Yours very sincerely,

BERTRAM B. BOLTWOOD

P.S. Will you be so good as to ask Geiger [7] to send me one of his reprints on the counting expts. Would he care to have me send him separates of my recent papers?

P.S. I got a letter some time ago from a Charles H. Walter, 16 Heathfield Gardens, London, asking me if he might have my

name in a list of collaborators to a journal to be called "Ion." [8]
Can you give me any information about this person?

1. Joseph Sweetman Ames, successor to Henry Rowland and as director of the Johns Hopkins physical laboratory and later president of the university.

2. Ira Remsen, the first professor of chemistry at Johns Hopkins and Ames' predecessor as president of the university.

3. ER and Geiger, "A method of counting the number of α particles from radio-active matter," *Mem. Proc. Manchester Lit. Phil. Soc.*, 52:9 (1908), 1–3; "An electrical method of counting the number of α-particles from radio-active substances," *Proc. Roy. Soc.*, *81A* (27 Aug. 1908), 141–61; "The charge and nature of the α-particle," *Proc. Roy. Soc.*, *81A* (27 Aug. 1908), 162–73. There is no other paper in collaboration with Geiger and presumably Boltwood was referring to ER, "Experiments with the radium emanation; I. The volume of the emanation," *Phil. Mag.*, *16* (Aug. 1908), 300–12. It is also likely that Boltwood did not see the first paper listed here (which, in any case, is an early announcement of the second), and the fourth paper for which he congratulated Rutherford was ER and Royds, "Spectrum of the radium emanation," *Phil. Mag.*, *16* (Aug 1908), 313–17.

4. ER, "The succession of changes in radioactive bodies," *Phil. Trans.*, *204A* (1904), 169–219.

5. Max Abraham, an authority on the electrical nature of matter, was formerly a lecturer at the University of Göttingen; later he was professor of physics at the Technisches Hochschule in Munich.

6. William Duane, a fifth generation descendent of Benjamin Franklin, left his professorship of physics at the University of Colorado in 1907, and spent six years in Mme. Curie's laboratory. On his return to the United States he was appointed to a professorship at Harvard, where he achieved fame for his work on X rays and on the radiological treatment of cancer.

7. Hans Geiger, a German physicist, was first employed by Arthur Schuster as his librarian and assistant. When Rutherford took over the Manchester laboratory, he inherited also the services of Geiger, who was an extremely clever and indefatigable experimenter. His work with Rutherford on electrical counting led to the famous "Geiger counter" and "Geiger-Müller counter," while counting by another method, scintillations, with Ernest Marsden, led to Rutherford's theory of the nuclear atom. Before World War I he took a post in the Physikalische Technische Reichsanstalt in Berlin, and later held professorships at the Universities of Kiel and Tübingen.

8. Soddy long had felt that there should be a journal in English devoted

to radioactivity and related studies. With Walter, who seems to have had a publishing, rather than a scientific background, he founded *Ion*. The impressive list of contributing editors included almost every well known person in radioactivity, but the venture failed in about a year. Rutherford describes why in a later letter.

8 NOVEMBER 1908

17 Wilmslow Road
Withington, Manchester

My dear Boltwood,

I was delighted to get your long letter—it was like an Atlantic breeze & I am glad to feel that we agree on a good many points about men & things. I recd. your package of radioactive material safely & will make use of it soon. You will have seen ere this our paper in the Phil Mag re the non-production of neon.[1] I hope the last sentence pleased your critical eye.[2] I wonder what line our nimble friend will take. I don't think I left a hole for him to crawl into. I quite agree with your remarks re our nimble friend. He is now absolutely unreliable in everything he publishes. I have a secret to let on to you but don't breathe a word of it till it sees the full light of day. Royds[3] who is working with me is small physically but has a very keen nose for spectra & such things & knows a good deal about them. I had a look over C. & R. spectrum of Ra Eman which appeared with emendations & corrections in Proc. Roy. Soc & gave it over to Royds to find out what he had got in the emanation. After a few hours, Royds had sniffed it out. His final corrected spectrum only contains at a maximum 15 emanation lines—the other 70 odd are *Xenon*—a mixture of the jar & spark spectrum. Not a strong line is absent except one & that is nearly coincident with a hydrogen line. I feel the Lord has delivered him into my hands but now have qualms about rubbing it in too hard. I have held it over for a month as ammunition in case R. broke out in any direction but I suppose we shall publish it soon. The paper as it reads is a most coldblooded damning production & does'nt leave him a leg to stand on. There is not a doubt about the Xenon but how it got there is the question—probably from contamination with pump or mercury used in previous Xenon expts. We have, I need hardly tell you, *made sure* it does'nt naturally come from the emanation. Devil a line of Xenon can we get. The beauty of it is that R. states his spectrum is in *excellent agreement* with ours—in order to claim priority. "The wheels of god grind slowly but they grind exceeding small."

Next as to our further work. We have settled the α particle question in favour of Helium in my mind conclusively. We got very thin glass tubes blown which were thick enough to withstand atmospheric pressure but thin enough to let all the α particles through. The pure emanation was compressed in this tube & the α particles expelled into a vacuum surrounding tube & the gas tested for He. After 4 days we got a complete He spectrum. In order to be sure *He* had not *diffused* through, eman was removed & He put in thin glass tube & a new outer vessel fixed up. No trace of He, however, got through; Eman added, He spectrum again. This is conclusive I think. We have the last few days shown we can get the He spectrum after 3 hours from a thin lead tube placed over the emanation tube. The lead tube is fused & gases collected & tested for He by charcoal method; have done it a dozen times with blank tests in between. It make[s] a darned fine expt. to see the way a ZnS screen lights up when brought a few cms away from an emanation tube; really gorgeous with 150 mg Ra emanation. We hope to test in this way for the α particles from Rad C separately. We have communicated a preliminary acct. of this work to the Manch Lit & Phil Soc this week.[4] Also an account of the neon work & a note on the absorption of the Ra Eman by charcoal [5]—showing that 1 gram of charcoal cannot absorb more than 1/10 c.mm of emana-

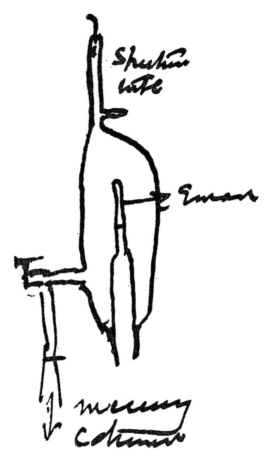

tion at $-40°C$. By the way, it is not an easy matter to blow the fine glass tubes. Baumbach our glass-blower managed it after a time.

Next as to things in general. I quite agree with you that the bigger problems of Radioactivity can only be solved by the people with lots of Ra but there is still lots to be done with homeopathic doses. As a matter of fact, it is not very easy to run expts. in the same Lab on the large & the very small scale. I have avoided all contamination so far but occasionally somebody

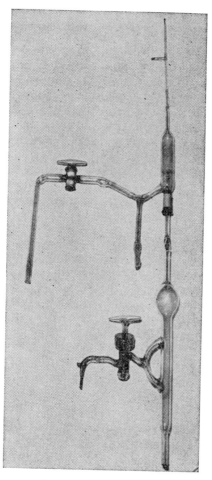

knocks over an emanation tube downstairs when the Laboratory
hums like a beehive with excited workers wanting to know what
has gone wrong with electroscopes. I work upstairs & every
thing goes up & not down & we very seldom let any emanation
loose.

Now I have a proposition to make to you which I hope you
will consider seriously. Why not come over next year & put in a
year's work with me? I will give you the run of the radium & the

actinium we have just separated from the R.S. residues & generally do what I can to give you a chance for tackling some of the
bigger questions. I would be delighted to have you. I think we
could make things hum.

I think I could arrange to get you the John Harling
Fellowship—it is £125 but would provide bread & butter. I
daresay Dana could arrange to get you a year's leave—tell him it
is for the good of your scientific soul. Bumstead would have to
be sacrificed but a years absence (as in the case of a wife) would
make him appreciate your virtues even better than at present.
Do consider the question seriously.

Manchester's climate is pretty tough in winter but does'nt
worry me as I work in a dark room half the time. I am in first
class form—running if anything to adipose tissue but in excellent fighting form if anyone feels inclined to bump against me
—if one does, as Stephenson puts it "it will be bad for the coo."

I note what you say re actinium. The stuff I have separated is
not very active—about 400 (150 grams of it). I shall write to
Exner[6] of Vienna to see whether they can spare any for you.
My wife & Eileen are just recovering from colds but are other-
wise flourishing. My wife sends kind regards. Give my regards to
Bumstead Dana & Wheeler & Schwill. Yours ever,

E. RUTHERFORD

P.S. Geiger would like to have copies of your papers.

1. ER and T. Royds, "The action of the radium emanation upon water," *Phil. Mag., 16* (Nov. 1908), 812–18.
2. The last sentence of the above paper read: "Consequently, the experiment described by Cameron and Ramsay is quite inadequate as a
proof of the production of neon from the emanation."
3. After studies at Manchester, Tübingen, and Berlin, Thomas Royds
was appointed assistant director of the Kodaikanal Observatory, Madras,
India. In 1923 he became director of the observatory.
4. ER and Royds, "The nature of the α particle," *Mem. Proc. Manchester Lit. Phil. Soc., 53:1* (1908), 1–3.

5. ER, "Some properties of the radium emanation," *Mem. Proc. Manchester Lit. Phil. Soc., 53:2* (1908), 1–2.

6. Franz Exner was professor of physics at the University of Vienna and one of Rutherford's closer contacts with the Academy of Sciences.

12 DECEMBER 1908

Sloane Laboratory, Yale University
New Haven, Connecticut

My dear Rutherford,

Just a line to convey to you my sincere and hearty congratulations in the matter of the Nobel Prize. There have been unofficial rumors for some days in the American press that you were to be one of the recipients, but it was only a couple of days ago that the official announcement appeared and it was certain enough for me to feel that I could write and congratulate you. I am *perfectly delighted* over it, although I have believed for some time that they could not possibly pass you by very many times. Well it certainly is a bully X-mas present and I wish you many happy returns of the day. I think that it was very fine their giving you the "chemistry" prize, for you certainly have done a great thing for the chemists *in more ways than one,* but I think that they might have thrown in the physics prize too without overdoing it.[1] Perhaps they are holding that over until later! Any way my dear friend and *chemist* (because you can't avoid that title now even if you want to) it is matter to be joyful over and I can assure you of the cordial and sincere satisfaction which it has brought to all your friends.

I thank you ever so much for your good letter full of the most interesting news. That experiment with the radium emanation in which you capture the escaped alpha-particles is a fine one and definitely settles the whole matter. I am also glad to see by the announcement of Royds' paper before the R.S. on the

10th [2] that you are going to let the facts come out about that emanation spectrum of Ramsay's. It would have been entirely wrong to have suppressed it, wrong from a moral as well as a scientific standpoint.

The proposal which you make in your letter relative to my coming over to Manchester next winter is certainly an attractive proposition and I can not think of anything that would give me greater pleasure than [to] accept it. There are so many factors entering into a final decision, however, that I have not yet been able to make up my mind definitely. I want to see first what they will do for me here, they will grant me leave of absence for a year at half pay without doubt, but there is a possibility that as I only get less than half pay now, that they will be willing to continue that ($1000), in which case I shall be able to go. I will let you know definitely just as soon as I possibly can.

With regards and best wishes to you and to Mrs. Rutherford, wishing you all a very merry Christmas, I remain, Yours very sincerely,

BERTRAM B. BOLTWOOD

1. The 1908 Nobel Prize in physics went to Gabriel Lippmann, for his work in color photography. Coincidentally, Lippmann was Marie Curie's research adviser at the Sorbonne and president of her thesis examining committee in 1903.

2. Royds, "A comparison of the radium emanation spectrum obtained by different observers," *Proc. Roy. Soc., 82A* (16 Feb. 1909), 22–25.

11 JANUARY 1909

17 Wilmslow Road
Withington, Manchester

My dear Boltwood,

I read your letter with the greatest pleasure and must thank you for the rose-coloured view you take of my virtues. I thoroughly appreciate the good wishes of a brother-chemist who is in such an excellent position to judge of my deficiencies. Really, I was very startled at my transformation at first but afterwards saw that it was quite in accord with the disintegration theory. J.J.T. was greatly tickled. I was able to attend the "Sir Joseph" dinner given by the Cavendish men on my way to Stockholm & thoroughly enjoyed it. The boys gave me a royal reception and sang a special song on the "α rays" in my honour which went very well.[1] I must send you a copy of it later. My wife went with me to Stockholm & we had a right good time but had no time to think while we were there. The function started with a formal recitation of the prize winner's virtues & a presentation of the medals & diplomas by the King. Then a banquet beginning at 6 & ending god knows when where I had to speechify. I chose to joke them on my transformation into a chemist & I think they all were pleased. I was feeling in excellent form & let myself go a bit. Next day was my lecture on the "*Chemical* nature of the α particle," [2] then a dinner with the King & Queen at the Palace & numerous other festivities which would be much too numerous to mention. Arrhenius [3] was in excellent form & looked after us well. We returned via Berlin where I was most kindly received. Rubens [4] gave a farewell supper to us at which most of the physicists & chemists were present. I saw over Nernst's & Fischer's [5] Laboratories. The latter impressed me as a really big man. Nernst was very cordial & trotted me round with all his research people bringing up the rear. It was embarrassing but amusing. Marckwald [6] presented me with some "ionium" & was very cordial. He is very distressed that the Austrian Ac of Sci will not allow him their polonium residues to see if lead appears. I saw Regener [7] at work counting the scintillations in the diamond. He seems a keen fellow. I returned via Leyden & saw Lorentz [8] & Onne's laboratory. Onnes was too unwell to see me. By the way Hahn took charge of us in Berlin & made all arrangements. By a fortunate chance he was giving a paper the last evening on "The radio[?]-activity of actinium" at the

Physikalische Gesellschaft. He proved that the stuff of Meyer & Schweidler was actinium α fired out as a result of the breaking up of radioactinium. I spoke to the paper. Lise M[e]itner [9] is a young lady but not beautiful so I judge Hahn will not fall a victim to the radioactive charms of the lady. I am just getting down to work again but I feel devilish slack after a dose of exam papers. I am going to try to get the condensation point of the Ra Eman at atmospheric pressure. It will be rather a job as there is only 1/10 cubic mm of Eman. available.

Geiger has repeated Bronson's results by scintillations & confirms the fact that actinium eman blows off $3\ \alpha$ & Th Eman $3\ \alpha$. He so far finds *no* evidence that *two* appear together & can get no difference in the range. It is looking rather strange but we may get down on it somehow. It is an important point to solve what happens in these cases. Schuster is back & has invested in a £1250 motor car. [10] He is keen on things physical & meteorological still. Strutt I understand is having trouble with his students. He was stuck in to lecture for the first time to the rowdiest lot of students in South Kensington. Soddy's you will have seen has got out of the "Ion" journal. I think the latter will collapse. Soddy as the result of an enquiry of mine found he [11] had stuck down names wholesale without permission & so pulled out to avoid responsibility.

I shall be awfully glad if you can manage to honour the John Harling Fellowships. Make a good try to pull out for a year. Yours ever,

E. RUTHERFORD

1. The version sent by Rutherford is as follows:

AN ALPHA RAY
Air 'A Jovial Monk'

1. An alpha ray was I, contented with my lot;
From radium C I was set free
And outwards I was shot.
My speed I quickly reckoned,
As I flew off through space,
Ten thousand miles a second

Is quite a fine old pace.
　For an alpha ray goes a good long way
　In a short time t, as you easily see;
　Though I don't know why my speed's so high,
　Or why I bear a charge $2e$.

2. And on my wild career, as swiftly on I flew,
A rarefied gas wouldn't let me pass,
But I shoved my way right through.
I had some lively tussles
To make it ionize,
But I set the small corpuscles
A buzzing 'round like flies.
　For an alpha ray hasn't time to stay
　While a low down gas of inferior class,
　Scarce conducting sound, goes dancing round
　And plays the goat when I want to pass.

3. An electroscope looked on as I made that gas conduct;
Beneath the field the gas did yield
And the leaf was greatly 'bucked'.
But I murmured Botheration!
(A word that's most obscene),
And I made a scintillation
As I struck a zinc-blende screen.
　For an alpha ray makes a fine display
　With fluorescence green on a zinc-blende screen,
　When the room's quite dark you see a spark
　That marks the spot where I have been.

4. But now I'm settled down and I move about quite slow,
For I, alas, am helium gas
Since I got that dreadful blow.
But though I'm feeling sickly,
Still no one now denies
That I ran that race so quickly
That I've won a Nobel prize.
　For an alpha ray is a thing to pay
　And a Nobel prize one can not despise,
　And Rutherford has greatly scored,
　As all the world now recognise.

Alfred A. Robb

For a variation, see the song as printed in J. B. Birks (ed.), *Rutherford at Manchester* (London, Heywood, 1962), pp. 362–63.

2. Rutherford's Nobel Lecture, "The chemical nature of the α-particles from radioactive substances," was delivered before the Royal Academy of Science at Stockholm, 11 Dec. 1908. It is printed in James Chadwick (ed.), *The Collected Papers of Lord Rutherford of Nelson* (New York, Interscience, 1963), *2,* 137–46.

3. Svante Arrhenius, recipient of the 1903 Nobel Prize in chemistry and director of the Nobel Institute for Physical Chemistry.

4. Heinrich Rubens, professor of physics at the University of Berlin.

5. Emil Fischer, professor of chemistry at the University of Berlin and 1902 Nobel prizewinner.

6. Willy Marckwald, chemistry professor who worked on radioactivity in Emil Fischer's laboratory.

7. Erich Regener, physicist at the University of Berlin, pioneered in the method of counting alpha particles by their scintillations.

8. Hendrik Antoon Lorentz, professor of physics at the University of Leyden and 1902 Nobel prizewinner.

9. Lise Meitner received her doctorate in 1906 from the University of Vienna, then moved to Berlin for further study under Max Planck. In addition to her theoretical interests, she soon began research on radioactivity, in collaboration with Otto Hahn. Although she too found academic positions for women very scarce, in 1912 she became Planck's assistant. In 1917 she was appointed head of the physics department at the Kaiser Wilhelm Institute for Chemistry in Dahlem, near Berlin, and there continued her association with Hahn, who headed the institute's chemistry department. This team of Hahn–Meitner was broken in 1938, when Hitler's racial policies forced her to flee to Sweden. Nevertheless, Hahn immediately notified her of his experimental results late that year and it was Meitner, together with her nephew Otto Frisch, who correctly interpreted the phenomenon as nuclear fission.

10. According to Sir Arthur Schuster's daughter, he purchased the very first automobile produced by the firm of Rolls-Royce.

11. Soddy's co-editor, Walter.

21 FEBRUARY 1909

Sloane Laboratory, Yale University
New Haven, Connecticut

My dear Rutherford,

Thank you ever so much for your fine letter of January 11th.

I was immensely interested in your account of your trip to
Stockholm and your visit to Berlin and Cambridge. What a
splendid time you must have had and how proud you must have
been of your *transformation* into a chemist! Thanks also for the
copy of the Cavendish dinner song which is very amusing.

Well the die has been cast and I have decided (D.V.) to
spend next winter with you in Manchester. I was able to make
the necessary arrangements here and what with the John Harling (have I the name right?) Fellowship to help out I think
that I shall be able to get along respectably. I am planning to
bring my mother along with me, for we have been unseparated
for so many years that to leave her on this side would have been
quite impossible for both of us. We are planning to sail on the
Baltic on July 17th for Liverpool and I plan to go directly to
Manchester in order to get acquainted with the place and to
make arrangements for the winter. Unless you advise me to get
busy right away, which I shall be very glad to do if there is anything to be gained by it, I think that we will loaf around a bit in
the British Islands and possibly spend a few weeks in Holland,
returning to Manchester for the opening of the fall campaign. A
few weeks vacation wont do me a bit of harm although I am not
at all in need of a rest.

I have been very busy indeed since the first of January working up nearly sixty pounds of thorianite which was loaned to me
by the Welsbach Co. They turned the mineral over to me under the condition that I would work it up and send them back
the thorium which it contained. I have extracted the helium,
about a hundred and fifty liters, the radiolead, the polonium
and the uranium. I am now working at the residues in order to
obtain the radium (about 4.4 mg $RaBr_2$) and particularly the
mesothorium. The thorium and alas also the ionium, has already been returned. It has been something of a job and although I have been doing the work in the chemical laboratory
the equipment there is not at all adequate for the proper and
convenient handling of such large quantities of material. I hope
ultimately to extract mesothorium equivalent to about 15 kilos

of thorium oxide. One of the impressive facts which has come out in working up this material is the almost complete absence of both bismuth and barium in the mineral.

Things here are going on much as usual. Bumstead is in rather poor health and I am trying to persuade him to cross with us in the summer and spend a few weeks in travel. Two of our men are working on alpha rays and a third on ultra-violet light, which by the way is a devilish mean form of radiation to try to do anything with. I was much interested in that paper by yourself and Royds in the last Phil. Mag.[1] It certainly settles things.

With regards, remembrances and best wishes to you all, Yours very sincerely,

BERTRAM B. BOLTWOOD

1. ER and Royds, "The nature of the α particle from radioactive substances," *Phil. Mag., 17* (Feb. 1909), 281–86.

7 MARCH 1909

17 Wilmslow Road
Withington, Manchester

My dear Boltwood,

I was delighted to hear you will be able to come over for a year's work. I will at once propose you for the John Harling (it is quite correct) but as the Vice-Chancellor is away for some time, it may not be possible to officially inform you of your election for a month or more. However, I don't think you need worry about the matter as I think they are inclined to take my recommendations as final. I would not, however, mention the matter of the Scholarship until you are officially notified. It has to go through the Senate and the Council & these things take time.

I think we may look forward to have a lively year. I would like you & Mrs. Boltwood on your arrival to come over at once to Manchester & stay with us quietly for a few days. You know I have to go to Winnipeg as president of Section A [1] & we start on Aug 13. I was hoping to see you there but I don't repine under the present conditions. Next as to work we might do. If you are inclined, I would like to use your services for a few days after your arrival to get ready for experiments in October. As I cannot leave my radium making about 40 cc of H & O per week without attention, I am thinking of removing it, precipitating with H_2S to remove radiolead & polonium. We can then put the radium aside dried until October to produce *helium* & thus measure rate of production of He. We can put aside Radiolead & Po also for rate of production of He & examine them as soon as we start. There will then be a dose of radiolead & polonium to play with & I think that your fertile mind will grasp possibilities there. I think that if we have a glass blower at hand to fix up for us as the chemical operations go along, we ought to be in position to have a holiday with the full knowledge that a research is in progress notwithstanding. You will have seen that I have been getting the boiling point of the emanation. I am delaying concluding this for a week or two on account of another effect that has come to light. I have a Finn here Tuomikoski [2] whom I set to measure accurately the rate of decay of Ra Eman in sealed tubes by the γ rays with the intention of getting the constant over a range of a million or so. He is a very reliable man with an electroscope & takes infinite care. He found that his different samples did *not* decay at the same rate. When I gave him some of my purified emanation, it started decaying $\frac{1}{2}$ value in 3.6 days & then after a week or so slowed down to 3.75. Another sample of gas from the pump direct decays over a fortnight exponentially with a period 4.3 days. There is no doubt about it for he has a dozen samples under test. It is very funny and it looks at first sight as if there were *two* emanations one of which was partially separated from the other by my methods of purification. I think, however, that other data are against two successive emanations, although it may be possible I have got another emanation in my impure radium. What appears to me probable for the moment is that the emanation varies in properties according as it breaks up at once or in a weeks' time & that one can use this difference in properties to partially separate the emanations into one decaying slower than the average & the other faster. You will appreciate the bearing of this view if it turns out correct. I noticed one funny fact in the condensation experiments at various pressure. When condensation started, it did not all condense at constant pressure as it ought to do but required 5 or 10 degrees lower temperature to condense most of it. This would be explained in the above view if the condensation point of the emanation had an average value with two extreme values. The work is jolly difficult as it takes so long to be quite sure of a change of period in different samples for a difference of 5 hours in the decay period requires some care to bring out with certainty over a period of a week.

I am thankful that I have such a reliable rock of support as Tuomikoski who measures steadily about 14 hours a day & never gets wearied. Don't mention anything about this for it may take us some time to get it cleared up. It interests me mightily at present, for I am sure something really interesting will come out of it.

Geiger is hard at work with your samples of Ur & minerals counting scintillations. It looks as if it is coming out alright & that Ur gives two scintillations for 1 of Ra. By the way, I can't find your letter where you give the corrected values of the Ra/Ur constant. Was it 3.4×10^{-7}. Give me details if you can.

The paper of Danne on radiouranium [3] made me tired. Like all these French fellows, you don't know anything about it when you have dug through the paper. What is its period? Does it give α or β rays? Danne apparently does not worry about such trivial matters.

I have just written to Soddy to tell him to treat a man of Eve's

solidity with a little more care (see last Nature) [4] unless he
wants a cyclone to strike him. Soddy makes me tired when I
read his stuff. He can never state his own results without hitting
somebody else. As a matter of fact, I am sure the difference in
absorption constants is largely one of experimental conditions
in these days. I have got more work of various kinds than I can
tackle so I am ruthlessly throwing cargo of least value over-
board. It is devilish difficult to keep things going full steam
ahead & to find time to run your own little engine as well.
Needless to remark, people regard a Nobel Prize winner as a
Carnegie to support the impecunious & wasters.

Soddy always reminds me of a cock crowing on his own dung-
hill.

You will have seen Hahn's new method of finding stray products works out pretty well.[5] I am glad he does well for he has
the real stuff in him—and withal a thoroughly good fellow.

The life of a professor is no sinecure.

We are all well & flourishing. I was down in London last
week & chatted in a friendly way with the great Ramsay. He
amuses me immensely but I cannot enter into a discussion of his
mental attitude—it is too funny for words. He is mentally the
most unbalanced scientific man I ever ran across.

By the way, I think you know that Manchester in winter is
not an ideal resort for tourists. Your mother must expect to find
the absence of sun rather depressing at first. Write soon. Yours
ever,

E. RUTHERFORD

1. The Mathematical and Physical Science section of the British Association for the Advancement of Science.

2. Y. Tuomikoski.

3. Danne, "Sur un nouveau produit radioactif de la série de l'uranium,"
Comptes Rendus, 148 (8 Feb. 1909), 337–39.

4. Soddy and A. S. Russell, "The γ rays of uranium," *Nature, 80* (4 Mar.
1909), 7–8.

5. This is the method of radioactive recoil: when an alpha particle is

ejected from an atom it carries a great amount of kinetic energy. The residual atom experiences an equal reaction or recoil, often sufficient to free it from its surrounding atoms and transport it a short distance. See Hahn and Meitner, "Ein neue Methode zur Herstellung radioaktiver Zerfallsprodukte; Thorium D, ein kurzlebiges Produkt des Thorium," *Verhandl. Deut. Physik. Ges., 11* (15 Feb. 1909), 55–62. See also Sidney Russ and Walter Makower, "The expulsion of radio-active matter in the radium transformations," *Proc. Roy. Soc., 82A* (6 May 1909), 205–24.

1 MAY 1909

17 Wilmslow Road
Withington, Manchester

My dear Boltwood,

I have forgotten whether I wrote to you some time ago that you have been elected John Harling Fellow. You no doubt have heard officially before this.

I have been expecting to hear from you but I expect you are like myself averse to correspondence & it is only occasionaly the spirit moves you. I wrote to you some time ago about arrangements [and] suggested for a few days' work as soon as you arrive in order to put things in train for the next term when you start work. I hope these will suit you.

You will have seen my paper on the emanation in the Phil Mag [1] & how Ramsay & Co tried to cut in before the publication of my paper.[2] He has no conscience whatever. I have become quite philosophic & do not now worry myself about him. He is pretty discredited already among his brethren & his retiring address as president of the Chemical Society fell I understand on very stony ground. We are hard at work on the decay of the emanation. The results we get are very startling & peculiar. There is a great deal to do & it is slow work as it takes some time to get a decay curve.

By the way, can you spare the preparation of pure thorium in equilibrium to complete the scintillation experiments? I wrote to you about it last time.

I have got a heavy grind in front of me for the next few months for I have to prepare my B.A. address amongst other things.

I was feeling fagged out the end of March & my wife & family went to Italy for a month's sunshine. I have just returned a week & am endeavouring to overhaul my correspondence. I am now in good form again & maintain a cheerful attitude before the world. How are things with you? I hope Bumstead is in good form again.

There is nothing of much interest going on here at present. Spring is with us & a fair amount of bright sunshine. Lord Morley[3] came down & opened the new Union Building for the students—which should prove of great utility. You will soon become acquainted with the smoke room alloted to the staff.

My wife & Eileen are both flourishing. With kind regards to your mother. Yours ever,

E. RUTHERFORD

Take up your pen & write! You are worse than I am.

1. ER, "Condensation of the radium emanation," *Phil. Mag., 17* (May 1909), 723–29.

2. As reported in *Nature, 80* (20 May 1909), 347–48, Ramsay exhibited liquefied radium emanation at the Royal Society's semiannual *conversazione,* 12 May 1909. The conversazione was a scientific social event at which members attempted to display the striking features of their work to colleagues and their ladies.

3. John Morley was chancellor of Manchester University. An author, editor, Member of Parliament, and Secretary of State for India, he received many honors, including the Order of Merit (which Rutherford would someday receive) and creation as a viscount.

30 MAY 1909

Sloane Laboratory, Yale University
New Haven, Connecticut

My dear Rutherford,[1]

I am honestly ashamed of myself for not having more promptly answered your very good letters of March 7th and May 1st, but the fascinating prospect of spending next winter in Manchester has completely disturbed my former equilibrium and the last three months have rushed by with startling rapidity. They have gone by all the more rapidly because I have taken it rather easy this spring, really loafing to tell the whole truth, and in this respect time is very much like money, one can waste it much faster than one can make it. As a matter of fact I have really been distinctly stale this spring, which is not surprising when you consider that I have had my nose steadily on the stone for the last seven years. But by taking it easy I have gotten around into first class shape again and by the time I get to Manchester I shall be ready for anything.

Your suggestions as to work are very attractive and I shall go directly to Manchester from Liverpool (where we ought to arrive about July 25th) in order to get things started as promptly as possible. It is very kind indeed for you to ask us to stop with you in Manchester and the invitation is very much appreciated, but as you are going to see a good deal of both of us during the coming winter and as we don't want to begin by too severely testing Mrs. Rutherford's good nature I think that it would be best for us to take quarters by ourselves, possibly somewhere in the neighborhood of the laboratory.

I am enclosing in this letter two samples of material the one a sample of pure thorium oxide, just separated from thorianite. It

has been completely separated from radium and other radioactive products of the uranium series except ionium and
uranium-X. The thorianite was of the variety containing 78% of
ThO_2 and 10% of U. The thorium oxide should then contain
ionium sufficient to contribute about 4.5% of the total alpha ray
activity when the thorium products have come into equilibrium, which will be about July 1st. The oxide has been prepared by igniting with the hydroxide to a very high temperature and is therefore in a very dense and non-emanating form. I
did not have any normally active salts of thorium at hand when
your letter was received and so I had to prepare the material
which you asked for. I would have sent it sooner only the material which I separated first was lost just as I was about to send it
on to you. I am also sending you a small sample of thorite which
is unique in that it contains only about 0.44% of uranium and
52.0% of ThO_2 (45% of thorium). Only about 3% of the alpha
ray activity of this material is due to products other than thorium and it is in complete equilibrium. I hope that I am not
sending these substances too late to be of use to Geiger in his
counting experiments.

I have been much interested in your account of the surprising
results which you have been getting on the rate of decay of
radium emanation, and greatly at a loss to explain them. I suppose that you know that Giesel claimed to have observed a very
slowly disintegrating emanation evolved by some of his actinium preparations (Ber. d. chem. Ges., 40, 3011, 1907). I never
took much stock in this observation of Giesel's but there may
be something in it and your radium salts may contain the same
parent material, what ever it may be. I shall be very glad to
learn the explanation when you get it. Your friend Ramsay
seems to be butting into you rather strongly in that matter of
the liquifaction of the radium emanation. If the supplemen-
tary volume of the Century Dictionary soon to appear is actually issued before next winter I am afraid that it will not be

safe for me to be in the same town with Sir W., for I have been doing the radioactivity portion and I have touched him up rather strongly on certain matters.

We are having a very strenuous time here over a new physics laboratory. The donors of the present Sloane building are anxious to do something very much better for the institution and have offered to present a fine, new building to be used as a University Laboratory, that is for both the College and the Scientific School.[2] We are now having a fine, friendly scrap over the question of location, the president and secretary (who have had nothing whatever to do with getting the gift, which was obtained by Bumstead working alone) wanting to put it about a mile from the Campus, on some new land recently acquired by the University, and Bumstead and the rest of us doing all that we can to have it put nearer to the College. It is very fortunate that the whole matter came up after my plans for being with you had been settled or I should never in the world have been able to get away for next winter.

With kindest regards and best wishes. Yours very sincerely,

BERTRAM B. BOLTWOOD

1. This letter exists only in a typed copy, RCC.
2. This was the means by which the vested interests of Yale College and the Sheffield Scientific School were overcome and their separate physics departments consolidated into a single university department.

1 JULY 1909

17 Wilmslow Road
Withington, Manchester

My dear Boltwood,

I hope this will reach you before you leave New Haven. Come along to Manchester as soon as you can & wire me when you expect to arrive. I was hoping to be able to put you up but

I find the date of your arrival coincides with the visit here of Professor Elliot Smith [1] of Cairo & his wife who has just (the former) been appointed to the chair of Anatomy here. They are staying with us & I am afraid our house has no more accomodation. If it would suit you, Mrs. Rutherford would look at some rooms for you for the few days you are likely to stay here.

I have just got off my British Ass address & feel greatly relieved. We have Degree Day on Saturday & the King visits the University Tuesday—great doings. With kind regards. Au revoir.

E. RUTHERFORD

1. G. Elliot Smith, a noted anatomist and anthropologist, was professor of anatomy at, successively, the Government Medical School, Cairo, the University of Manchester, and University College, London.

BOLTWOOD'S YEAR IN MANCHESTER

The only time Rutherford and Boltwood worked in the same laboratory was during the 1909–10 academic year. It proved to be a very happy collaboration, for Boltwood had access to larger quantities of radioactive materials than ever before, Rutherford had the services of a first-class radiochemist at his side, and the two enjoyed each other's company immensely. Since both their research papers decreased considerably in quantity during this year, one may wonder, in fact, whether more time was spent in the laboratory or the local pub. (Boltwood, at least, seems to have had a large capacity for beer, and this thirst could not have been quenched in Rutherford's home because of Mary Rutherford's strong temperance beliefs).

This apparent research slowdown, however, does have other than bacchanalian explanations. Boltwood, in his letter of 30 May 1909, admitted to relaxing somewhat before going to Manchester and, considering the normal delay between submission of a manuscript and its publication, his dearth of articles is more a measure of his activity at Yale. By the same token, the work he accomplished in Manchester did not appear in print until after his return to the United States. Another reason for a lag in publications is that, for both Boltwood and Rutherford, this was a time of transition. Research projects had been successfully completed and new ones undertaken. Boltwood's long search for the parent of radium had ended with his discovery of ionium, while Rutherford had proven that the alpha particle is a charged atom of helium and had determined the properties of radium emanation. Their work during 1909–10 was a logical continuation of these interests, but at the same time distinct. Rutherford grew increasingly fascinated by scattering studies with "his" alpha particles (conducted largely by Geiger and Ernest Marsden), and this led, in 1911, to his concept of a nuclear atom. Now that he knew that helium and the alpha particle were the same, he and Boltwood measured the production of helium by radium. And Boltwood further concerned himself with the separation of ionium and actinium from certain residues and the production of helium by ionium.

The year was not without unhappiness, for Boltwood's mother died a few months after their arrival in England. There is some evidence that Rutherford asked him to remain as a permanent member of the laboratory staff, but a counter-offer from Yale brought Boltwood back across the Atlantic. Yale, fearful of losing one of its most eminent scientists, created a new professorship in radiochemistry for him. Though Boltwood remained in the physics department under Bumstead's chairmanship, the name of the chair had been carefully contrived to allow him a foothold in the chemistry laboratory.

But before he returned to America Boltwood visited Germany, for which his fondness dated from his student days. Rutherford's next few letters are therefore addressed to the Continent.

20 JULY 1910

17 Wilmslow Road
Withington, Manchester

My dear Boltwood,

Am glad to hear you are still disenchanted of Munich and its waters. Why don't you choose a fraulein of domestic tastes to take back to America with you? She could even brew the beer to keep her lord in good condition. I have been loafing along writing testimonials & doing a little paper writing. We spent three days in the Lakes & had beautiful weather & not a puncture for over 300 miles. We are off directly to Chester to see the pageant & fireworks in the evening. Altogether I feel life is worth living even in Manchester. I am sending herewith a letter which came to the Lab for you.

Elliot Smith says he can't afford to go to Munich so goes to Ireland instead to live on potatoes.

Send the helium paper along as soon as you can but I am doubtful whether I shall get it before September—so much faith have I in the Munich waters.

Mrs. Rutherford sends her kind regards. Yours ever,

E. RUTHERFORD

21 JULY 1910

17 Wilmslow Road
Withington, Manchester

My dear Boltwood,

Your postcards "beer beer glorious beer" came regularly and I am glad to see you send the more respectable of them to my private address. The motor car with the correct number from you & Geiger was much appreciated.

Re my projected visit to Munich &c, will you advise me the best route to take & how I shall get my tickets. Will it be best to get return for Vienna returning via Brussels or return to Munich via Brussels?

You will be interested to see the latest communication of the great chemist in the Comptes Rendus [1] apropos of density of the emanation for which five concordant numbers differing only by a few per cent are given & a final value 222. It is great. There are no details of weighings but the paper is mostly taken up to say I, Ramsay, determined the volume, the spectrum, the everything of the emanation & I give it the name "niton"—shining—with my fatherly blessing. It is a most admirable piece of boom I have seen for some time. You remember of course the maximum volume of emanation dealt with is 1/10 cubic mm.—a truly great piece of work.

I enclose postcard from Daniel [2] about abstracts of papers—attend to it. We are all well. Boyle,[3] Gray [4] & Wilson [5] still remain. The motor shed is up & used. Yours ever,

E. RUTHERFORD

1. Ramsay and Robert Whytlaw Gray, "La densité de l'émanation du radium," *Comptes Rendus, 151* (11 July 1910), 126–28.

2. J. Daniel, a Belgian engineer, was secretary-general of the International Congress of Radiology and Electricity, held in Brussels, September 1910. As members of the committee on radioactivity standards, Boltwood and Rutherford planned to attend.

3. Robert W. Boyle had worked under Rutherford for some years at McGill, receiving his Ph.D. degree from that institution in 1909. The next two years were spent at Manchester as an 1851 Exhibition Scholar, after which Boyle returned to McGill as a staff member. In 1912, however, he was appointed professor of physics at the University of Alberta, leaving there in 1929 to become director of the physics and engineering division of Canada's National Research Council.

4. Joseph A. Gray became interested in radioactivity while a student of R. J. Strutt at Imperial College of Science, London. An 1851 Exhibition Scholarship then permitted him to spend three years (1909–12) in Ruther-

ford's Manchester laboratory, after which he joined the physics staff at Mc-Gill University. In 1924 he was appointed to a professorship in Queen's University, Ontario.

5. William Wilson, a physicist who received his B.Sc., M.S., and D.Sc. degrees from Manchester, taught briefly at Toronto and then worked for Western Electric Company and Bell Telephone Laboratories.

22 AUGUST 1910

West Head Farm
Wythburn, Grasmere

My dear Boltwood,

Your tardy letter was received here a few days ago where we at present hibernate in the wet weather with occasional spins in the motor for fresh air. Never a puncture for the last 1000 miles so my heart & pocket rejoiceth.

I received your numerous post cards to the refrain of "beer beer glorious beer." I can see the effects on you in your correspondence & absolute laziness. It is about time I came along to wake you out of your slothful dream.

I am intending to leave here Monday 29th or next day & motor to Manchester—then next day to Harwich & should then arrive 10.20 Munich on Wednesday but will write later when my plans are more matured. I tried to bring Lamb [1] along but he finally failed me. I hear from Hahn he is stationed or staying with Von Baeyer [2]—20 minutes from Munich & wants to call on us when I arrive, so I will give him your address.

I note what you say about routes & will follow your advice. Please arrange for a room with you & we will fix our plans later. I got a gorgeous photo of Geiger mounted on his war-steed [3]— really fine & imposing & a devil of a looking fellow.

By the way, remember my walking must be strictly limited in my travels. My knee has again been giving me trouble but I hope will be reasonably right before I leave.[4] Mrs. R. is away climbing rocks. Eileen is as bully as a cricket. Yours,

E. RUTHERFORD

See last week's Nature. Campbell is on nomenclature & whacks at Ramsay & also at you in the same old style.[5]

1. Probably Horace Lamb, who had been professor of mathematics in Manchester since 1885.

2. Otto von Baeyer, of the Physical Institute of the University of Berlin, collaborated on radioactivity studies with Hahn and Meitner. His father, under whom Hahn had once studied, was Adolf von Baeyer, a Nobel Prize winning chemist at the University of Munich.

3. Geiger was an officer in the army reserve.

4. Soon after his arrival in Cambridge in 1895, Rutherford slipped on a banana skin, damaging his knee. The injury bothered him periodically, and in the latter part of his life he obtained some relief from the massages given by a Cambridge butcher who worked part time as a "manipulator." Shall we draw the conclusion that one of the world's foremost scientists inclined toward nonscientific medicine, or that a great empiricist simply appreciated the talents of another man with talented hands?

5. Norman R. Campbell, "The nomenclature of radioactivity," *Nature, 84* (18 Aug. 1910), 203–04. For many years Campbell was a fellow, first at Trinity College, Cambridge, then at the University of Leeds. In 1919 he became a physicist at the General Electric Company's London laboratory.

27 SEPTEMBER 1910

17 Wilmslow Road
Withington, Manchester

My dear Boltwood,

You will probably have arrived by this time in New Haven and be studying the new conditions. I got back to Manchester on Saturday afternoon feeling rather miserable, as I had a fine bulge due to a tooth on one side of the face and a bad cold. However, I am now pretty fit again. A good many people at the

Congress were suffering from relaxed throat, due I presume to endeavours to talk German.

I have not yet started definitely to work, am finishing up Examination papers, etc.

You will be interested to hear what happened at the Congress after you left.[1] First of all I may mention that we read the conclusions of the Committee [2] at the final meeting of the Congress in French, German, and English, and the report was adopted without any discussion. We suggested in the report that the name Curie should be given to the mass of emanation in equilibrium with one gramme of Radium, and we left over the question of giving names to small standards of Radium and Emanation. The report otherwise was as you know it.

Mme. Curie left on Friday. She had a bad cold; I sat next to her at the Opera on Thursday and found she was not well, and took her home halfway through. She was very miserable next day and could not attend the Dinner; but was well enough next morning to leave with Perrin [3] for Paris. I think she has been overworking, and some of the medical fraternity consider she is in a very bad nervous state.

I took the chair the whole of Wednesday's meetings. Perrin gave a good paper about his experiments on the Brownian movement, and was very lively and jumped about like a jack-in-the-box. I made the only joke of the meeting by saying that Professor Perrin himself was an admirable example of the Brownian movement. Perrin, Becquerel, and some of the other Frenchmen took a whole hour talking of work about three years old. They are incorrigible in the matter of length. The secretarial arrangements throughout were rotten, and even the Belgians were very angry at Daniel's mismanagement, or rather laziness. There was a group of about twelve radio-active papers that I specially arranged with Daniel to be put down on the last morning of the Congress. For example, the papers by Bragg, Kleeman, Barkla,[4] Hahn, Makower, Eve, Moulin,[5] etc. I arrived a little late and found that the papers were not down on the programme at all, although it was the last morning. I took the matter in my own hands and formed a section straight away, and had it going in five minutes, each being allowed a quarter of an hour for expression of his views and then ordered off the platform. We had a very good meeting, in fact the best of the Congress, and there was plenty of discussion on each paper, mostly in English. I found that Wertenstein,[6] one of the Frenchmen who had worked on recoil, seemed to think that he should be allowed half an hour or more for telling of some poor experiments; but finally I got him to sit down. Moulin, on the other hand, showed great sense and got through in his quarter of an hour. Eve gave a paper on "Penetrating Rays in Earth" on which there was a good deal of discussion. We had quite a good section and practically all the radio-active people were present. The final closing meeting was a regular bear-garden. De Heen [7] and the Belgian Commissioner and Mme. Curie were on the platform. The Standards Report was first of all read in three languages and adopted. Professor Riecke [8] then got up and proposed the names of an International Committee to arrange for the time and place of the next Congress.[9] This Committee included Mme. Curie, Professor Wien,[10] Righi,[11] and yourself, as well as several representatives of the medical side, and Righi proposed that I should be President of this Committee. Only two Belgians were put on it, but De Heen and Daniel were left out. There was at once a row and the Belgians wanted to incorporate the whole of their Belgian Organising Committee. The audience was very hostile obviously to the Belgians on account of their mismanagement of the Congress, and there were dozens of speeches in every language at all parts of the hall. In order to smooth matters over I suggested De Heen should be added. This was done but obviously the audience showed disapproval. De Heen was hopeless as a Chairman and either did not know what to do or was afraid to move. The audience got out of hand and started whistling and boo-hooing. Finally Professor Hallwachs [12] went up by the platform, waved aside the President

and put the resolution throwing out the Belgian Committee
and instituting the new one. In the course of the meeting
Daniel had fled and rushed off to Ostend, leaving all the final
arrangements to be looked after by other people. Finally as an
act of grace I suggested that Daniel be put on the Committee in
order to preserve continuity, but obviously the audience would
have been quite willing to bury him. Finally I and several
others thanked the Belgian people for their hospitality, but the
audience did not receive it in too cordial a manner. The session
closed at last in a reasonably amicable state. I understand the
Belgians were as bitter against Daniel as anyone. They say that
he was paid by the Government to make arrangements, and instead of that stayed at Ostend and left it to the underlings. One
of the Belgian professors got up at a meeting and spoke very
strongly of the demerits of his countrymen in managing the
Congress. I have since got a letter from Daniel stating that he
left the meeting in order to attend his father, who was ill at
Ostend!

We had a very pleasant dinner the same evening and a reception at the Hotel de Ville, which was very well managed. I understand, however, that some of the excursions the next day or
two were hopelessly mismanaged, and everybody was feeling
that the Belgians were the limit.

I went on Friday morning to have a look at the Exhibition,
and looked over the German scientific apparatus, which was
very good, and left that evening for Harwich via Antwerp. The
boat was very full but the weather was fine. We have had good
weather since I have been in Manchester, and we have been out
in the country by motor several times.

Kovarik [13] and Geiger are back and hard at work. Geiger's
mother had a breakdown a day before the marriage of his sister,
and I understand from him will have to be kept very quiet for a
year or two.

I am writing up a brief account for "Nature" in regard to the
standards and nomenclature,[14] and Makower is writing up an

account of the Congress,[15] and I have arranged for Soddy to write an account for the 'Times.' You had better arrange to give the matter some publicity in Science and in your own papers.[16]

By the way your countryman, Becker,[17] was very incensed at his treatment by the Belgians at the Congress, and damned them all most heartily. We gave him an opportunity of talking at the last meeting and he spoke very sensibly about the arrangements for the next Congress, so I hope he felt better after it.

I hope to hear from you before long as to your progress with the authorities. Give my kind regards to Bumstead and Dana. My wife and Eileen are both very flourishing.

I have omitted to mention that Bateman[18] has been appointed Assistant Professor of Mathematics at Bryn Mawr, and leaves to-morrow for Philadelphia. He was very amusing for he seemed to think at first that Bryn Mawr was a mixed institution of men and women. I pointed out the dangers of his situation. I should be glad if you could show him any attention at any time in America. I think he will attend the Physical Society's meetings.

I have just been to see Lamb to-day. He is just back & looking well. Elliot Smith is flourishing. Did you hear that Wood-Jones (his old demonstrator) married the daughter of Ross (King of Cokos)[19] (¾ Malay stock) with a ready-made family of five.

You will see how my handwriting has improved. My amanuensis is responsible. Write as soon as you can. Yours ever,

E. RUTHERFORD

1. Boltwood had to leave the International Congress of Radiology and Electricity, Brussels, before the last sessions in order to sail home in time for the start of the school year.

2. Members of the International Radium Standards Committee were Boltwood, Marie Curie, André Debierne, A. S. Eve, Hans Geitel, Otto Hahn, Stefan Meyer (secretary), Rutherford, Egon von Schweidler, and Frederick Soddy. Because comparison of results from different laboratories was difficult without a standard of radioactivity, there had long been a de-

sire for its establishment. Though some committee members were unhappy at the large size of the standard chosen (they preferred a quantity of the order with which they usually worked; no one had a full gram of radium), they authorized Marie Curie to prepare a standard of about 20 milligrams which would be preserved for comparison purposes.

3. Jean Perrin, professor of physical chemistry at the Sorbonne, and 1926 Nobel Prize winner in physics.

4. Charles G. Barkla, professor of physics at King's College, London, later at the University of Edinburgh, and 1917 Nobel Prize winner in physics.

5. Marcel Moulin, head of physics laboratory instruction in the Municipal School of Industrial Physics and Chemistry, Paris, a position once held by Pierre Curie.

6. Ludwig Wertenstein, at this time a student in Paris, later professor of physics and radiology in Warsaw.

7. Pierre de Heen, professor of physics at the University of Liège and president of this congress.

8. Eduard Riecke, professor and director of the physical institute at the University of Göttingen.

9. The first congress, in 1905, had been held in Liège and, presumably, the Belgians wished to continue as hosts for these meetings. The arrangements committee, however, chose Vienna for the 1915 Congress, but World War I caused its cancellation.

10. Wilhelm Wien, professor of physics at Würzburg, then Munich, and 1911 recipient of the Nobel Prize.

11. Augusto Righi, professor of physics at the University of Bologna.

12. Wilhelm Hallwachs, professor of physics at the Technisches Hochschule in Dresden, and an interesting transition figure between the nineteenth and twentieth centuries, having been assistant to Kundt, Wiedemann, and Kohlrausch.

13. Alois Kovarik was a physics professor in a small school in Iowa for twenty years, during which time he earned a Ph.D. from the University of Minnesota and succeeded Boltwood as John Harling Fellow in Rutherford's laboratory. In 1916 he joined the Yale faculty, rising eventually to full professorship.

14. ER, "Radium standards and nomenclature," *Nature, 84* (6 Oct. 1910), 430–31.

15. Unsigned article by Makower, "The International Congress on Radiology and Electricity," *Nature, 84* (13 Oct. 1910), 478–79.

16. BBB, "International Congress of Radiology and Electricity," *Am. J. Sci., 30* (Dec. 1910), 415–17; "The International Congress of Radiology

and Electricity, Brussels, September 13–15, 1910," *Science, 32* (2 Dec. 1910), 788–91.

17. George F. Becker, chief geologist of the United States Geological Survey.

18. Harry Bateman, a mathematical physicist who helped Rutherford formulate the equations of radioactive decay, remained at Bryn Mawr two years, then went to Johns Hopkins and finally to the California Institute of Technology as Professor of Aeronautical Research and Mathematical Physics.

19. The Cocos Islands, part of the former British Straits Settlements, southwest of Java.

2 NOVEMBER 1910

New Haven, Connecticut

My dear Rutherford,

You were very good to write me that long and interesting letter of Sept. 27th and I really appreciated it very much. I have been putting off answering it from day to day in the hopes that I too might find time for writing a correspondingly long reply, for I have a lot of things I want to tell you, and I wanted to be able to tell them all at once. However, if I don't write you now there is no telling when I shall get a chance to do so. So here goes and I shall do as much as I can!

I had a very comfortable and uneventful trip back on the Baltic and reached New York on schedule time. I spent a couple of days there with my relations and then came on here to New Haven, where I found everything much as I had left it. There was one notable exception, however, and that was the big hole in the ground on Prospect Hill, the future site of the New Sloane Physical Laboratory! [1] (I hope you were duly impressed by the red ink on the previous page!) It, the new lab., is certainly going to be a beautiful, fine building, but Oh Lord, what a devil of a mess there is going to be in this department before it is all done. There are hopes that it may be ready for use by Jan-

uary 1912, but I am willing to offer odds that it will not be occupied before September of that year at earliest!! And I am very
much afraid that I shall be rather mixed up in it all before it is
done.

Bumstead is in about his usual form although I think his general condition is somewhat better.[2] He is taking things fairly
easily and promises to hold out. He seems very glad to have me
back and I have been having a very pleasant time stopping with
the family. They took me in until I got a satisfactory place to
live in and I am only leaving them at the end of this week.

It is a difficult matter to explain just how I find my own position under present conditions. Hadley[3] is away galavanting
around the Continent of Europe and will not return until late
this month. As I want to talk business with him first of all I
haven't made any definite moves as yet, but I have made a few
indirect, strategic advances on the Stokes[4] Camp and my scouts
report that his earthworks are not invulnerable. I think that if I
can get a chance to buy a few tons of good uranium ore, either
pitchblende or carnotite, and can go to them with a definite
proposition I have a good chance of getting them to do something for me.[5] But I am not counting any of my chickens before
they are hatched.

The papers I have to write are getting along all right. I have
engaged a stenographer, typewriter and private secretary (all in
one, female-plain and perfectly safe-) and I am beating them
out in great shape. I think they ought to be ready to send on by
next week.

The apparatus I ordered from Baumbach has just come. He is
none too prompt in his deliveries and Cook[6] is evidently worse.
The things I ordered from Cook in August have not yet put in
an appearance. But I have hopes that they will get here before
Christmas.

The effect of your amanuensis on your handwriting is certainly wonderful. It adds a new pleasure to the receipt of your
letters, that of being able to read them on the first trial.

231

Please give my best regards to Elliot Smith, Fiddes, Chaffers, Lamb and all the other good people who were so kind to me in Manchester. Remember me to the men about the laboratory and give my warmest personal regards to Mrs. Rutherford and Eileen. I wish I had time to write all the many things I have in mind but the hour is growing late and this has been a very busy day for me.

With very best wishes and many thanks for all your kindnesses, I remain, Yours very sincerely,

B. B. BOLTWOOD

P.S. Could you manage to send me the data about the relative strength of the Austrian, the Curie and the Rutherford standard as I should like to have it at hand. Also the strength of the Dewar specimen in terms of your standard.

APPENDIX!!! My note at the end of the last page reminds me that I have failed to mention one matter of importance about which I should say something at this time. This is the matter of the International Radium Standard. I had a talk with Rosa [7] in New York, at the Physical Society Meeting, and he suggested that the Radium Standards Committee should approach the International Bureau of Standards at Paris with a view to finding out whether the I.B.S. would not be willing to defray the costs of the preparation of the New Curie Standard. He said that he thought that the International Bureau would probably be willing to defray the cost if they had the necessary funds at their command, if the New Standard was ultimately to be deposited with them, which as I understood it was the general plan which the Committee had in view. I am expecting to write the Congress up and give an account of the Committee's action in the columns of SCIENCE [8] and the American Journal of Science.[9]

Another matter has come up on which I should like to have your opinion. Bumstead has made what seems to me to be an excellent suggestion. He suggests that the term "Curie" be used to denote the amount of any radioelement in the uranium-radium series in equilibrium with one gram of radium. Thus one curie of uranium would be the amount of uranium in equilibrium with one gram of radium, and one milli-curie of ionium would be the amount of ionium in equilibrium with one milligram of radium, etc. I think that the use of this term (or unit) in this manner would be of great practical advantage in many ways. I do not think that I have to go into any further details to make it quite clear to you. What do you think of it? Yours again,

B.B.B.

1. The administration won the "battle" for the location of this laboratory. See Boltwood's letter of 30 May 1909.

2. The reference is to Bumstead's frail health.

3. Arthur Twining Hadley, president of Yale.

4. Anson Phelps Stokes, secretary of the university.

5. University budgets customarily contained no funds for research; monies for this purpose had to be requested from general funds on each occasion.

6. Cook was an assistant in the mechanical workshop of Manchester University. Apparently he engaged in private business also.

7. Edward B. Rosa, chief physicist at the National Bureau of Standards.

8. BBB, "The International Congress of Radiology and Electricity, Brussels, September 13–15, 1910," *Science, 32* (2 Dec. 1910), 788–91.

9. BBB, "International Congress of Radiology and Electricity," *Am. J. Sci., 30* (Dec. 1910), 415–17.

14 DECEMBER 1910

17 Wilmslow Road
Withington, Manchester

My dear Boltwood,

I received your good letter some time ago, and have been waiting for the paper to appear, but apparently your angle of lag is large. I wish you could send it over as soon as possible, as I want to send in another paper on the Decay of the Emanation with it. I have forgotten to look up the data about Dewar's and the Curies' radium; but if I remember right Curies' standard was 90 per cent of mine, and Dewar's a few per cent higher. But of course the measurements of the big quantity are very uncertain.

I received a copy of *Science* with the excellent account you wrote of the Congress, with all of which, of course, I cordially agree. I note what you say in regard to the extension of the term "Curie," but I suppose we can not do anything definite about it just yet. The difficulty is that it would require for some time a definition in every case, but it will undoubtedly be very useful.

I received a few days ago the copy of Mme Curie's two volumes on radioactivity.[1] They are very heavy and very long, but she has got a great deal of useful information collected together. I think she makes a mistake of trying to include all the work, old and new, with very little critical discussion of its relative importance. I have not had time to read more than parts of it, but, as a whole, it would appear that she has been reasonably generous in the recognition of those outside of France. At any rate, I should judge that I have not been neglected. In reading her book I could almost think I was reading my own with the extra work of the last few years thrown in to fill up. Some of the chapters start in very much the same way, and the subject-matter is divided in much the same manner. I am glad to see that she has shown great discrimination in dealing with Ramsay's discoveries, and such delicate questions as the spectrum of the emanation. I think as a whole she is much better, as one would expect, on the chemical side, but shows rather a lack of grip on the physical side, especially in her discussion on radiations.[2] It is very amusing in parts to read where she is very anxious to claim priority for French science, or rather for herself and her husband. Long quotations are given to show their mental attitude at the times under consideration. By the way, I see a table of minerals appended which she says she took from the

Jahrbuch which bears an extraordinary resemblance to the list you gave in my second edition. She evidently knows good material when she sees it! Altogether I feel that the poor woman has laboured tremendously, and her volumes will be very useful for a year or two to save the researcher from hunting up his own literature; a saving which I think is not altogether advantageous.

As for myself I am getting ahead with my own book [3] and trying to keep it within reasonable volume. I have got five chapters well in hand, and hope that another six months will see me through the greater part of it. I feel it an unmitigated bore, and I am afraid the book will suffer for that reason.

As to the Laboratory, things are going very well. We are going to have the extension for the Electrical Engineering at the back of the dynamo house, a new lecture room for Physics, and I have also got another floor of about five rooms for special research as well as a small Chemical Laboratory to be built outside, with a draught cupboard and other accessories, to await your next arrival. I hope that the building will be ready by next October, although the work is not yet started. With the Electrical Engineering rooms, we ought to be able to research in comfort. I have been working at the delta rays [4] from the emanation preparatory to having a look for the positive electron, [5] and have been doing a good deal of calculation on scattering. I think I can devise an atom much superior to J.J.'s, for the explanation of and stoppage of α and β particles, and at the same time I think it will fit in extraordinarily well with the experimental numbers. It will account for the reflected α particles observed by Geiger, and generally, I think, will make a fine working hypothesis. Altogether I am confident that we are going to get more information from scattering about the nature of the atom than from any other method of attack.

I have one of the students working at a compensation method for a comparison of γ rays, and I think we shall get over the difficulty of comparing large and small standards. The method is to balance the γ ray effect against uranium and adjust the distance of the radium for balance in each case. This can be done very accurately. I am calibrating the scale, although from theory it can easily be calculated what the error is likely to be. Geiger and Kovarik are in good form, and working on the question of the number of β rays from different products. I daresay you heard that Geiger's mother died suddenly in the middle of the term. He intends to go home for Christmas. Gray seems to have discovered that β rays set up γ rays under certain conditions. This is very interesting, and looks to me all right. Boyle is working at the absorption of the emanation in water, and is happy up in the attic. Royds has just got an appointment to the Observatory at the Kodikanal in India, and goes out there shortly. I have a new man working on radium C, who has confirmed Hahn's results of its complexity. I am working at several other things, and generally the laboratory is very busy.

I have unfortunately been appointed a member of the Council of the Royal Society, and will have to go down to London once a month. This will keep me from becoming too bucolic.

Other items of news are that Lang is to be married in a week or so, while Elliot Smith has just been presented with a bouncing boy, initial value 10 pounds. He has kept away from the Refectory for the last few days in consequence. Dr. Wilde [6] has been playing up all last term with a shower of writs on the Literary and Philosophical, but we are still out of jail.

The motor car still behaves admirably, and we make a good deal of use of it even in winter. To-day is beautifully bright and balmy, and I am sure is a contrast to your own depressing climate. I may say that we had a very bad November, even worse than last year.

I cannot remember any items of special importance with the exception that Ramsay has not popped up for the last six months. One of the minor financial papers has been attacking him for his connection with the Radium Company. If I can find the copies I will send them on to you, as they will keep you from becoming too sad.

We are all well at home and find life quite reasonable. I forgot to mention that I went down to Cambridge to attend the celebration in honour of J.J.'s 25th anniversary. A memorial "volume de luxe" of the History of the Cavendish was presented to him in the afternoon, and we had a dinner of old and present researchers in the evening, about sixty in all. I occupied the chair and dispensed even justice. It went off very well with the exception of one or two rather awkward breaks by some of the speakers, for some of J.J.'s original rivals for the Chair were present.

I shall be glad to hear how things are getting on with you and to impress on you the necessity of getting to work, and sending over the MS. of your papers. If it does not come soon I will use you as an awful warning!

Give my kind regards to Bumstead and all my friends. Yours ever,

E. RUTHERFORD

1. M. Curie, *Traité de Radioactivité* (Paris, Gauthier-Villars, 1910).

2. Though trained as a physicist, Marie Curie's work in radioactivity was, to a great extent, chemical. This was due, in part, to the early division of labor she arranged with her husband.

3. ER, *Radioactive Substances and Their Radiations* (Cambridge, University Press, 1913).

4. Delta rays are relatively slow-moving electrons, usually emitted from surfaces exposed to alpha ray bombardment.

5. The positron was not found until 1932, by Carl Anderson, who detected the particle in cosmic rays.

6. Henry Wilde, a pioneer in the electrical industry, made his fortune manufacturing generators of his own design and also using such equipment to produce plated tubes by the electro-deposition of copper. He retired early and devoted his many remaining years to scientific research and to philanthropy. The Manchester Literary and Philosophical Society, of which he was president from 1894 to 1896, received substantial funds from him for various purposes, including the prestigious annual Wilde Lecture.

237

The substance of his controversy with the Society in 1910 is unknown, for their records were lost during World War II bombings. Wilde, however, had a great fondness for litigation and was frequently engaged in patent and personal suits.

11 JANUARY 1911

Sloane Laboratory, Yale University
New Haven, Connecticut

My Dear Rutherford,

Your letter of December the 14th was duly received and very highly appreciated. Considering my somewhat protracted silence and the delay in sending you the papers on helium etc., it was very good of you to write me such an interesting and lengthy epistle. I have to congratulate you on the enormous improvement which has taken place in your hand writing and contrary to my previous experience I was able to make out everything in your letter on the first reading. Every time I look at that letter I feel that the year which I spent in Manchester was certainly not wasted. I expect some day to receive a substantial testimonial contributed in my behalf by your other correspondents.

I havn't seen Mme Curie's new book as yet, but I expect to get it before long. I am anxious to know what she has done towards collecting purely chemical data but I do not suppose that the book contains very much along that line outside of her own work. I am glad to learn that you are getting ahead on the third edition of "Radioactivity." I should be greatly pleased to read the manuscript over for you if you care to have me do so. I mention this because you spoke about it last September. It is very pleasant to think of the additions which you are planning for the Physics building, and I am very glad that you are going to have a better place for the research students. I shall be much in-

terested to learn more about your model atom. I suppose the
paper will be out before very long.[1]

I sent yesterday by registered mail the manuscript of the article on the Production of Helium by Radium.[2] I have had a
devil of a time getting this into shape, and even now it seems to
be a good deal longer than is desirable. If any desirable changes
occur to you please make them without any hesitancy. I have
left a page for you to fill in with a sort of general summary
pointing out the bearing of the results on other matters such as
the accuracy of your earlier counting experiments, etc.

With this letter I am sending you the manuscript of the report on the Separation of Ionium and Actinium and on the
Production of Helium by Ionium for the Royal Society.[3] I have
left certain blanks on the first and third pages which you can fill
in for me if you will be so kind as to do so. Page 7, foot note at
bottom of page, you might fill in the reference to the Helium
from Radium Paper if you happen to know in time when and
where it is likely to appear. The same is true with regard to the
statement on page 8 where the production of helium per gram
of radium is taken as 0.107 cubic millimeters per day. A foot
note here referring to the other paper might be desirable.

I have just received about 230 pounds of pitchblende ore
containing approximately 25 per cent. of uranium which I purchased in Colorado for about $250.00. I am planning to work
this up in the next month or so and should get out quite a reasonable quantity of ionium and actinium. Also about sixteen
milligrams of radium bromide.

The University is still promising to supply me with materials
and laboratory facilities for chemical work, and the Treasurer
has recently been in Colorado where he has been trying to get
some of the Yale Alumni there interested in these matters. He is
not yet back and so I do not know how successful he has been,
but I am rather afraid that nothing very much will come out of
it.

Wellisch [4] has arrived in New Haven. He got here about ten days ago. He seems to be a very good sort of fellow and will certainly be an addition to the department.

Your reference to the weather in your letter calls for some comment on my part. I have been back here now for something over three months and the weather has been so fine that until ten days ago it was really a serious matter. There wasn't any rain for months and the water supply from the City got so low that we all had to stop drinking water. That is to say, we had to add as little water as possible to the national beverage. I have really never seen finer weather in the autumn and early winter and it brings tears to my eyes to think of my poor smoked-up friends in Manchester.

Things here, in general, are going along much as usual. Bumstead is in exceptionally good shape and now that he has a laboratory assistant is spending a good deal of time on research work, which is always good for him. The new laboratory on the hill is progressing slowly and the innumerable details of its construction are constantly being impressed upon us. I suppose the darn thing will be done some day, but I am afraid it will be a year or two before we get into it.

I received about $100.00 worth of mesothorium from Knoefler. They appear to have given me very decent measure for the stuff has a gamma-ray activity, if anything a little higher than that at which they sold it. I also got about $100.00 worth of actinium from the Braunschweig people. They wrote that this was particularly selected for me by Giesel and I dare say that he gave me good measure, but at the rate that I paid, that material which I separated for you last winter must be worth about $2000.00 or $3000.00.

There isn't any scientific news that I can give you. In this respect it is about as dead around here as one could well imagine, and unless I get out of town occasionally I don't hear much about anything. I spoke very frankly in regard to our friend Ramsay in one of the Lectures that I gave in Brooklyn in December.[5] Several men in the audience came up and spoke about it later and from what they said I gather that public opinion is beginning to size him up more correctly.

Please give my very best regards to my Manchester friends. With warmest personal regards to yourself and Mrs Rutherford and with love to Eileen. Yours very sincerely,

BERTRAM B. BOLTWOOD

1. ER, "The scattering of the α and β rays and the structure of the atom," *Mem. Proc. Manchester Lit. Phil. Soc.*, *55* (1911), 18–20; "The scattering of α and β particles by matter and the structure of the atom," *Phil. Mag.*, *21* (May 1911), 669–88.

2. BBB and ER, "Production of helium by radium," *Phil. Mag.*, *22* (Oct. 1911), 586–604. Before this was published the paper was translated into German and appeared as "Die Erzeugung von Helium durch Radium," *Sitzber. Akad. Wiss. Wien, Math. Naturw. Kl. Abt. IIa, 120* (Mar. 1911), 313–36.

3. BBB, "Report on the separation of ionium and actinium from certain residues and on the production of helium by ionium," *Proc. Roy. Soc., 85A* (14 Mar. 1911), 77–81.

4. Edward M. Wellisch, an Australian, became assistant professor of physics at Yale in 1911. Four years later he returned to Sydney as lecturer, then professor, of mathematics.

5. Boltwood gave five lectures before the Brooklyn Institute of Arts and Sciences, in November and December 1910.

1 FEBRUARY 1911

17 Wilmslow Road
Withington, Manchester

My dear Boltwood,

I received safely the two papers you forwarded and have been busy getting them ready to send off for publication. I have added a page at the required point in the helium paper,[1] and am adding a somewhat long footnote to your "Residue" paper,[2] giving the connection of myself with the same. I am sending it off to-day to the Royal Society, but am not quite sure whether they will feel inclined to publish the chemical details. If there is any difficulty I will arrange that the "Production of helium by radium" shall be published separately and immediately.

We have had a very good winter so far and a good deal of dry fine weather; but there is an epidemic of colds about. A good many in the Laboratory have been affected and Evans[3] has gone away for a few days to recuperate. I fortunately have kept pretty free of such troubles.

As to work, Gray has proved completely that the β rays from radium E produce a considerable quantity of γ rays when they fall on matter, and there seems to be little doubt that a small quantity of γ rays ordinarily observed are mainly secondary. His paper will be sent in a few days to the Royal, and I think is a good piece of work.[4] It is possible that the γ rays from uranium X and possibly from actinium may in the same way prove to be secondary. On the other hand there is no doubt that the secondary γ rays from radium C, thorium D, etc. are difficult to detect, so that there is no appreciable error in employing γ rays as a standard for measurement of radium and thorium. Geiger is examining the distribution of the α particles which suffer a large deflexion. As far as experiments have gone, the results agree well with the distribution deduced from my special atom. I think that this type of work will ultimately throw a great deal of light on the intensity and distribution of the electric field within the atom. Kovarik is working away on the comparison between the number of α particles and β particles expelled from various products, but they are having difficulty with the weak β ray products. Another man is doing recoil from radium C, and is getting some interesting results which are at present rather difficult to explain. I am working at odds and ends and trying a number of things, but mainly working to get the value of e/m accurately for various radioactive sources, and to see whether it varies with speed. I gave a lecture soon after Christmas to the Röntgen Society on Mesothorium, etc. as a substitute for radium. I think they were interested and I showed a number of experiments. I have agreed to write a short pamphlet for the Akademische Verlagsgesellschaft on the radium standard. They were rather pressing, and I thought it worth doing to put the case forward in a simple way to prepare the way for the adoption of the standard.

Geiger has been approached to take a position in the Reichsanstalt in Berlin as head of the Radioactive Testing Department. I do not want to lose him, and am seeing what can be done to retain his services.

You will have seen by this time Ramsay's paper on niton in the *Proc. Roy. Soc.*[5] It is better written than usual, but there are a good many points in which I take leave to differ.

You will have seen that Mme. Curie was not elected to the Academy.[6] I do not suppose it will worry her much.

Estimates and tenders are at present being prepared for the extension of the Physics, and I hope the matter will be finally settled in a month or so.

I was interested to hear about your investments in radioactive material. Have you had time yet to look into the separation and concentration of radio-lead? Some one will have to tackle that before long. Mme. Curie gives an account of the methods so far adopted in her new book, but none seem to be very effective.

I understand Antonoff [7] has been amusing himself with the English Law Courts. He and some friends took some rooms in a Welsh boarding house for a fortnight. They left next day on account of the number and ferocity of the fleas, and refused to pay. The landlady had them up in the Courts and Antonoff gave evidence in a most graphic manner, illustrating with appropriate gestures the number, colour and habits of the fleas and his endeavours to "execute" them, and finally as a touch of comedy offered to strip and show his wounds. I understand it was all very amusing, and he enjoyed himself thoroughly. The magistrate has deferred giving judgment, so I do not know whether they will have to pay.

The motor is going much better than ever it did, and we go out when the weather is not too cold. Lamb and Elliot Smith are both in good form. The latter is putting on flesh and looks quite rosy—another advantage of the English climate. We are all pretty well, and there is little to record domestically.

I have got well into five chapters of my book, but have gone rather easy the last month, as I have so many other things on. It is a laborious task. I do not think I shall be in a special hurry to put it through at once as there is no object in coming out so soon after Mme. Curie's book, but I hope to have it well in hand by the end of the summer. When I have completely prepared the number of chapters I will send them over to you for perusal if I have time. Yours ever,

E. RUTHERFORD

Give my kind regards to Bumstead, Dana, & others in your Lab.

1. BBB and ER, "Die Erzeugung von Helium durch Radium," *Sitzber. Akad. Wiss. Wien, Math. Naturw. Kl. Abt. IIa, 120* (Mar. 1911), 313–36.

2. BBB, "Report on the separation of ionium and actinium from certain residues and on the production of helium by ionium," *Proc. Roy. Soc., 85A* (14 Mar. 1911), 77–81.

3. E. J. Evans, a spectroscopist, later furnished strong evidence for Bohr's theory of the atom. After World War I he became professor of physics at Swansea.

4. J. A. Gray, "Secondary γ-rays produced by β-rays," *Proc. Roy. Soc., 85A* (11 Apr. 1911), 131–39.

5. R. Whytlaw Gray and Ramsay, "The density of niton ('radium emanation') and the disintegration theory," *Proc. Roy. Soc., 84A* (26 Jan. 1911), 536–50.

6. The French Académie des Sciences is a far more limited society than those of other countries, having only a few positions for each scientific specialty. Thus, in the intense competition for the occasional vacancies, Marie Curie's sex was a distinct handicap, for the academicians were loath to break tradition by inviting a woman to their ranks.

7. George Antonoff, born in Warsaw, received his D.Sc. degree from Manchester and then held several positions in Russia, including professor

of chemistry at the Ural Mining Institute. In 1938 he became professor of physical chemistry at Fordham University in New York.

15 FEBRUARY 1911

17 Wilmslow Road
Withington, Manchester

My dear Boltwood,

I have sent on your paper to the R.S. with my blessing and an explanatory footnote, and it has been accepted for publication and so should appear before long. I took a copy of the helium production paper and have sent it on to the Vienna Academy, and I presume they will publish it very soon.

I have arranged to get Geiger a rise and put him definitely on the staff, and he is very satisfied.[1] Those old buildings at the back and in front of the Physics are coming down preparatory to a new erection. Things as a whole are going very satisfactorily.

We have had an excellent winter and I feel in very good form. This is just a short letter as you owe me one. Yours ever,

E. RUTHERFORD

1. This merely delayed Geiger's departure for a year, however, for in August 1912 he accepted a post in the Physikalische Technische Reichsanstalt.

11 APRIL 1911

17 Wilmslow Road
Withington, Manchester

My dear Boltwood,

I have not heard from you of late but trust that your energy will return to you in the spring. You no doubt will have re-

245

ceived before this the reprints of your paper to the Royal Society.

There is one question on which I would like your advice and assistance. Can you tell me the chemical state of the actinium preparations in the two glass tubes, whether hydroxide or chloride or what not? I should be glad also if you could tell me what you think would be the best compound to make the actinium give off a maximum quantity of emanation. I want to use the actinium as a source for a production of a very strong active deposit. Please drop a line as soon as you can.

We have just returned from a motor tour in the South of England. We had a pleasant enough time, but the weather was very cold in the latter portion. We are going up to the Lakes for another short holiday in a few days. The house is at present in the hands of decorators, and the study is the only room inhabitable in the house.

I will tell you some time later the scientific work that is going on. Geiger and Marsden [1] are hard at work counting scintillations in order to see how far my theory of scattering fits in with the facts. I hope in another year or two to say something fairly definite of the constitution of the atom.[2]

I was much amused recently to read the Carnegie Institute report by an engineer on efficiency of Physics teaching. It struck me as being pretty crude, and I see that Maclaurin has been satirising it in *Science*.

Give my kind regards to Bumstead and Company. I hope that you are as well as I am. Mrs. Rutherford sends her kind regards. Yours ever,

E. RUTHERFORD

P.S. (Afterthought) Elliot Smith grows rosier every day. His two boys have had measles and also a cousin who was visiting them, but the baby has escaped. Smith is very proud of the physical dimensions of this infant. Tout had an attack of pneumonia a short time ago, but is recuperating slowly. Lang is married to a Scotchwoman, while the great Miss Stopes was married to a Dr. Gates, Botanist of Chicago, an event which created quite a flutter of amusement in our University circles. Her wedding announcement was certainly of the most humourous character, including the statement that in order not to lose her identity, all future scientific publications will be published under the name of Marie C. Stopes. She is an original character any way. I trust that this gossip will put you in touch with your friends here. I forgot to mention, Makower is engaged to a Manchester lady. I have'nt seen her but I understand her parentage is quite respectable and the two may be able to help a little financially. I gather that he is to be married before long. I admire the courage of these young people in marrying on small incomes.

1. Ernest Marsden, at this time a student of Rutherford, later became professor of physics in Wellington, New Zealand, and then secretary of that country's Department of Scientific and Industrial Research.

2. While Rutherford did publish more on the constitution of the atom, the subject received its next major advance from Niels Bohr, whom Rutherford had interested in the problem during a visit to Manchester. Bohr's paper, in three parts, appeared as "On the constitution of atoms and molecules," *Phil. Mag.*, 26 (July, Sept. and Nov. 1913), 1–25, 476–502, 857–75.

25 APRIL 1911

Sloane Laboratory, Yale University
New Haven, Connecticut

My dear Rutherford,

Replying to your letter of the 11th, for which I am greatly obliged and which I shall answer at greater length presently when I get the first opportunity, let me say now—

The actinium preparations in the two glass tubes consist, in all probability, chiefly of oxides. The material was precipitated with ammonium hydroxide (see "Report," Proc. Roy. Soc. page 80, end of second paragraph), and then ignited at a moderate heat. There may be a little phosphoric acid or silica in the preparation as it was separated from a rather large weight of the residual ammonium salts.

The stuff ought to be almost completely soluble in moderately dilute hydrochloric acid (half strong acid and half water) on warming. Any active material remaining undissolved should be decomposed by fusion with sodium bisulphate. Once in solution the actinium can be separated with the rare earths present by precipitating with oxalic acid. This will give the oxalates containing the actinium, and if these are *very gently* ignited, just sufficient to destroy the oxalic acid, the purer oxides will remain in a much more porous form than the material exists at present, and these should evolve the emanation very freely.

If you would care to have me fix the stuff up for you, which I can do very easily here, send the preparations on to me as soon as you get this letter. I am going to sail for England on the Baltic leaving New York on July the first and ought to be in Manchester by the 8th or 9th. I can bring the purified material over with me at that time and you will not be delayed by having to wait for it, because it will not have produced the equilibrium amounts of radioactinium and actinium X much before the middle of July, even if you work it up yourself in Manchester.

As I said at the beginning of this letter, I hope to write you more fully within a few days, but I am sending off this letter in order to supply you with the information that you want as promptly as possible.

With kindest regards to Mrs Rutherford and my Manchester friends. Yours sincerely,

B. B. BOLTWOOD

16 MAY 1911

17 Wilmslow Road
Withington, Manchester

My dear Boltwood,

I have received your note, but by the time I got your letter
we had succeeded in getting as much effect from the actinium as
was needful for the experiment. I will not bother you by sending it over just now but will talk to you about it when I see you.
I am expecting to get that letter from you which you promised,
as I like to know how things are going with you. We of course
expect you to come straight to Manchester on your arrival, and
to stay with us for a week if you can. I shall be up in Edinburgh
on July 7th, adding another to my scalps in the way of Honorary Degrees.

We have had beautiful weather here for the past fortnight,
and everything is looking its best. I had to work hard on Saturday at a party we gave to young University people, and feel I
deserve a week's rest after it.

I have nothing very interesting to record scientifically. I
went down to the Soirée of the Royal Society and saw Ramsay's
famous balance, and Strutt's experiments on the after glow. He
gets his effects on a very large scale, and seems to open up a line
for a good deal of work. Lewis seems to have anticipated him in
some of the work. Between ourselves I understand Dewar
kicked up a fuss about the matter on the general lines to which
I am now accustomed.

I saw the proofs the other day of our paper for the Vienna
Academy. Geiger says it has been very well translated. You will
have seen that Hahn is finding that the β ray problem is more
complex than at first appeared. Geiger and Kovarik have been
investigating the matter in another way, and find that while

there is some indication of order in the β rays, there are some very notable exceptions. The whole problem is very peculiar. Antonoff, who has been working like a slave for the last year, reckons he has found a new product emitting α rays of period about 1.5 days, in purified uranium. He has done a great deal of work, and it looks as if it may be correct. I have a number of the chemists, including Holt and Lapworth, doing courses in radio-activity. Professor Farr of New Zealand is also with us here picking up radioactive tips.

I saw Wood in London the other day. He tells me he surveyed the ground at Stockholm last Christmas from the point of view of ultimately playing the principal part.[1] He seems to have been making the Germans work, and I understand left several of them in a fit state for the hospital.

Our new building is going up apace, and we expect to be in it in October.

Excuse this short letter as I have got a lot to do. Barnes of Montreal comes over to-day or to-morrow. Yours ever,

E. RUTHERFORD

1. Probably Robert W. Wood, professor of physics at Johns Hopkins University and a noted authority on optics. While he received numerous honors and medals during his long career, the Nobel Prize was not among them.

15 JUNE 1911

17 Wilmslow Road
Withington, Manchester

My dear Boltwood,

Just a line to remind you we are expecting you to come at once to our house when you arrive in England.

It is possible we may not have arrived home from Edinburgh

by the time you come but make yourself comfortable & at home. We leave Edinburgh at 2.30 & should be back in time for dinner. Yours ever,

E. RUTHERFORD

25 JUNE 1911

New Haven, Connecticut

My dear Rutherford,

Your letter of June 15th reached me this morning. If all goes well I shall sail from New York on the Baltic on next Saturday (the 1st). I should then reach Liverpool on Sunday, the ninth, and leaving for Manchester should get there before Sunday evening.

I have lots of things to tell you but shall keep them until I see you. My plans for the summer are very indefinite but I shall be glad to spend a week with you in Manchester in order to see all my friends again. I will telegraph you from Liverpool in order to let you know when to expect me.

With kindest regards, Yours sincerely,

B. B. BOLTWOOD

15 SEPTEMBER 1911

Göttingen

My dear Mrs. Rutherford,

Your letter of Aug. 29 reached me at Eisenach and, of course, I immediately began to play a series [of] 200 games of "killing time" in order to disprove your theories as to the difficulties of obtaining a solution. The results of my observations are not in "good agreement" with yours and are scarcely of "the same order of magnitude." I consider the conclusions of Rutherford, Rutherford & Co. as distinctly lacking in *quantitative* significance and attribute their erroneous outcome of their experiments to an incomplete mixing of the ingredients (in other words: the pack was not properly shuffled!)

I append to their table (which is enclosed herewith) the results of my own observations and trust that before "rushing into print" they will undertake a new series of measurements exercising greater precautions and avoiding the errors in judgement of which they have previously been guilty!!!!

I came in here yesterday afternoon and joined Oertel,[1] who came up from Munich. Together we go on to Bremen to take the steamer which leaves on Tuesday.

To refer once more to the patience game let me tell you of a modification which I have found very interesting. One *shuffles* the cards, and then puts them down (face up) in four rows of thirteen each. Then one begins anywhere one chooses to take cards out according to the same plan as in the ordinary game. Instead of removing the cards, they are simply pushed up (or down, as one chooses). When no more progress can be made, the cards are all pushed back into their proper rows again, and a new trial is made. It is a very interesting study to see how many cards can be taken out in this way. It is best to have "matching" cards on top & bottom of pack to start with; that is—to start with a possible solution not altogether excluded.

I give below a combination which I found very puzzling, but which can be solved. Try it!

"D" for diamonds; "H" for hearts; etc.

"J" for knave (as you call him).

3D, 2H, 1H, 4H, 9D, KD, QS, 5H, QC, QD, 4C, 5C, QH, JS, 2C, KS, 8S, 10H, 5S, 5D, 3S, 7C, JC, 10D, 9H, 6S, 8H, JH, 2D, 1C, 7D, KH, KC, 3H, 9C, 6H, 6D, 3C, 7S, 2S, 10C, 8D, 10S, 1D, 7H, 8C, 9S, 4S, 6C, 4D, 1S, JD. (Note—I have just checked this up by playing it out and am sure it is right.)

Rutherford   19 September 1911

I enclose a key which you may consult if you get stuck!
With regards & best wishes. Sincerely,

B.B.B.

1. Karl Oertel, professor of geodesy and astronomy at the Technische Hochschule, Hanover.

19 SEPTEMBER 1911

17 Wilmslow Road
Withington, Manchester

My dear Boltwood,

This note will reach you shortly after your arrival in God's own country, and I trust that you will reach it in a suitably religious frame of mind. My main object of writing is to inform you that a postal official called on me to-day to ask for your address, as two registered letters sent by you were considered by the German officials "inadmissible," and I presume that that official ridden country will return you these letters. I imagine the letters contain the voluntary offering which you told my wife you would send to her and to Mrs. Elliot Smith, and of which ours at any rate has not arrived so far. I trust that your language will be suitable to the occasion, and that this will still further increase your belief in the efficiency of the great German nation in making trouble for others.

Next, in regard to the probability curve. I am surprised at a man of your reputed ability imagining that you can determine such a probability curve with a mere 200 observations without the use of the scientific imagination, which is so unusual in your chemical brethren. In order to redeem your reputation I suggest that you employ the services of the University Club to play 10,000 games, and send me the result. I will then pay some little attention to your "scientific results."

Next to speak of more peaceful subjects. We have been back a

253

fortnight and I have been working on the distribution of the heating effects of the emanation and its products. The experiments have gone well, and I hope soon to have them completed and to make measurements with an accuracy of at least one per cent. You will be interested to hear that Gray and Geiger and Marsden are back and ready for work. I am afraid I shall lose to a large extent the services of Lantsberry [1] the next few years, for he has decided to go through the Honours course of this University and take a degree. However, I expect he will be able to help distribute emanation and to make a few α ray tubes. I shall have a couple of new men, at any rate this year, besides a dose of my own students.

Schuster leaves for America next Saturday. You will probably see him in Baltimore. My wife, no doubt, will write to you about the puzzle you sent her. Your key appears to me far more difficult to interpret than the puzzle itself. I spent half an hour without success in endeavouring to decipher the tortuous processes of what you are pleased to call a mind.

I trust that this letter will act as an irritant. Let me know how things are going with you. We are all well and fit for work. Yours ever,

E. RUTHERFORD

1. W. C. Lantsberry, at this time a "laboratory boy" under Rutherford's chief assistant, William Kay, took his degree at Manchester and later accepted a post in Baltimore, Maryland, where he had charge of preparing radium emanation for medical use.

21 OCTOBER 1911

17 Wilmslow Road
Withington, Manchester

My dear Boltwood,

I have not heard from you yet although I sent you a letter which probably was awaiting you on your arrival.

I would like to hear from you confidentially how the radium separation is going on, for I expect I will have to start some negotiations before long with the Vienna people.

There is one item of news that I am sure will interest you. Hahn informed me a short time ago that Soddy had taken out a patent for the separation of meso- and radio-thorium. In a letter I received yesterday, he told me that Knöfler and Co. are going to contest it, for they consider that the method was common knowledge at the time of the patent. I know it was as far as you and I were concerned, and I must say that I was very sorry to hear of Soddy taking such a line. I hope that the matter will be amicably settled, for it would be an awkward matter if it came into the courts. I think it is a great pity when radioactive people start squabbling on the financial side of radioactivity. Hahn, of course, is very anxious to hear my opinion on the subject. While I feel that he has justice on his side, I am naturally not disposed for many reasons to take sides on the matter. I shall let you know if I hear how the matter progresses.

I understand from Russell,[1] who is working with me, that Soddy was very annoyed because Hahn would not publish the methods employed in the separation; but it would appear to me that any one of sense would understand Hahn's position in connection with Knöfler and Co.

I have been laying hard into experimental work and also into my book, and am making very good progress in both. The Laboratory is full, and work is in full swing. You will have seen that the last number of the *Phil. Mag.* was unusually radioactive.

Apart from a cold I am feeling in pretty good form. I am going at the end of next week to Brussels to take part in a small Congress, about fifteen people, on the Theory of Radiations. Some wealthy man in Brussels pays a thousand francs each for our expenses.[2] This is the sort of Congress I have no objection to attending. Planck,[3] Lorentz, Nernst, Jeans,[4] and others will be present, and I am hoping also to meet Mme. Curie and find out how the standard is getting along.

I am hoping to hear from you soon when you have settled down to the bracing climate of your country. By the way, we have had the first rain for an age, and I trust that the water famine is broken. Our water has been turned off for the last three months between 7 p.m. and 6 a.m. Yours ever,

E. RUTHERFORD

P.S. I have received the reprints of our paper in the *Phil. Mag.*[5] and will send you thirty for distribution.

1. Alexander S. Russell was probably the only person to work with both Rutherford and Soddy. A chemist, who spent most of his career at Oxford, he published a paper early in 1913 that contained a close approximation to the group displacement laws shortly presented by Fajans and Soddy.

2. This was the first Solvay Congress, which began an impressive series of such meetings over the years. In 1911 the theme was the theory of radiation and quanta, and the list of about two dozen invited participants included Einstein, Langevin, Onnes, Perrin, Poincaré, Sommerfeld and Wien, besides those mentioned in Rutherford's letter. The patron of these meetings was the Belgian chemist, Ernest Solvay, who devised and made a fortune from the commercial method of preparing sodium carbonate.

3. Max Planck, professor of physics at the University of Berlin, received the 1918 Nobel Prize for his discovery of energy quanta.

4. James Jeans, mathematician, theoretical physicist, astronomer, and one of the outstanding popularizers of science in the first half of this century. After a year as a university lecturer at Cambridge, in 1905 he became professor of applied mathematics at Princeton. Under its recently appointed president, Woodrow Wilson, Princeton was then endeavoring to transform its provincial, ingrown faculty into one of international reputation by hiring brilliant younger men from abroad. The appointment of Jeans, and of O. W. Richardson to a chair in physics, may be seen in this context. Jeans returned to Cambridge in 1909 as Stokes Lecturer, but after 1912 held no academic position, supporting himself largely by his writings.

5. BBB and ER, "Production of helium by radium," *Phil. Mag.*, 22 (Oct. 1911), 586–604.

20 NOVEMBER 1911

17 Wilmslow Road
Withington, Manchester

My dear Boltwood,

I have come to the conclusion that getting a letter out of you is like pulling your best tooth, for I think I have sent two or three without even the courtesy of a reply.

I have just received the first proofs of part of my new Edition, and if you are prepared to go through them I can send them out regularly. If possible, I would like you to attend to them as quickly as possible and return them promptly to me in order that there shall not be too much delay. I may mention that Geiger is reading the MSS for me and verifying references, etc. so that I hope that not too many glaring mistakes will pass both of us. I will send you two copies of proof, one of which you will retain for reference and forward the other when corrected to me.

There is an important matter I have to talk to you about, viz. the radium standard. I was over in Brussels about a fortnight ago at the Radiation Conference, an account of which you will see I gave to *Nature*.[1] It was a pleasant affair but they worked too hard at meetings for my comfort. Mme. Curie was there, Perrin and my old friend, Langevin.[2] You may have heard that there have been some scandalous references in the French Press in regard to Mme. Curie and Langevin. I am sure it is all moonshine; but it must be rather a miserable business for both of them. I had some conversation with Mme. Curie at 12 o'clock at night about the standard matter. She has prepared a standard at 24 mg $RaCl_2$ but wishes to retain it in her Laboratory partly for sentimental reasons and partly to continue observations on its activity. I pointed out to her that the Committee could not allow the international standard to be in the hands of a private person. As you know she is very obstinate, but after some discussion she suggested that it might do to place a duplicate in one of the French Bureaus to be taken as a standard. On the other hand, I wrote to Soddy about it, and he objects to any such arrangement, for he says that the Committee's standard must be a weight standard and no duplicate involving possible errors of γ ray measurement. Mme. Curie has suggested that a fee of a thousand francs should be charged for the preparation and testing of each standard apart from the radium, and commissioned me to ask Meyer whether the Austrian Government could provide the radium at a reasonable price. I wrote to Meyer about the matter, but our letters crossed and I found that he had written to me at the same time outlining what they had done in the preparation of a pure radium standard, and he is desirous to compare their standard with Mme. Curie's. I forward for your private reading his second letter to me in answer to mine, as it brings out clearly the main points at issue, and the difficulties in the way of a satisfactory settlement. Please regard this letter as confidential and send it back to me when you have finished. I have written to Meyer that I quite understand his position, and sympathise with it, and suggested that the first thing to do is to arrange for a comparison of his and Mme. Curie's standard. I personally do not feel that a meeting of the Committee would accomplish much until such a comparison had been made, for otherwise if any marked differences were found the whole question would be in the melting pot again. I think, however, that it may be desirable to hold a meeting later, but when or where I do not know. I am sure it is going to be a ticklish business to get the matter arranged satisfactorily, as Mme. Curie is rather a difficult person to deal with. She has the advantages and at the same time the disadvantages of being a woman.

I think you will gather from these two letters the general state of affairs. I am sure Mme. Curie is likely to be far more reasonable now that she knows that another standard is prepared. By the way, I am hoping to have Mme. Curie over here in February at the opening of the new extension Laboratory, when we shall give her an Honorary Degree. I think that these little things will help to smooth matters over. I was very glad to see that she got a Nobel Prize,[3] but I had thought Richards[4] would be the nominee. He certainly deserves it, but I hope will not have to wait long.

I have completely finished seven chapters of my book, and have two more nearly ready, and am driving through it now at express speed. It is the only way to get things done. Work is going on very well in the Laboratory, and the outlook is promising. I hope you saw Schuster in America. We are expecting him back early in December.

We are all well and flourishing, and have Dr. Newton[5] staying with us. With kind regards. Yours sincerely,

E. RUTHERFORD

1. ER, "Conference on the theory of radiation," *Nature, 88* (16 Nov. 1911), 82–83.

2. Paul Langevin was a former student of Pierre Curie, who succeeded him as professor of physics at the École Municipale de Physique et de Chimie Industrielles, and eventually became director of this school. Later he was professor of physics at the Collège de France.

3. Marie Curie's first Nobel Prize, in physics, was shared with her husband and Henri Becquerel. Eight years later, in 1911, she received the chemistry prize alone.

4. Theodore W. Richards, chemistry professor at Harvard University known for his accurate determinations of atomic weights, was awarded the 1914 Nobel Prize, but had to await the war's end before he received the medal.

5. Charles Newton, a physician, was Mary Rutherford's brother.

5 DECEMBER 1911

Sloane Laboratory, Yale University
New Haven, Connecticut

My dear Rutherford,

I hope the Schusters have given you some account of me and

my doings. It was a great pleasure to me to see them and I wish I might have been able to have gone down to Baltimore while they were there.

I have never been more busy and occupied in my life than I am at present. First of all there was the new laboratory with a lot of things requiring my attention when I got back here in September. Then Bumstead broke down completely and had to go to the Johns Hopkins Hospital for an operation which was performed on the 10th of November. This left a lot more things for me to do. In addition, I got desperate and bought a house early in November and the work of getting this settled has taken even more time than I expected. Then I have a contract to work up 150 pounds of pitchblende from a Colorado mine for a commercial concern, and this is now under way and must be completed in ten days or there will be somebody greatly disappointed. There are a number of other things, but they are too unimportant to mention.

Now I mean to write you a longer letter very soon, just as soon as I get a chance to do so, but this is to tell you that I am still alive and *kicking*. Mme Curie is just what I have always thought she was, a plain darn fool, and you will find it out for certain before long. Meyer is quite right in the position he takes and altogether justified. Will send you back his letter and write more about it later. The radium situation is still unsettled and I can give you no definite encouragement at present. Will write about this also when I get a chance.

But PLEASE send on the proof of your new edition for it is fun to read it and I really need a little fun and recreation. It is fine. I will return it promptly and enclose the first installment with this letter.

Please apologise for me to Mrs. Rutherford and explain the circumstances. I have enjoyed her letters immensely and am extremely indebted to her for writing. But—Lord how many things I have left undone.

If I live through it I shall write again, and perhaps soon?

With warmest personal regards to you all, Very sincerely yours,

B. B. BOLTWOOD

14 DECEMBER 1911

17 Wilmslow Road
Withington, Manchester

Dear Boltwood,

I enclose herewith three sections of proof, from page 33 to page 80. I am afraid you will find them dull reading.

I received back your first section of proof this morning, and also your letter. I heard from Schuster that you were very busy, but I should have thought that even a busy man could find time, with the aid of a secretary, to write a letter of decent size. As, however, you state that you are still alive and 'kicking', I will not say more at the moment.

I was sorry to hear of Bumstead's illness, but I hope that he is proceeding satisfactorily. Give my kind regards to him. His paper in the *Phil. Mag.*[1] was excellent, and I am inclined to believe his explanation.

I am driving at my book with the accelerator down. I am practically through to Chapter X, so you may expect heaps of proof before long.

With best wishes for a happy Christmas time. Yours sincerely,

E. RUTHERFORD

1. Bumstead, "On the emission of electrons by metals under the influence of alpha rays," *Phil. Mag.*, 22 (Dec. 1911), 907–22.

18 March 1912

17 Wilmslow Road
Withington, Manchester

My dear Boltwood,

My wife received a long letter from you this week giving an account of your doings for the past year. I can appreciate that you have had a pretty hard time of it and that you have been doing some pretty heavy kicking. I am very glad to hear that Bumstead is all right again after his operation, and is fit to take up work again. I hope he will be much stronger in the future.

Yes, the condition of affairs in regard to your Laboratory is very much what you anticipated; but I would certainly make a heavy bid for research funds, for otherwise it appears to me there is no advantage at all in having a new Laboratory.

In regard to my own little show, you will have received a pamphlet before this indicating what was on view. We had a very successful time of it, and had between 20 and 30 visiting professors. Experiments were going on not only on Friday evening but on Saturday morning, and I think it was the best physical show we have had in this part of the world. It was a heavy business arranging everything for it took about six weeks of my time; but fortunately everything passed off like clockwork, and everybody was very pleased. I gave a dinner to about fifty people before the reception and that also went off very well. The new Laboratory looks very well, very bright and comfortable, and the new Physical rooms are already proving very useful. I have a little Chemical Laboratory attached, which is now being used by Russell. The new Museum building is pretty well up, and the new archway over Coupland Street improves the whole appearance of the Laboratory very much. All the old houses are pulled down and things generally look much more academic. You can imagine what a rush I have had of it this year, what with my regular work, the opening, and the new edition on my hands, not to mention a number of other very important matters. It is quite on the cards that Beattie will be appointed a Professor. Reynolds of the Technical School has retired and William *Maxwell* Garnett has been appointed in his stead. He is a young fellow (son of Garnett, Demonstrator of Maxwell), not much over thirty, but will probably do very well. We are also appointing a Professor of Electrical Engineering to the Technical School tomorrow.

You may have heard that within a week three of the University people pegged out, including Osborne Reynolds, the former Professor of Engineering, Young, the former Professor of Anatomy, and, most serious of all, Hogg, whom you will remember. He got influenza and pneumonia and there was very little chance for him. They are collecting a fund to assist Mrs. Hogg, for they were left very poorly provided for. I think they have got over £1500 collected for the children. I understand it is quite likely that Mrs. Hogg will be appointed to a position in the Women's Residential College, so that things will be arranged fairly comfortably for her. It is a sad business about Hogg, and was a great blow to us all. Recently Capper was thrown on his head from a horse and made a partial recovery; but I heard a couple of days ago that he is now down with pneumonia in London at his brother's house. I gather that there is not much chance of his pulling through, and I am not sure that one should desire it, for I understand there is grave doubt whether he will ever recover his sanity completely. [*Added to typed letter:* (Later) I hear, today, he is pulling through alright.] I do not know whether you have heard that H. W. Schmidt of Giessen had a similar accident about six months ago, and is now in a private asylum. His wife writes that he shows occasional gleams of sanity, but it is a very bad business. You will remember that Schmidt was with me in the Laboratory for six months, and was a very good fellow. He has several young children, but I understand they are financially in a reasonable position. I am afraid this is rather a catalogue of disasters, but I thought you would be interested to hear as you knew them all. Fortunately the rest of us are still alive and kicking, but we are all very glad that the term is at an end.

Next as to my own intentions. I go over on Saturday next to Paris to take part in the comparison of the Vienna and Paris standards, and probably also Ramsay's. Meyer and Schweidler, and also probably Soddy and Hahn will be there. Mme. Curie is, I understand, not well enough to take part, but Debierne will be her representative. She was anxious to postpone the meeting, but Meyer felt that it would delay matters very much, and there was some doubt as to how long the delay would be before she could hope to attend. I have not much doubt but that the two standards will be found in very good agreement, but it will be a devil of a mess if they are not. That is one of the reasons why I must be there to act as arbitrator between the two parties. I have developed a balance method of a γ ray comparison,[1] with which I think I can compare two nearly equal standards [to] an accuracy of 1 in 1000. I suppose, however, we shall not worry if the agreement of the two standards is within 1 in 300 or 400. I leave Paris on the following Thursday morning and go to Havre where I am to meet my wife, the chauffeur and the motor, and also Professor Bragg, who is coming with us. We then intend to make a beeline for the South of France, skirt along the Pyrenees and return homewards, a distance in all of 1800 miles in a little over three weeks. I hope the weather will be good and that we shall have plenty of sunshine. I am pretty well tired out and want a good holiday with no cares or worries, although I anticipate plenty of a mechanical kind.

I have been endeavouring to keep my work going with Robinson[2] helping me, and I think we shall get something very interesting out of the distribution of the heating effect of the active deposit. We have also been experimenting on the velocity of groups of rays from radium, for you will see in *Nature* that I have found that there is some apparent connection between the energies of a number of the groups.[3] A very interesting paper will soon appear in the *Phil. Mag.* by Hevesy [4] on the electro-chemistry of the active deposits. He is a very able fellow, and I think his experiments are a notable advance, and put the matter in a very clear light. He has a number of other results to publish, but at present he is away in Graz nursing himself. You know that he suffers a good deal from indigestion troubles, but he hopes to be back again early in the summer. You will have seen that Geiger has got out the two ranges of uranium.[5] Schrader is working on the volatility of the active deposits and is getting very interesting results.[6] He can obtain definite evidence of the formation of oxides, chlorides, and bromides, etc., and generally the subject is clearing up in good style. Russell is tackling the nature of the scattered radiation set up in wood, etc. and under my direction is tackling the origin of actinium. It is probably a forlorn hope, but worth trying. Several other people are investigating the range of recoil atoms, range of α particles from thorium products, and recoil generally. Marsden has been tackling the nature of the anomalous breaking up of thorium C and has obtained a number of interesting results which will soon be published.[7] Miss Leslie is comparing accurately the diffusion constants of the thorium and actinium emanations.[8] She has found, as I long ago anticipated, that the first values I found for the diffusion constants of radium emanation are much nearer right than all the later values. I think she will also find that the diffusion constants of thorium and actinium are not very different. Florance [9] is back and is just starting work, while Bohr,[10] a Dane, has pulled out of Cambridge and turned up here to get some experience in radioactive work. Moseley [11] is working away and has got plenty of ideas. Geiger and I are preparing to count the number of α particles from radium accurately, and re-determine the charge. We are at present making experiments of the best conditions of the ionisation chamber. We have had the string electrometer working in great style and intend to photograph the kicks.[12] If all goes well, we should get the number well within one per cent. You know that Geiger is leaving us at the end of the summer to take up a position in Berlin, so we are anxious to get it through before he leaves. You will see from the above the general activities of the Laboratory, and that we have not stopped work. I should mention, by the way, that we have made comparisons of our standard with Meyer's, and find that his is about 5 per cent *higher* than mine. This is rather unexpected, and shows by the way that your 2000 years is probably too high after all.

You will see that J.J.T. has been given the Order of Merit. We are all very pleased about it, for it is a great feather in his cap considering that other notabilities like Ramsay, Lockyer [13] and Dewar would not have refused it. It looks after all as if merit was occasionally recognised.

By the way, you have been singularly uncommunicative about the radium business. I hope that things have not gone too badly in that direction. I shall be very glad to hear if you have any confidential information to impart.

I hope you are enjoying the reading of the proofs. I have finished writing all but the three last chapters and am sending in a batch of three chapters before I leave. I find it a tremendous business getting it through, and shall sing the Old Hundredth when it is finally off my hands. I think after Geiger and yourself have looked through it not many errors of importance should be overlooked. I, of course, pay the greatest attention to all your corrections, and I think you will find them all in the page proof. I have written now 17 chapters, and I hope the book will not be more than 150 pages longer than the Second Edition. It will be a long time before they get me to tackle another one. I have come to the conclusion that one ought to have a year free to undertake a task of that character. The book is to be published in Germany by the Akademische Verlagsgesellschaft, who have offered very good terms. Marx is to be the translator. I am very much indebted to you for the trouble you have taken over the matter. I suppose I read the things about ten times before they are through, but the author is the worst possible person to correct proofs.

No doubt Mrs. Rutherford will write to you and give you more of the domestic news. I am in reasonably good form, but thoroughly tired of work. Give my kind regards to Bumstead, Wheeler, and any other friends of mine who may be with you. You had better make a point of coming over this year even if you cannot visit your beloved Munich. Yours very sincerely,

E. RUTHERFORD

PS I have just heard from Soddy from whom I gather Ramsay is anxious to get his standard compared. I think we shall do so. It will be amusing for one who has *not* a standard to compare the results.

1. ER and J. Chadwick, "A balance method for comparison of quantities of radium and some of its applications," *Proc. Phys. Soc., 24* (1912), 141–51.

2. Harold R. Robinson began research under Rutherford while still an undergraduate at Manchester. He remained there about a dozen years, becoming assistant director of the physical laboratory after Rutherford departed for Cambridge in 1919. Robinson later held posts at Cambridge, Edinburgh, Cardiff, and finally Queen Mary College, University of London. His many administrative responsibilities included the vice-chancellorship of the University of London.

3. ER, "The origin of the β rays from radio-active substances," *Nature, 88* (29 Feb. 1912), 605.

4. Georg von Hevesy, "The electrochemistry of radioactive bodies," *Phil. Mag., 23* (Apr. 1912), 628–46. Hevesy, recipient of the 1943 Nobel Prize in chemistry for his work in radioactive tracer techniques, was a lecturer at Budapest, then professor at Copenhagen, Freiburg, and Stockholm.

5. Geiger and J. M. Nuttall, "The ranges of the α particles from uranium," *Phil. Mag., 23* (Mar. 1912), 439–45.

6. Hans Schrader, "On the existence of chemical compounds of short-lived radioactive elements," *Phil. Mag., 24* (July 1912), 125–34. Schrader received his Ph.D. degree from the University of Berlin, having worked under Emil Fischer. After a year in Manchester, he returned to Germany and a post at the Technische Hochschule in Berlin-Charlottenburg; after World War I he worked in the Kaiser Wilhelm Institute for Coal Research, Müllheim.

7. Marsden and C. G. Darwin, "The transformations of the active deposit of thorium," *Proc. Roy. Soc., 87A* (26 July 1912), 17–29.

8. May Leslie, "A comparison of the coefficients of diffusion of thorium

and actinium emanations, with a note on their periods of transformation," *Phil. Mag.*, 24 (Oct. 1912), 637–47. Miss Leslie was one of several female workers in Rutherford's laboratory at various times.

9. D. C. H. Florance.

10. Niels Bohr, later professor at the University of Copenhagen and recipient of the 1922 Nobel Prize in physics for his investigations of the structure of atoms and their radiations, spent several months in Manchester in the spring of 1912. He had first been attracted to Cambridge by J. J. Thomson's ideas on the electronic constitution of atoms, and then absorbed Rutherford's enthusiasm for the nuclear atom. He returned to Manchester in the 1914–15 academic year as Schuster Reader in Mathematical Physics, a position Rutherford's predecessor had created to aid the theoretical work of the laboratory. For a complete biography, see Ruth Moore, *Niels Bohr* (New York, Knopf, 1966).

11. H. G. J. Moseley was considered by Rutherford as perhaps his most brilliant student, and his death in Gallipoli during World War I was regarded as a tragic and needless loss to science. Had he lived, his work with X rays showing a characteristic spectrum for each element, which thereby indicated the more profound significance of atomic number over atomic weight in the ordering of the elements, would probably have been rewarded with the Nobel Prize.

12. Rutherford was quick to see the value of new instruments and he early adopted the string galvanometer for photographic recording. This device was perfected by Willem Einthoven as part of his electrocardiogram apparatus.

13. Norman Lockyer, an astrophysicist who first detected lines of the new element helium in the solar spectrum, was professor of astronomy and physics and director of the solar physics observatory, Royal College of Science. He was also widely known as a popularizer of science.

25 MARCH 1912

Sloane Laboratory, Yale University
New Haven, Connecticut

My dear Rutherford,

On page 164 of the paged proof in the table of "Ranges of α-particles, etc." I notice that the range of the α-particle from

Radium A (4.75 cm) is greater than the range of the particle from the Radium Emanation (4.16 cm). I am quite sure that this is an error, for so far as I know the only data on this matter is that in my paper "Radioactivity of Uranium Minerals, Am. Jour. Sci., XXV, 284, 1908," and this indicates that the range of the particle from the Emanation is the greater of the two. Bragg never decided this matter and left it an open question as to which substance the particle came from. In his papers you will find a bracket always used, thus:

Emanation	Range
or	4.23
Radium A	
Radium A	
or	4.83
Emanation	

Is there any other reason for taking them in this order? Yours sincerely,

B. B. BOLTWOOD

22 APRIL 1912

17 Wilmslow Road
Withington, Manchester

My dear Boltwood,

We have just returned from a three weeks' tour through France, thoroughly sunned and in good shape for work. We took Bragg with us and had a thoroughly pleasant time, with three weeks' sunshine marred occasionally by cold wind. We saw a good deal of the Pyrenees and of France generally. I am now feeling in a very fit state to tackle work again and finish my book.

You will have received from Meyer an account of the pro-

ceedings of the Committee in Paris and of the resolutions proposed. I hope that they will meet with your approval; I think
that they will serve their purpose. The agreement between the
Vienna and Curie standard was as close as the measurements
were possible within a limited time, at any rate, to 1 point in
300, and may have been closer. Soddy brought over a small standard of about 3 milligrams, made by Ramsay and Gray.[1] Rough
measurements showed that it was within about 2 per cent of the
others; but we did not have time to measure it with great certainty, and in addition it was much smaller than the other
standard and was not in a very suitable form. The meeting
passed off very pleasantly and without any friction. Debierne
had made excellent arrangements for the apparatus for testing,
and proved himself a very sensible person. We all had lunch
with Mme. Curie and her family. She looks rather feeble and ill,
but no worse than she did at Brussels two years ago. We held a
short meeting in her house and then retired to the Laboratory
to make the final arrangements, with which she was quite satisfied. I think we perhaps got through matters very much quicker
without Mme. Curie, for you know that she is inclined to raise
difficulties. I raised the question in the Committee about paying
for the standard, and we all thought it very desirable that the
money should be raised in some way by the Committee, and we
pledged ourselves individually to raise the money required.
Very fortunately, however, Soddy spoke to his father-in-law, Dr.
Beilby F.R.S.,[2] and he and Mrs. Beilby agreed to finance the
matter. I am very glad that the donation has come from the English section and not from France, as in the latter case there
would have been a tendency to consider the standard as belong-
ing too much to their country. The gift will remove many difficulties, for if the governments had been asked to pay a fraction
of the cost they would undoubtedly have wanted to be represented by some Government official on the Committee, and that
would have been impossible. As it is the standard will remain in
the possession of the Committee, and we are an independent
body to suggest what we think fit.

Hahn was in very good form, and Soddy made himself useful. You will see that we bridged over the difficulty between the Vienna and Paris group by arranging that the Meyer standard is to be a subsidiary standard and to be preserved by the Vienna Academy. This will please the Vienna people and will strengthen Meyer's hands in dealing with them. I am very glad that the whole matter is now definitely arranged, for it would have been a very difficult matter if the standard had proved to be in serious disagreement. We shall soon proceed to circularise the governments about obtaining duplicate standards.

I have no doubt that Mrs. Rutherford will write to you in more detail about our journey.

I have found some proofs of my book from you awaiting me, and shall push on with the book as rapidly as possible. I find it a nuisance that new papers are continually appearing to which reference ought to be made. I wish people would stop work for three months to relieve me of this trouble.

I have very little scientific news of interest to detail to you. You may have seen that Ramsay went down to Bath and gave a lecture on the Bath waters. This was a great advertisement for the Bath people and I wonder how much Ramsay got out of it. It appears to me that it is not quite playing the game for a President of the British Association to go in for that sort of thing, for of course the Bath people recognise that it is the best puff they have had for generations, although, of course, he did not make any definite statement about the curative properties of his niton; but that went by inference. You will have seen that Ramsay has retired and Donnan [3] has been appointed in his place. He is, I think, a fairly good man but in rather orthodox physical chemistry. It seems to me that we are rather hard up for a good chemist in this country, and I have been rather surprised at several recent appointments.

I have forgotten to remark on your letter about the ranges of radium A and the emanation. I have no doubt that radium A has a longer range, and I was under the impression that H. W. Schmidt had settled the matter. However I shall look into the matter to see what the evidence amounts to. Geiger's rule would be rather upset if your view were correct.

The Elliot Smiths have just returned from a holiday and are in good form. The Government have given Manchester an extra £5000 a year, so we shall not be worried financially for a year or two.

We are all well and flourishing and spring is now well with us and also sunshine. Yours very sincerely,

E. RUTHERFORD

1. Robert Whytlaw Gray received his Ph.D. degree in 1907 from the University of Bonn, worked with Ramsay for several years, and later became professor of chemistry at Leeds.

2. Sir George Beilby was an industrial chemist who served as managing director of the Cassel Cyanide Company plant in Glasgow. A man of wide-ranging abilities and interests, he devised a successful retort for shale oil distillation, was an early advocate of the microscopic study of metals, and strongly supported the departments of science in the several Glasgow educational institutions.

3. F. G. Donnan, a former member of Ramsay's staff, was appointed to succeed Ramsay at University College, London, but delayed his departure from the University of Liverpool for a year until his own successor there could be selected.

3 JUNE 1912

17 Wilmslow Road
Withington, Manchester

My dear Boltwood,

I have not heard from you for an age with the exception that the steady return of the proof with corrections shows that you are still alive and kicking. I am just trying to finish the last three chapters in the book, on Helium and Heating Effect, General Discussion, and Radioactivity of the Earth and Atmosphere, and find it very hard work; but I hope to push it through within the next month. If you can manage to overcome your objection to writing, I want your opinion on the following question.

The University Press is anxious for fairly obvious reasons that I should give a new title to the present volume. The changes are so considerable that it practically constitutes a new volume, and they would like to have a new title to start fresh with. The only title that I can think of is "Radioactive substances and their radiations." This included the subject matter of the book pretty well, and Geiger thinks it has a good Germanic roll about it. What is your opinion on the matter? Do you think it desirable to retain the old title or to make a change? Let me hear your views on the question.

I also want to ask you whether you think it is desirable to more or less repeat your Appendix on Radioactive Minerals? If it is to go in it must go in the Appendix.

We are all very well and in good form. Recently I had my sister and her husband and three children from New Zealand staying with us. It made quite a houseful. I have recently seen Webster [1] and Millikan,[2] who have come over for the summer. Barnes had also been here and is making quite a stir over his micro-thermometer for iceberg detection. The new rooms in our Laboratory are proving very serviceable as they have a low natural leak.

Let me hear from you as soon as you can. Yours very sincerely,

E. RUTHERFORD

P.S. I hope you are coming over this summer if only for a short time.

1. Arthur G. Webster, professor of physics at Clark University, Worcester, Massachusetts.

2. Robert A. Millikan, professor of physics at the University of Chicago, was then on a six months' European work-holiday. The major purpose of this trip was to find the free time to work up all his data on the famous oil

drop experiment, from which he derived the charge on the electron. This research brought him the Nobel Prize in physics in 1923.

19 JUNE 1912

Sloane Laboratory, Yale University
New Haven, Connecticut

My dear Rutherford,

I enclose the last of the proof that I have received up to date, and I hope you will forgive me for not having attended to it more promptly. These have been strenuous times; we have been engaged in moving into the new laboratory for the last three weeks and began the packing nearly five weeks ago. We are all tired out, every thing is topsey-turvey, and to add to the complications I have had to participate in a reunion (the 20th) of my class, which was almost the last straw.

The greater part of the work of getting up there has now been accomplished, but there is still a good deal to be done including the moving of the storage battery, which unfortunately falls to my lot. The new building is as yet incomplete in many of its minor details, so that it is going to be some time before it is decently settled. Bumstead leaves today for a two week's outing and I shall have to stay on the job as long as I can stand it. Fortunately we are having very fine, cool weather, a much appreciated blessing.

I can well appreciate what a hard task you find it to complete your book for it all means an awful amount of work. However, you can comfort yourself with the thought that you are certainly putting it through in fine shape. I do not like the idea of a change in title. I am afraid I am too conservative for these times, for I like to see a few good things remain as they are. "Radioactivity" seems to me to be the only proper name; I might be willing to accept "A Text Book of Radioactivity," which would perhaps imply its broadened scope. But honestly I do not like the title you mention—"Radioactive substances and their radiations." It is altogether too much of a change.

I am very much afraid I shall not be able to get over to Europe this summer however much I should like to do so. I do hope to be able to get time to write you before long and really give you some news and information.

With best regards and kindest wishes to you all. Yours very sincerely,

BERTRAM B. BOLTWOOD

15 AUGUST 1912

17 Wilmslow Road
Withington, Manchester

My dear Boltwood,

Just a line to inform you that I have got the MSS. of the book finished and the proofs corrected up to about page 500. I have asked the Press to forward you direct the proofs of the last two chapters with the accompanying Appendices and Tables. I shall be glad if you can find time to correct them and send them back promptly, as I hope to send the corrected proof to the Press as early as possible in September so that the book may come out in October. I have fully decided to call the book "Radioactivity" and to leave out "Third Edition." I think after all it will not make much difference.

Geiger and I have been very hard at work counting the α particles and recoil atoms, but are unable to finish before he leaves for Berlin. We are presenting him to-day with a gold watch as a testimony of our good will. I shall miss him a great deal, but I hope he will soon get a good University place. You know that Taylor [1] is coming over to me next year. He will probably be here in the first week of September.

You will be interested to hear that Russell and Rossi [2] have determined the spectrum of your ionium preparation with the large Rowland grating, but did not observe a single line that could not be attributed to thorium. If ionium had a period of 100,000 years the thorium should contain 16 per cent ionium, while experiment showed that at least one per cent of another substance should have been detectable by its spectrum. The most plausible conclusion is that ionium has a much shorter life than is supposed, and that probably another substance intervenes between uranium X and ionium. This by the way is quite private, as the paper will not be published for some time.

My wife and Eileen have been for a fortnight's holiday at Robin Hood's Bay on the Yorkshire coast. I went down by motor last Sunday and brought them back on Tuesday. We are hoping to leave on Saturday by motor for a fortnight in the South of England. The weather in England this summer has been atrocious; the temperature of the Arctic circle accompanied by tropical rain. I trust that our meteorological instability will be transferred either to your part of the world or to the southern hemisphere.

I am feeling in very good form considering that this is the end of a very heavy year. I hope to be at the British Association in Dundee for a few days, and then homeward bound to correct final proofs.

I may mention that you seem to have lost your powers of writing letters this year, but I trust that you will some time let me know how your various interests are progressing. I gathered from your last letter that the transference of your high potential battery weighed heavily on your mind. I can imagine your carrying the cells to the new quarters one in each hand like pots of home made jam. I trust that your system has recovered its normal tone after this exciting experience.

By the way, you will be interested to know that the Vienna people have given me another radium lease for two years, so I am again in an equable frame of mind. I have little news to record as most of my friends are holiday making, but we are all well and flourishing. Elliot Smith and his family are growing apace, and he is now much worried over educational problems. He looks very fat and rosy notwithstanding his troubles. Yours ever,

E. RUTHERFORD

1. Thomas S. Taylor received his Ph.D. degree in physics from Yale in 1909, taught at the University of Illinois, and then spent the 1912–13 academic year in Rutherford's laboratory. Upon his return to the United States Taylor joined the Yale faculty, but in 1917 became a research physicist at the Westinghouse Electric and Manufacturing Company.
2. A. S. Russell and R. Rossi, "An investigation of the spectrum of ionium," *Proc. Roy. Soc., 87A* (13 Dec. 1912), 478–84. Russell was the chemist in this investigation, while Rossi, an Englishman, was the spectroscopist.

23 SEPTEMBER 1912

17 Wilmslow Road
Withington, Manchester

My dear Boltwood,

I was waiting to get an address from you and finally I wrote to Brown and Shipley to ask whether they were forwarding letters. They replied that they were at intervals. However, I got your post card this morning and am glad that you are still in the land of the living.

I have not bothered to forward you the last proofs as I do not want to work you too hard during the vacation. Everything in the main part of the book is now in print, and I am correcting the last proofs. I am busy preparing the Index, which is rather a long business.

We have fortunately had very good weather for the last fortnight, sunny and not too cool. I have had a rotten cold, which I have not yet got rid of, and a stiff knee, and so have felt an object of pity for the past fortnight. We went for a week end on Saturday to Grindelford, a beautiful valley near Sheffield, and arrived back yesterday. Most of the research men are back in the Laboratory, and the Taylors have arrived. They are staying for the first week in your old quarters, and have got rooms to suit them near by. They seem an interesting couple, and I hope they will have a pleasant time here. Perkins called to see me on his way over to America. I saw Webster, Millikan, and McLennan in Dundee, where I had a good time.

We are, of course, expecting you to stay with us before you go back. You must make a point of coming to see us before you leave in any case. I shall consider it an unforgiveable discourtesy if you do not. In any case you must be pretty sick of Germany by this time. Let us know if you can when you expect to arrive. I am going over to Brussels on September 30th, and stay there two or three days in order to settle up the conditions of a new foundation, the Solvay International Physical Institute. I will tell you all about it when I see you. I have got many things I want to talk over with you, especially in connection with standards, radium, etc.

By the way, my lease of the radium has been extended another two years, so I am free from worries on that score. Our mutual friend Ramsay has kept pretty quiet recently with the exception that he has a finger in every doubtful commercial speculation going. He has retired from his Professorship as you know, and they have not filled his place yet.[1]

We are all well and reasonably contented. Yours ever,

E. RUTHERFORD

1. See note 3 to Rutherford's letter of 22 April 1912.

6 OCTOBER [1912]

Prinzregentenstr 18/0
München

My dear Rutherford,

Your letter of Sept. 23rd, forwarded by Brown, Shipley & Co., reached me last Wednesday in Dresden. I could not answer it any sooner because I was not quite sure that I should be able to get over to Manchester, but particularly as I did not know just *when* I would get there.

It should be needless for me to say how much I want to see you all. My present plan is to leave here on Friday morning (the 11th) and cross via Hook of Holland that night. I shall want to stop for a couple of hours in London but should reach Manchester on Saturday afternoon. I will telegraph you from London as to just when I shall reach Manchester and of course inform you if for any reason I am unable to get through. I shall probably go up on the Midland.

Although the Holland Am. Steamers touch at Plymouth on the eastern passage, they do not call at any English port in going west. I'll therefore have to come back to Rotterdam again to get the boat which sails on the 19th at 7.30, o'clock. This will mean leaving Manchester on the 17th at the latest.

I have been having a very pleasant and restful vacation notwithstanding the "somewhat inclement" weather. Best regards.
Yours sincerely,

B. B. BOLTWOOD

20 NOVEMBER 1912

Sloane Laboratory, Yale University
New Haven, Connecticut

My dear Rutherford,

I got back here safely on October 29th after a comfortable, interesting but not very eventful trip after leaving Manchester. While I was in London on my way over to Rotterdam I got a letter from Bumstead telling me of the discovery of the body of my Japanese servant in my house, the poor fellow having apparently died some days before as a result of a hemorrhage from the lungs. So when I arrived here I stopped for about 10 days with the Bumsteads and have since been at the Club, as I have been too much occupied with other matters to be able to bother about getting the house in running order again. As it is now I think I shall wait until after the Christmas vacation before I attempt to start housekeeping again.

I have been unpacking my laboratory equipment and getting my quarters in shape at the new building. I found a good many things had been done while I was out of the way, for which I am duly thankful. The two months vacation did me a lot of good and I have come back in a much more comfortable frame of mind than I was in when I left. Bumstead is in better shape this fall than he has been in for years, and altogether things seem much brighter than they did a year ago.

One of the first things I intend to tackle is the separation of the actinium from some pitchblende from Colorado that I began work on last winter. I want to separate the ionium as well as the actinium and have a plan for getting a line on the genetic relations by a new method, if it will only work!

I hope that the Taylors are getting along more comfortably in the matter of lodgings. Please remember me to them and to the men in the laboratory. With best regards to Mrs. Rutherford, love to Eileen and best wishes to all, Yours sincerely,

B. B. BOLTWOOD

23 NOVEMBER 1912

17 Wilmslow Road
Withington, Manchester

My dear Boltwood,

I have not heard of you since you left these shores, but I presume you turned up on the other side in your usual good health.

I am enclosing herewith a copy of my book, which is just appearing. I need hardly say how much I appreciated your help in getting the book ready. I think it looks very well, but I do not know whether you will like the title. I arranged to call it "Radioactivity, Third Edition," but at the last moment it was found advisable to change, since the German publishers were very much afraid that they would have trouble in consequence with the German translators of my Second Edition. To overcome this difficulty, it was necessary to give it a new title, and I think the present one will do well enough.

Work is going on in good shape in the Laboratory, and I think we shall manage to get some interesting work done this year. I find I have now much more time for research, and am laying into work pretty hard.

Let me hear from you when the spirit moves you. I have no great objection whether it is of the beer or cocktail variety.

Give my kind regards to Bumstead and Dana. Yours very sincerely,

E. RUTHERFORD

5 MARCH 1913

17 Wilmslow Road
Withington, Manchester

My dear Boltwood,

I hope you are still alive and kicking, but it seems a long time since I heard from you.

I have received notice that the International Radium Standard has been deposited in the Bureau International des Poids et Mesures at Sevres. The Director asks me to collect the signatures of the International Committee to inscribe in the record. Please send me your signature on a slip of paper as soon as you can.

Arrangements are now well in hand for the English standard and we hope to have the matter through in a few weeks.

You will have seen of the new outburst of Ramsay,[1] and the papers of Collie and Patterson.[2] Also J.J.'s letter in *Nature* in answer.[3] Collie is a careful worker and I have no doubt many of his observations are correct, but J.J.'s explanation rather knocks the wind out of his sails. You will have seen that Ramsay took the opportunity of resurrecting all his old experiments, which I regarded as long since dead.[4]

Work is going on very steadily in the Laboratory, and we have a lot of interesting things on hand. Taylor works steadily and I think enjoys his life here. He is conscientious but by no means brilliant.

Give my kind regards to Bumstead and Co. Yours very sincerely,

E. RUTHERFORD [5]

P.S. I have heard today that Ramsay's outburst in the Daily Mail, where he took all the credit that was [due] in Collie's experiments, has resulted in the disillusionment of Collie who has stuck to him through all his vagaries. Ramsay must have advertisement even at the expense of his best friends.

1. Ramsay, "The presence of helium in the gas from the interior of an x-ray bulb," *J. Chem. Soc.*, *103* (1913), 264–66. Ramsay read this paper to the Chemical Society on 6 February 1913, and a report on it appeared in *Nature*, *90* (13 February 1913), 653–54. The work attracted attention for it seemed that transmutation had been effected by the use of cathode rays. Ramsay had found helium and neon in the glass of some X ray tubes that had been deeply colored by long use, and concluded that "its source is, of course, a matter for conjecture; it may be that under the influence of the cathode discharge helium and neon are able to penetrate the walls of the bulb, which exclude oxygen and nitrogen. Or it is possible to imagine another explanation less likely to be received without challenge: that these gases are in some way the product of the cathode rays."

2. John Norman Collie and Hubert Sutton Patterson, "The presence of neon in hydrogen after the passage of the electric discharge through the latter at low pressures," *J. Chem. Soc.*, *103* (1913), 419–26. This paper, presented at the same meeting as Ramsay's, above, also was summarized in *Nature, 90* (13 February 1913), 653–54. The authors reported finding neon, and at times helium, in hydrogen, although these gases were rigorously excluded from their apparatus. Again, it seemed to them that the most logical explanation was that a transformation had occurred. Collie, who many years earlier had been Ramsay's assistant for a decade, and then was professor of chemistry at the Pharmaceutical Society College, London, was at this time professor of organic chemistry at the University of London. His colleague, Patterson, received his B.Sc. degree from the University of London, and later was at Leeds.

3. J. J. Thomson, "The appearance of helium and neon in vacuum tubes," *Nature, 90* (13 February 1913), 645–47. Thomson argued that the gases are present in the metal electrodes of the tubes and are merely liberated by the cathode ray bombardment. Simple heating of the apparatus will not expel all the gases. In his own work on positive rays, he had frequently experienced the appearance of helium and neon and had traced their origin to the metallic parts of the tubes.

4. In his paper Ramsay recalled his earlier, skeptically received experiments on the emanation-induced production of argon from copper, and declared himself pleased that these new transmutational experiments did not require rare radium, but could be repeated by anyone with cathode ray tubes and chemical facilities.

5. It is curious that neither Boltwood nor Rutherford exchanged comments on the group displacement laws and concept of isotopy early in 1913. These discoveries, in which the decay series were explained and the radioelements placed in proper sequence and proper boxes in the periodic table, were of profound interest to both. Yet, Boltwood's research career effectively had ended and his letters after 1910 contain little scientific detail, while Rutherford's remarks about work done outside his own laboratory were largely restricted to critical comments that would amuse Boltwood.

2 APRIL [1913]

Dear Dr. Boltwood,

What a dreadful procrastinator you are! That photo needless to say did *not* come with or after your letter which I got a week ago. We are delighted to hear you are coming over & want you to promise to come to us first, as soon as you arrive in June, as we may not be here early in September. I am trying to work Ern up to motor in Tyrol in August. If I succeed we may meet you in Munich! I may tell you that Mrs. [illegible] thinks you treated her very badly over the call you didnt make—your excuse was too thin I fancy. She thought you might have telephoned to say you weren't coming.

You seem to have been doing a two men's job this winter. I forget if you have heard we went to the Riviera & had a good time at Xmas. We are going for a week to Lake Thirlmere, next Wed. & hope to get some good motoring. Mr Schuster & Margaret sail today I think for America—some celebration at Washington. They will only be 10 days on shore. I shall have to order Eileen's photo for you so will wait till you come & can choose which position you like best. She is very well. We have given her a parrot for her 12th birthday just past, & we are all greatly interested in it. So far he doesn't talk, but tries to, & is very friendly & amiable. We all feel quite fit, not at all a bad winter. A break in the middle is quite a success I think. By way

of dissipation I have taken up skating (ice) with Mrs Nugent, &
like it immensely. It has not been an exciting winter socially,
we have gone out very little. The Samsons are very jolly. She
was in today, & has booked us for one evening when you are
staying with us in June, so you see it is all settled.

Eileen sends her love, & with kind regards from Ern & myself
I am Your sincere friend,

MARY   RUTHERFORD

12 SEPTEMBER [1913]

The Hague

My dear Rutherford,

I arrived here on Wednesday, coming through from Munich
as far as Nijmegen the day before. I leave here for Rotterdam
this afternoon, go aboard the steamer this evening and should
sail shortly after midnight.

I had a very interesting and pleasant visit to Vienna last
week. I went down there from Munich on Thursday, spent Friday there and came back on Saturday. I had the good fortune to
find Meyer in town, he had come up from Ischl for a few days to
get Fijans [1] started. I also saw Fräulein Meyer and of course
Honigschmidt.[2] They all treated me very well and I was very
glad I went down there. The Radium Institute is a very fine
place indeed, most attractive and admirably suited for the purpose for which it is intended. Fijans and all the others wished
to be remembered to you.

I have a piece of news that will interest you. Mlle. Gleditsch [3]
has written that she has a fellowship of the American Scandinavian Foundation (I never heard of it before!) and wishes to
come and work with me in New Haven!! What do you think of
that? I have written to her and tried to ward her off, but as the
letter was necessarily delayed in forwarding to me, I am afraid

she will be in New York before I get there. Tell Mrs. Rutherford that a silver fruit dish will make a very nice wedding present!!!

I hope that everything went well during the end of your motor trip and that you got back fine and fit to Manchester.

With very best wishes to all. Yours sincerely,

BERTRAM B. BOLTWOOD

1. Kasimir Fajans, born in Warsaw and educated at Leipzig and Heidelberg, spent the 1910–11 year in Rutherford's laboratory. After returning to Germany, he held several positions at Karlsruhe and Munich before becoming professor and director of the institute for physical chemistry at Munich. In 1936, as a result of the policies of the Hitler government, he accepted a professorship of chemistry at the University of Michigan. Fajans' best known contribution to radioactivity was the discovery in 1913, independently and slightly earlier than Soddy, of the group displacement laws and the concept of isotopy.

2. Otto Hönigschmid had studied under Theodore W. Richards and was himself one of the world's outstanding atomic weight experts. This talent was brought to bear upon the different isotopes of lead shortly before World War I. At this time Hönigschmid was at the German University in Prague; later he was professor of chemistry at Munich.

3. Ellen Gleditsch, who earlier had worked for several years in Madame Curie's laboratory, returned to Norway after her year in America and eventually became professor of chemistry at the University of Oslo.

6 OCTOBER [1913]

Dear Dr. Boltwood,

The photographer has kept me waiting for ages but I have now posted Eileen's photograph to you. We were so glad to hear of the pleasant time you had after you left us. Did you hear anything more of your friend Mr Henderson? Are you engaged to the charmer yet, I forget who she was—in your last letter which I unfortunately destroyed in mistake for an earlier one. Wasn't she going to work with you? I am getting *some* decent photos, but a good many not much good, which of course I should never have taken. Do you remember my lens being loose? That affected several. My Dolomites are pretty good. I'll send you some to see later & you might do likewise if you will. I should not want to keep them, one's own bad ones endear themselves after you have laboured over them. Eileen is awfully well, she gained ¾ inch in height in 8 weeks & 3 lbs in weight. Miss Martin got a post on the boat going over & stayed a month at it when the people announced they could not afford any more help! However it was just as well, for Maurice got another bad fit of depression & went off to Vancouver (70 miles) where she followed him & was just in time to prevent another disaster. A Dr. told her that she must get work near him, & if there was anymore must take him to N.Z. at once. She had a very nice post in a Women's Hostel when she wrote & the Committee were interesting themselves to get the two work together. I haven't heard for a month, but hope to hear they are going back to N.Z. We went over to the Braggs on Sat for a night. Their sons are such delightful boys, I had never seen them before. Mrs Bragg does paralyse one with the loud & voluminous gush she indulges in. Ern sends his kind regards & Eileen her love. Yours very sincerely,

MARY RUTHERFORD

7 NOVEMBER 1913

17 Wilmslow Road
Withington, Manchester

Dear Sir,

You will remember that, at the last Radiology Congress at Brussels in 1910, you were elected a member of an International Committee to make arrangements for the next Congress. In the normal course of events this Congress will be held once in five years, and the next Congress is consequently due in 1915.

It has been suggested to me that the next Radiology Congress should be held *in Vienna towards the end of June 1915*. I know that the authorities in Vienna interested in that subject would be prepared to extend a cordial invitation to the Congress for that date. During the past year I have had an opportunity of speaking personally with a number of members of the Committee, and find that they are agreeable to this proposal. I personally am strongly in favour of it.

As Chairman of the International Committee, it is my duty to lay this proposal before you, and obtain your opinion upon it. I shall be glad of an early reply, as it is important that the arrangements for the next Congress should be begun as soon as possible. If the majority of the Committee are in favour of the proposal to hold the meeting in Vienna, it will be the duty of the Committee to make the necessary arrangements for organisation of the Congress as promptly as possible. Believe me, Yours very sincerely,

E. RUTHERFORD

This is a formal letter. I hope to write you personally a little later about our doings at the Solvay Conference in Brussels.

ER

28 NOVEMBER 1913

Sloane Laboratory, Yale University
New Haven, Connecticut

Dear Sir: [1]

Your letter of November 7th in regard to the next Congress of Radiology to be held in 1915 has been received. I note the suggestion that the next Congress be held in Vienna towards the end of June, 1915 and, as a member of the International Committee on Arrangements for the next Congress, I desire to state that I heartily approve of holding the Congress at the suggested time and place. I should be glad to hear further from you in regard to the arrangements to be undertaken in connection with the organization of the Congress. Yours very sincerely,

BERTRAM B. BOLTWOOD

N.B. This is a formal letter in reply to your own. I hope to get the other letter promised from you before very long and to hear how things are going in Manchester. I hope Mrs. Rutherford got the photograph and that every thing is going well with you and your family. With kindest regards and best wishes.

1. This letter exists only in the carbon copy preserved at Yale.

11 JANUARY 1914

New Haven, Connecticut

My dear Sir Ernest and Lady Rutherford,

(Phew! Doesn't that look magnificent?) I have just been shown a note in the "Literary Gossip" column of the Athenaeum and I can not possibly express my delight at the well-deserved honour (notice the *u*) which has been bestowed upon you by his Royal Highness, our noble King and Protector— Long may he reign—God bless him! The list of New Year's honours as published in the hopelessly incompetent newspapers of this country, did not include your name, although they gave an impression of completeness, and so the information that you had been elevated to this *exhalted* rank came all the more as a surprise to me. No more, My dear Sir Ernest, can our old friends Sir William, Sir James and Sir Joseph put it over you as not being one of the fold, no more can they push you away from the manger or boo at you for trying to share their victuals. Thank Heaven! That's all over now.

Please thank Lady Rutherford for her kind letter and for the photographs which were very fine indeed and many of them much better than the ones I took of the same subjects. Some time in the near future I hope to settle down and write you a longer letter, but just now my chief desire is to tell you how delighted I am at this splendid piece of news that has just reached me.

With kindest regards and heartiest congratulations. Sincerely yours,

BERTRAM B. BOLTWOOD

27 JANUARY 1914

17 Wilmslow Road
Withington, Manchester

My dear Boltwood,

Many thanks for your very kind congratulations which were much appreciated by both of us & also Eileen, who read the letter several times & concluded it was the right sort of letter to write to her distinguished daddy. Such a form of recognition is rather ridiculous is'nt it? But I hope you will sympathise with me as a martyr in the cause of science. I have of course received shoals of letters & telegrams from England, America & Australasia. I have no sooner got the English letters in hand, than the Canadian ones descend upon me & I am soon expecting the New Zealand ones. Eileen is of opinion that her parents have not that natural "swank" to carry off such a decoration with dignity but I am afraid such distinctions make little difference to yours truly, for I have enough democratic tendencies to see the humorous side of this business. I shall have to go to a Levie before long to be properly knighted—velvet breeches & coat, cocked hat—a sword & buckles in galore! I am now in the hands of the tailor to fix me up—dam'd expensive but highly humorous.

Next in regards to items of more interest. I am visiting the "Land of the Free" early in April to deliver a couple of "pop" lectures before your National Academy of Sciences on April 23–25 in Washington—subject "evolution & structure of atoms"—the first of the "Hale" Lectures. I am looking forward with much pleasure to seeing you & a good many of my American friends. It will be a hurried visit but I hope to spend a fortnight in "Gods own Country" to acquire the proper religious flavour. This is a very illeligble [sic] & hurried note but give me all the advice you can how to enter & leave with safety your highly protected land.

With best wishes from us both. Yours ever,

E. RUTHERFORD

17 MARCH 1914

17 Wilmslow Road
Withington, Manchester

Dear Boltwood,

I told you some time ago that I was expecting to visit you some time about the middle of April, but have not heard a word from you. I trust you are not in the middle of preparations for matrimony, for if that is the case, I shall make a point of descending upon you to investigate your condition.

My plans now are pretty well fixed. I travel over to Halifax by the Tunisian leaving Liverpool on March 28th and go straight to McGill. I will there spend three or four days with Eve and will then start South visiting Boston for possibly a couple of days, and then going on to New Haven, if you are prepared to put up with me for a few days. I shall then go on to

New York, where I have more or less promised to give a lecture of some kind, and probably leave for Washington about the 19th, to make arrangments for my lectures before the National Academy. If you are not too busy, I expect you had better come down and look after me. I shall not have an umbrella with me but there will always be an overcoat and a handbag or two to keep watch on. I have to get back to Manchester as early as I can after the lectures, as the term is in full progress; but there have been so many changes in the sailings from New York that I am not quite sure what day I will leave. You know that we are all leaving for Australasia on July 1st, so I expect to have a pretty rushed time.

You will be interested to hear that we have Bragg over on Wednesday to lecture before the Lit. and Phil. Soc. on X ray spectra and crystals, and we give him a dinner in the evening. I then go down to London on Thursday to introduce a discussion on the structure of the atom. I am speculating whether J.J.T. will turn up, because he knows that I think his atom is only fitted for a museum of scientific curiosities. The ideas of a nucleus atom are really working out exceedingly well. You will have seen the work of Bohr and Moseley. The latter has still further results, and as far as they go, it looks to me that the X ray spectra of the atoms will tell us definitely how many possible atoms there are, and whether the industry of the chemist has missed any.

We are all in very good form, and work makes good progress. I saw a good deal of your friend, Dr. Kelly,[1] when he came to Manchester, and I understand he is arranging with you for a great blow out at Baltimore in connection with my visit to Washington. He is an enthusiastic chap and I was much pleased with him.

By the way, my wife told me to inform you that your photographs had not yet arrived for comparison with her own.

In case you want to communicate with me, my address in Montreal will be c/o Professor A. S. Eve, Physics Building, Mc-

Gill University, Montreal. I shall probably stay there till the 9th or 10th. Yours very sincerely,

E. RUTHERFORD

1. Howard A. Kelly, professor of gynecology at the Johns Hopkins University Medical School, and with Welch, Halsted, and Osler a member of the famous group of four doctors there, pioneered in the therapeutic application of radium to malignancies. This interest in radioactivity brought him into contact with Boltwood, who tested some of the active sources bought by Kelly, and through Boltwood, Kelly called on Rutherford when he visited Manchester.

20 JUNE 1914

17 Wilmslow Road
Withington, Manchester

My dear Boltwood,

I was very remiss not writing to you soon after my arrival. As a matter of fact I thought I had done so, but I had so much correspondence to attend to that I must have forgotten.

In the first place, we no sooner got out of the harbour than a dense fog descended, so that we had to anchor for fourteen hours in Ambrose Channel, so that I did not arrive till Tuesday morning. The trip, however, was quite a pleasant one, and I found several agreeable people on board. My wife and Eileen were down to meet me, and we arrived home in time for lunch. Since my arrival, I have been exceedingly occupied trying to get things ready for my departure, which takes place in about ten days' time.[1] I have a great deal of writing to do and many arrangements to make. The weather, fortunately, is very fine, and we are all feeling very fit.

With Andrade [2] I have just completed the examination of the γ ray spectrum of Radium B and Radium C, and devised a new transmission method for determining the wave length,

293

which shows some very pretty photographic effects.[3] We have also got a number of experiments going on X rays, which I hope will turn out all right.

I should mention that I think I got a mild attack of lumbago on my arrival on the ship, and felt pretty stiff for several days. I think it was just time that I had a rest after the busy time that I had had in America, but I felt very fit on my arrival in England.

There is very little news of interest to record. Professor Elliot Smith and his family left about a month ago for Australia via Suez, and should now be nearly in Sydney. Dixon,[4] Holland,[5] and Petavel are going on our boat, the Euripides, which is a new one of 15,000 tons, and I understand is really splendidly fitted up both as regards the safety and comfort of the passengers. Eileen is highly excited over her trip, and will probably have a great time.

I would like to take this opportunity of thanking you again for the way you looked after me in America. It was very good of you to come and see me off. I got a letter recently from Hale of a highly laudatory character over my lectures, which I hope were generally appreciated. I have not yet had time to write them up properly, as I want to do them well.

I am glad that you are getting Fleck [6] to work with you. I gather that he is a keen young fellow who has worked himself up from a subsidiary position. I understand from Miss Schmidt [7] that Miss Gleditsch is coming to stay with her some time next week.[8]

By the way, unless there is a consistent error in the same direction in the determinations, like the production of helium, heating effect, volume of the emanation and charge carried by the α particle, the life of radium must be very nearly 1700 years. I shall be much interested to know the value you get, but I am confident that 2000 is much too large. I am sending a paper to the *Phil. Mag.* correcting my data in terms of the International standard and am briefly discussing this question.[9]

You mentioned that you had got your uranium ore and were

working with it. I hope you will reserve a little for me. If so, I would like you to send it over some time after next January.

As you know I had a visit from Bumstead, and found him looking very fit and quite himself again. I think he is taking life quite easily at Cambridge and hopes to be able to settle down to hard work on his return.

By the way, your last letter was of a very melancholy character. You must buck up and not let your indigestion or the weather disturb your natural optimism. Yours very sincerely,

E. RUTHERFORD

I had a visit from R. W. Boyle the other day. He was looking fit.

1. Rutherford and his family spent the summer months visiting family and friends in New Zealand, and Rutherford also attended the British Association meetings, held that year in the Australian cities of Adelaide, Sydney, Melbourne, and Brisbane.

2. Edward Neville da Costa Andrade received his Ph.D. degree from Heidelberg and was at this time John Harling Fellow at Manchester. He later became professor of physics at Imperial College, University of London.

3. ER and Andrade, "The spectrum of the penetrating γ rays from radium B and radium C," *Phil. Mag.*, 28 (August 1914), 263–73.

4. Harold Baily Dixon, professor of chemistry at Manchester since 1886.

5. Thomas Henry Holland, professor of geology at Manchester and later rector of the Imperial College of Science and Technology, London, and then principal and vice-chancellor of Edinburgh University.

6. Alexander Fleck worked as a laboratory boy in both physics and chemistry departments of the University of Glasgow before taking a degree. He was encouraged in his education by Soddy, for whom he was assistant and demonstrator. Fleck became highly skilled in working out the chemistry of the short-lived beta emitters and this was the basis for Soddy's displacement laws early in 1913. Fleck arranged with Boltwood to continue his radioactivity investigations at Yale, but then decided instead to take a job in industry. Here he was outstandingly successful, rising to the chairmanship of Britain's largest corporation, Imperial Chemical Industries. For his contributions to science and to industrial chemistry, he was raised to the peerage as Baron Fleck and was elected vice-president of the Royal

Society, president of the Royal Institution, and president of the British Association.

7. Jadwiga Szmidt.
8. See note 3 to Boltwood's letter of 12 September 1913.
9. ER, "Radium constants on the International Standard," *Phil. Mag.,* *28* (Sept. 1914), 320–27.

28 October 1914

15 Bealey Avenue
Christchurch, New Zealand

Dear Boltwood,

As my estimable secretary is still in Manchester, you will have to decipher my writing which in my opinion has much improved by disuse. I am wondering whether you were in Germany at the declaration of war & how you got out and whether you still are a fervent admirer of German methods. They have certainly put up a good fight but I don't see how they have a ghost of a chance to succeed ultimately. N.Z. has sent off her 8000 men. They join with the Australians and are now on the high seas. Dr. Newton volunteered as medical officer & is now a Major. I saw him in Wellington in full kit & saw his quarters on the Troopship. There will be more than 40 Transports in all convoyed for part of the way by English & Japanese cruisers.

We have had a very pleasant holiday in N.Z. & found all our people well. The weather has been good & apart from the worry of occasional lectures have had a jolly time without worrying about science overmuch.

You will be interested to hear that we have decided to return via Vancouver—Montreal—New York leaving Auckland by the "Niagara" Dec 1st & should arrive in Vancouver about Dec 17 or 18 if all goes well. She is the fastest liner in the Pacific & should escape the Scharnhorst if she gets on our trail as the latter's bottom must be very foul by this time. We hope to be able to spend a day or two in New York about New Year before sailing & in that case hope you will be able to run down to see us. I expect the coasts of England will be pretty lively about the end of the year as no doubt the fogs will allow more German armed merchantmen & cruisers to make the blockade.

N.Z. & Australia have not been worried so far as the "Australia"—battle cruiser—is far too powerful & fast for the German cruisers in these seas. No boat has been captured within a radius of thousands of miles of Australia so far, so all the boats run as usual. The Emden & the Karlsruhe appear to have had a happy time on some of the trade routes. I expect it will be some time before they run them off the seas.

By the way, send me a line to Vancouver addressed to SS Niagara to let us know how you all are.

We are at present very blooming & lead a lazy life. Eileen goes to school to occupy her time. By the way, I met a good many American scientists in New Zealand. They made a very good impression & worked nobly at lectures.[1]

Notwithstanding the war, the B.A. meeting in Australia was very interesting & successful. Dr. Pringsheim [2] of Berlin who came out with us has not been allowed to leave Australia as he is a reservist. He us occupying his time in research in Melbourne.

My wife sends her kind regards.

E. RUTHERFORD

1. Some of the American scientists who attended the B.A.A.S. meetings in Australia were invited by the New Zealand government to lecture in the islands.

2. Probably Peter Pringsheim, who had received his Ph.D. degree in 1906 from the University of Munich, and was at this time an assistant in the physical institute of the University of Berlin. After the war he became a professor of physics there.

8 December 1914

Sloane Laboratory, Yale University
New Haven, Connecticut

My dear Sir Ernest,

Your letter of October 28th from New Zealand was duly received and I was glad indeed to hear from you. I had heard indirectly about you from Porter [1] of London, who went back by way of the U.S. and who spent a day here, and by Ernest Brown [2] who has returned from his trip with the B.A. We had a nice visit from Bragg who was over here for the Brown University lectures. He stopped for a couple of days with the Bumsteads and it was a great pleasure to all of us to see him once more.

Bye the way, what in the world ever made you think that my letter written last June [3] was such a gloomy one? You spoke of this in the letter you wrote before you sailed for Australia and Brown tells me you seemed quite impressed by it when you spoke to him about it! I was not conscious of being down in the mouth when I wrote you, and although I was a little disappointed that I hadn't any more to show for a years work, still I was not at all depressed nor was there any real reason for my being so. Perhaps I was tired when I wrote, and possibly it was written on one of those warm spring days. Something must have been wrong, but what was the trouble I have not the least notion.

I was on the Kronprinzessin Cecilie when the war broke out, having left New York for Germany on July 28th. As you have probably heard, we faced about when the news reached us in midocean, raced back to America through darkness and fog, and landed finally in Bar Harbor, Maine!!! Not at all a bad place according to my way of thinking to reach on that particular occasion. I spent several weeks with some friends of mine who were summering near where we landed.

You may feel grieved, but I don't think you can be justly disappointed to learn that I am considered here to be a PRO-GERMAN. No, I haven't grown any horns or hoofs or changed (so far as I am aware) in any particular. I have just remained where I was and all this excitement of the war with its discussions of morals and righteousness, and the protection of human interests has just passed over me. I don't think any less of the Germans or the English than I did before, my attitude on their relative merits and their way of doing things has not altered, and I can not be persuaded that everything the Germans have done is all wrong and everything the English have done is all right, or the contrary. I can not see why organizing your own citizens to make efficient fighters is any more reprehensible than organizing a lot of other nations to help you out to lick the other fellow. I suppose it is a moral defect developed through the intemperate consumption of German beer in German beer-gardens, but it has grown on me and some how or other I can not get rid of it! But I suppose they will go on killing each other until they all get sick and tired of it, and then they will start out on a peace basis once more and continue making the same old blunders. I can not see how the Germans have the slightest chance of winning, but they certainly have made a good fight of it and will continue to do so for some time to come according to my reckoning. And when they are licked, well, it won't be such a great victory for any one nation of the Allies, and they will probably have to scrap it out between them to decide which is entitled to laurels.

I am very glad indeed to hear that you are coming back by way of this enlightened country and the prospect of seeing you soon is truly a very pleasing one. I expect to be away from New Haven most of the Christmas holidays, but I shall make every effort to see you when you come to New York and I sincerely hope that nothing will prevent me from doing so. My address just before the New Year will be c/o W. C. Hammond, 231 Cabot St., Holyoke, Mass. When you get this you had better write me a couple of notes, one addressed here and the other to the address I have just given. I wish that we could have you declared a contraband of war and your re-exportation to England could be prevented.

With kindest regards to Lady Rutherford, and love to Eileen. Best wishes to yourself and hopes that you are having a pleasant and unexciting trip across the Pacific. Sincerely yours,

BERTRAM B. BOLTWOOD

1. Alfred William Porter, professor of physics at the University of London.

2. Ernest W. Brown became professor of mathematics at Yale in 1907, the same year in which he was awarded the Adams Prize. He had been a professor at Haverford College, in Pennsylvania.

3. Not preserved.

22 DECEMBER 1914

University Club of Montreal

My dear Boltwood,

Just a line to say we have arrived safely in Montreal where we will stay for a few days. We are all well & fit. I am staying at the University Club while my wife & Eileen are staying with Mrs. Pitcher (née Miss Brooks).[1]

We are expecting to sail for England on Dec 30 by either the Lusitania or Adriatic—not yet settled. We shall probably go to N.Y. by the night train (N.Y. Central) Dec 28 & stay over till the boat leaves. We shall probably stay at the Murray Hill Hotel in N.Y. as a travelling friend of ours wishes us to see him there.

I hope we shall be able to see you—we shall try & avoid the war as a topic of serious conversation. In any case, it will be a great relief to do so.

If you write or telegraph me to above address, it will be alright. Au revoir. Yours ever,

E. RUTHERFORD

P.S. I hear Pring,[2] Florance, Andrade & Walmsley[3] have commissions & are busy preparing for the front. Darwin[4] is censor of soldier's letters!

1. Harriet Brooks was one of Rutherford's research students at McGill. Her sister became the wife of A. S. Eve.

2. John Norman Pring, an electrochemist, worked in the Manchester physics laboratory from 1906. After a separate department of electrochemistry was established he was appointed professor.

3. H. P. Walmsley.

4. Charles Galton Darwin, son of the astronomer George H. Darwin, and grandson of the biologist Charles Darwin, was first a lecturer in physics at Manchester and, after the war, a lecturer in mathematics at Christ's College, Cambridge. In 1923 he was appointed professor of natural philosophy at Edinburgh, but returned in 1936 to Christ's as master of the college. When illness prevented Ralph Fowler from assuming the directorship of the National Physical Laboratory, the post went to Darwin, who held it for a decade.

22 DECEMBER 1914

University Club of Montreal

My dear Boltwood,

Just a line to say I have written to your university address with details of my movements.

I expect to travel to New York by the night train (N.Y. Central) on Dec 28 & stay over till my boat (either Lusitania or Adriatic) leaves on the 30th. We shall stop at the Murray Hill Hotel to meet a travelling friend.

We are all fit & well & hope to see you on Dec 29—if possible. Au revoir. Yours ever,

E. RUTHERFORD

9 January 1915

17 Wilmslow Road
Withington, Manchester

Dear Boltwood,

We had on the whole a pleasant journey over to England without any adventures and arrived in Liverpool on the 7th at 3 o'clock and were in Manchester just after 5. The first four days out were very calm but cold, followed by a two days' gale. We saw two cruisers at Sandyhook; one sent a boat on board with the mail and some of Admiral Cradock's personal effects. The only other sign of war was a cruiser off Cape Clear, and the search lights of Queenstown. We had a number of American doctors on board going to the American hospital in Paris.

We are all very well, and trying to get the house in order. Eileen goes to boarding school in a week's time and is in a high state of excitement. We found Moulsdale with his head tied up owing to a fall from a ladder, but he is getting along pretty well.

We do not start University work for a few days. Pring, Florance, Andrade, and Walmsley have commissions in Kitchener's Army in the Artillery, and I understand are enjoying themselves. Moseley has a commission in the Royal Engineers, and young Bragg, I believe, also. Everything in Manchester seems much as usual, and apparently business is pretty prosperous. We do not have lectures on Wednesday or Saturday, for nearly everybody goes drilling on those days. Holland is a natural warrior, and I understand runs the University under martial law of his own. Elliot Smith and family are well; I saw him yesterday. They had a narrow squeak of being caught by the Emden.

You will be interested to hear that most of the German people you know in Manchester are most violently anti-German.

Samson is, I believe, rather unwell—digestive troubles probably. You will be interested to hear that Baumbach's shop is
closed and he is interned. I gather that he was very indiscreet in
going about after war was declared telling the great things that
the Germans were going to do to England. The Chief Constable
will, I believe, not hear of his release; they probably are suspi-
cious of him. We have to get along with the services of a glass
blower who was the only English apprentice of Baumbach.[1]

Lantsberry has left for America, but nothing has been heard
about him here.

The Radium Department of the hospitals is now in full
swing. We have bought over 700 milligrams of radium element
from the Pittsburg Co., and it is now all ready for use. Marsden
has been very active getting the place in order. One of my
young men is in charge as physicist, and a radiologist has also
been appointed. Over £30,000 were collected for the purpose
just before the war.

I understand that the University is not much affected, with
the exception that 300 or 400 have got commissions; most of the
able-bodied of the residue are in the Officers' Training Corps.
There is a staff platoon of teachers under forty, of which I believe Lang is an ardent member. The Lambs are looking well
and cheerful.

It was very good of you to come down to New York to see us.
Give my remembrances to Bumstead, Wellisch, and the others.
Yours very sincerely,

E. RUTHERFORD

P.S. I believe Geiger was still at work in Berlin late in September. Chadwick [2] is, we understand, interned in Berlin. He
has only got one postcard through so far.

---

1. Otto Baumbach was the glassblower who constructed the thin tubes
used in the Rutherford–Royds experiment.
2. James Chadwick, after working under Rutherford at Manchester,
went to Berlin to spend a short time with Geiger. When war was declared

he was interned, but through the efforts of Geiger was allowed to continue some research activities. Chadwick then went to Cambridge when Rutherford became Cavendish Professor and served as his assistant director. In 1932 his experiments showed the existence of the neutron; this discovery was rewarded with the Nobel Prize just a few years later. Chadwick next became professor of physics at Liverpool, and upon retirement from this chair was elected master of Gonville and Caius College, Cambridge.

28 JANUARY 1915

Sloane Laboratory, Yale University
New Haven, Connecticut

My dear Rutherford,

I was very glad to get your letter of the 9th and to hear the latest news of yourself and my other friends in Manchester. I was also pleased to know that you and your family had enjoyed a comfortable passage without any unpleasant events in the course of it. I did not feel that you were running any serious risks, however.

Shortly after you were in New York I received a letter from Geiger. It was written in Erlangen. He wrote that he went to the front immediately after the war was declared and escaped all the more serious risks to which soldiers are exposed. He was taken down with rheumatism in October and sent back home, where he had been for some time in the Clinic of the Hospital at Erlangen. He anticipated a speedy recovery and hoped to be back on the fighting line early in the New Year. His letter was written on the first of December. He showed no bitterness about the war, took it hopefully as a matter of fate and expressed his confidence in the Germans being able to make a successful fight of it. He asked particularly to be remembered to you and sent his kindest regards to you and your family.

He said that Chadwick was with him at the outbreak of the war and that he had left him in charge of some of his (Geiger's) friends when he left for the front. Everything went very comfortably with C. until about the middle of November, then he had to be interned with the rest of the Englishmen "in retaliation for the action of the British authorities towards Germans in England." I think they have a good case against you there, and no one in England can object with justice to what was done in Germany.

Speaking of interning, I am very sorry to hear about Baumbach. Your officials must have had a pretty bad case of funk when they found it necessary to shut him up in order to preserve the integrity of Old England. Being a glassblower I supposed they feared he might "blow something up," or turn the X-rays on some diplomatic matters, or train a regiment of dachshunds to bite off the legs of the territorials. Well, anyway, I think it is a great pity and I wish that something might be done to exile him to this country and let us have the use of him for scientific purposes. Seriously, if you could possibly have it arranged to let him off to come over here, we would be very glad to employ him. I have talked with Bumstead about the matter and he is willing to pay him $1000 a year to work for us. I feel sure he could undoubtedly make more than that by outside work, which we would give him every opportunity of doing. Your officials would not have him on their hands, he would be able to earn a decent income for the support of his family, and the possibility of his going over to Germany to fight for the Kaiser would be rather remote, with your lovely, little warships haunting the threshold of New York Harbor. I am writing him a letter making him the offer and I wish you would do anything that might help us in getting him. He isn't any use to you now and is not likely to love England over much if they keep him shut up until Germany is vanquished.

There is not any news I can think of that might interest you. Everything here is just the same as it was when I last saw you. It was a great pleasure having that little chance to see you all and I would not have missed it for anything.

Bye the way, it strikes me as rather natural that my "German" friends in Manchester should be somewhat "anti-German." The atmosphere over there in England doesn't appear to be particularly favorable to political liberality or independent thinking just at present. I think my friends show good judgement in concuring in the popular demand as to opinions!

With regards and best wishes to all, Sincerely yours,

BERTRAM B. BOLTWOOD

1 MARCH 1915

17 Wilmslow Road
Withington, Manchester

Dear Boltwood,

I got your letter re Baumbach, and we have made enquiries about the possibility of his early release, as we are anxious to have him back to run his department. Although the Government is now releasing a considerable number of aliens, we have received a definite assurance that it is no use attempting to get the release of Baumbach for some little time. Baumbach's right hand man turned up from a detention camp the other day, and Dixon and I went surety for his good behaviour. He will be working at his trade, not far from the University. I think, from what I heard, that Baumbach lost his head and made a thorough ass of himself at the beginning of the war. He went round telling people that he hoped the British Army would be destroyed, and boasted of the definite dates when the Germans were to arrive in London and Manchester (long since past). I have heard from Cook [1] that he was in a terrible state of apprehension and terror in between. On seeing a lonely territorial marching down the street, he ran into Cook's office and asked him to protect him, as the territorial was going to shoot him. Whether the police have anything more against him than this, I do not know. The Chief Constable of Manchester has obviously made up his mind that the continued detention of Baumbach is necessary. The English father-in-law looks after his shop, and he practically says that Baumbach's detention is due to his own fault. Until the war is over, there is not the least possibility of Baumbach getting away from this country, even if he were released on surety; so that your plans for the moment must be in abeyance.

Whatever the intention, your remarks in your last letter make me feel tired. It is no use, however, referring to the subject.

As to ourselves, we are all in good health, and I am very busy with my University work and research. Barnes [2] of Bryn Mawr is with me, and we are doing some X ray work, while I have heard from Zeleny,[3] who is now in Cambridge, that he has been appointed Professor at Yale. I am hoping to see him later on in the summer before he returns.

We have been making substantial alterations to the house, including knocking down the wall between the drawing room and the back room, and a new window in the drawing room; also much decoration etc., so that the house for a month was a veritable pig-sty.

Robinson has got a Commission in the Royal Garrison Artillery; Andrade is now at the front in Belgium with a heavy battery. Yours very sincerely,

E. RUTHERFORD

1. Probably this is the same Cook referred to in note 6 to Boltwood's letter of 2 November 1910.

2. James Barnes, a Canadian who was an 1851 Exhibition Scholar at the turn of the century and then received his Ph.D. degree from Johns Hopkins, was associate professor, later full professor of physics at Bryn Mawr College, in Pennsylvania.

3. John Zeleny was professor and chairman of the physics department at the University of Minnesota before joining the Yale faculty.

16 MARCH 1915

Sloane Laboratory, Yale University
New Haven, Connecticut

My dear Rutherford,

Your letter of March the first reached me yesterday and from its justifiable tone of irritation I realized for the first time that I had unintentionally been putting my foot into things that I would much rather keep out of. Please accept the assurance that for one thing I did not have the slightest intention or desire of snatching Baumbach *away from you,* or of depriving you or your laboratory of his services. It simply occured to me on the spur of the moment that it might perhaps be possible for him to get away from England and work over here *now* at a time when he could not perhaps work in Manchester. Naturally we would be awfully glad to get him under any conditions which would not be undesirable from your standpoint. I had taken it for granted that the reason for his detention was simply that he was considered a person who could not be left at large in an English city. Therefore, I assumed that your authorities would be glad to get rid of him. I had also supposed that with the present strong feelings against the Germans in England you might not be willing to employ him if he were free to work for you, even if he cared to do so. The same post that brought me your letter also brought from him a reply to a letter I had written him asking whether there was any chance of his being willing to come over here. In his reply he states that there is at present no apparent prospect of his being released, which is even more apparent from your own letter. He states in his letter that he had previously written twice to me, but I did not receive the letters. I suppose my name was thought to be suspiciously German!

At all events, don't let us have any serious disagreements over the War.[1] My position is hard enough, because I find difficulty in getting along with either side since I agree completely with neither. You rulers of the waves are likely to cause us American scientists no end of trouble by cutting off our scientific supplies from Germany, but I suppose might makes right and all's fair in war! But my advice is, don't overdo it! This country has certainly stood by England very well thus far and we are likely to expect some consideration in return for it.

This isn't much of a letter and is hastily written. It is merely to acknowledge the receipt of your own and to apologise for anything I may have said in my earlier one that in any way annoyed you.

With best wishes, Sincerely yours,

B. B. BOLTWOOD

1. Boltwood's fondness for German efficiency and culture had grown during his many summer visits and longer periods of study there. His pro-German sympathies, therefore, were based on long acquaintance, but were largely of a nonpolitical nature, for Boltwood seems not to have been strongly politically oriented. These letters exhibit the one known occasion when his friendship with Rutherford was strained. As the war progressed, however, and as the United States was drawn into the conflict, Boltwood's sympathies shifted to the Allies' cause and he engaged in submarine detection research at the navy's New London, Connecticut, base.

1 APRIL 1915

17 Wilmslow Road
Withington, Manchester

My dear Boltwood,

I received your last letter in the south of England, where we had motored to bring Eileen back from boarding school. We had a pleasant if somewhat cold five days' journey, staying at the Schusters and the Perkins[1] en route. Eileen is looking blooming, and has gained nine pounds in weight and grown half an inch in her three months absence. She is very happy to-day, as she hopes to get a new bicycle.

I did not know that my last letter was so obviously irritable in tone. As a matter of fact, I had not the least objection to your suggestion of offering Baumbach a job, because I am not at all certain about what we shall do with him in the future. I was a little irritated at your rather facetious references to Baumbach's internment. As I told you in my last letter, I am doubtful whether Baumbach will be liberated until the war is over. I could never have believed that Baumbach would have made such an ass of himself as he is doing. He has been bombarding his chief man, who is now released, with letters of dismissal and threats of the intervention of the German Ambassador if he does this or that. As all these letters pass through the Censor, each one will be a black mark against him—and quite rightly too, in my opinion. He appears to misunderstand the situation completely, and his father-in-law obviously has the opinion that he is making a thorough ass of himself. Unless Baumbach returns in a somewhat chastened mood, it is not at all certain that the University will offer him the very great advantages he has had in the past.

I think I told you that Barnes of Bryn Mawr is with me, and we are working hard at some X ray problems. I wrote to Stefan Meyer and Geiger some time ago, and got a very cordial letter from the former, but so far have not heard from the latter. Apparently the Vienna people are all working away in the Academy as usual, and are doing some excellent work. Hönigschmid has found that the atomic weight of pitchblende lead is 206 as against 207 of ordinary lead, and they have also made experiments to test the physical properties of the radioactive lead.

Andrade is now at the front, and I expect was in the Neuve Chapelle affair.

Barnes showed me a letter he had received from New York about the glass supplies etc. in America. I can quite imagine that you are having fairly hard times, as all shipments from Germany have apparently ceased.[2] I am very sorry for you, but I think it is very good medicine for the Germans. I do not think that your country need be in the least alarmed at this country interfering with your trade too much. It is quite against our interest to do so, and in any case, in our wildest dreams we could not hope to emulate the drastic methods of our highly "cultured" enemies.

Things in Manchester are much as usual, with the exception that the streets are now darkened at nights. I think this is mainly to try and impress the population with the fact that we are actually at war. I think many people would like to see a Zeppelin attack, for it is the only chance of seeing anything of the war. I am sure they would turn out in crowds to view the spectacle and chance the bombs. By the way, as my friend Petavel puts it, the German submarines must be having a very "mouldy" time. It looks as if they would be destroyed as fast as Germany can build, for in addition to those published, there is good reason to believe that many more have been accounted for.

Give my kind regards to Bumstead. Yours sincerely,

E. RUTHERFORD

1. Probably William Henry Perkin who, after twenty years as professor of organic chemistry at Manchester, in 1912 was appointed to a professorship at Oxford.

2. It took this British blockade during World War I to point out the extent of the United States' dependency upon German chemicals and apparatus. The resulting efforts toward self-sufficiency led to the present strong chemical industry in America.

14 SEPTEMBER 1915

17 Wilmslow Road
Withington, Manchester

Dear Boltwood,

You will be very sorry to hear that Moseley was killed in the Dardanelles on Aug. 10th. You will see my obituary notice of him in *Nature*.[1] He was the best of the young people I ever had, and his death is a severe loss to science. I was wondering if you would feel inclined to write a brief notice on him for *Science,* as, if I remember aright, you knew him quite well personally.

You will also be very sorry to hear that Bragg's second boy, who had not yet graduated in Cambridge, died of wounds received in the Dardanelles. He was reported dangerously wounded, and died a day or two later at sea. A notice of his death has just appeared in the *Times,* Bragg was to have stayed with us for the British Association, but received the telegram the day before. Bragg's elder boy, Lieut. in the R.A., has been seconded for special scientific work in Flanders. My lecturer, Robinson (also in the R.A.) is with him. Pring (Lieut.) is at the front with the Chemical Corps, and looks forward to high times in the future.

The British Association passed off very well, and all the sections were as good, if not better than usual. The Physics Section met in my Laboratory, and we had very good discussions on isotopes, classification of the stars, and thermionics. Weiss [2] of magneton fame was here, and gave an address, while Bragg gave a report on crystal work. You will remember that Schuster was President. A small section of the Press attacked him with having a German name, but fortunately there was no disturbance of any kind in Manchester. His address, which you will read, passed off very well, although his voice was little weak. He got news the same day that his boy was wounded in the Dardanelles, but they have heard since from Alexandria that it is a comparatively mild wound in the forearm.

You will see by the *Phil. Mag.* that I have kept some research going.[3] I have also found a new long range set of alpha particles from thorium C, and have investigated the hydrogen atoms from emanation tubes, but it will be some little time before I publish the final results as I have been very busy the last two months on general war work. You may have seen that I have been appointed a member of the Board of Inventions and Research. I am especially connected with the question of submarines, and have undertaken some research on the acoustic detection.[4] The Navy, of course, has already done a good deal of work along a variety of lines, and the results are only too well known to our German friends, but I am doubtful whether they will ever make public a list of their losses. I should imagine that life on a German submarine at the present time is about as exhilarating as that of a criminal in prison condemned to the gallows. My brother-in-law, Major Newton, is in a dugout in the Dardanelles. He is head of a field hospital, and had a very tough time during the attacks from August 5th to the 10th, as the casualties were very heavy, and they are exposed to shell fire the whole time. New Zealanders have suffered very heavy losses, but have shown plenty of ginger. We have had a large number of the Australian and New Zealand wounded in Manchester, and my wife has charge of the general organisation for looking after the latter and the Canadians in the hospitals.

Manchester seems very little changed except that the streets have been darkened at night for the last six months. This city has provided over 108,000 men, so it has done pretty well. Of course the research men in the Laboratory are very much reduced, and it is difficult to get people to work very hard in these days, as most of them are engaged in munitions or other work. Cook is fully occupied with war work, and also the tinsmith. Baumbach is still interned and is likely to be so till the end of the war. His right hand man has been let out again, and is in work in the Chemical Laboratory. All the chemical laboratories in the country are at work producing special chemicals for therapeutic and other purposes. Weizmann [5] has got a big job in hand in connection with explosives, while Dixon is engaged by the War Office in testing the products of the different firms.

I think we shall about get up full speed in six months' time, when something will have to move. The country is still filled with troops, although we believe there is nearly a million and a half in France and the Dardanelles, but of course nobody knows the actual numbers.

I do not know what is your opinion of the present situation

between the U.S.A. and Germany. It looks rather ludicrous from this side, but of course we only get excerpts of the pro-Allies papers. I should think that the Government of this country are quite content with the submarine war on merchantmen, as it is very expensive to the Germans and diminishes their activities in other directions. I imagine, however, that the German Government has reached the conclusion that the game is not worth the candle. I am afraid the German public would be rather disturbed if they knew the real magnitude of their losses. The Navy is, I think, quite happy about it, as submarine hunting is their only relaxation from the routine of waiting for the German Fleet. London and the South of England is getting quite accustomed to Zeppelin visits. They usually manage to bag such a reasonable number of women and children as to send them home highly contented. I have so far not been in London at the time of a raid, but should like to have an opportunity of seeing one. I expect we shall bag them sooner or later, but they are rather difficult to get at in the darkness.

Give my kind regards to Zeleny, Bumstead, Wellisch, and Wheeler. We are all well at home; Eileen is on her holidays but goes to school again very shortly. I go to London to-night and then on to Scotland to try some experiments.[6] Yours very sincerely,

E. RUTHERFORD

1. ER, "Henry Gwyn–Jeffreys Moseley," *Nature, 96* (9 Sept. 1915), 33–34.

2. Pierre Weiss, professor of physics at the Polytechnic Institute, Zurich.

3. ER, J. Barnes and H. Richardson, "Maximum frequency of the X rays from a Coolidge tube for different voltages," *Phil. Mag., 30* (Sept. 1915), 339–60; ER and J. Barnes, "Efficiency of production of X rays from a Coolidge tube," *Phil. Mag., 30* (Sept. 1915), 361–67. These papers are among the few by Rutherford on topics other than radioactivity.

4. The employment of scientists during World War I was limited largely to acoustical problems: submarine detection and triangulation of enemy artillery pieces by sound ranging. It was because so few scientific opportunities were available that so many young scientists volunteered for service

in the trenches. Among the older (Rutherford was then 44) and better known scientists, W. H. Bragg and A. S. Eve also worked on anti-submarine problems.

5. Chaim Weizmann, then a reader in biochemistry at the University of Manchester, was a personal friend of Rutherford's. The big job referred to was the directorship of the British Admiralty Laboratories, a post he held until 1919. A leader in the Zionist movement, Weizmann's efforts won from the British government the Balfour declaration favoring establishment of a Jewish homeland in Palestine. Upon its creation in 1949, Weizmann became president of the new state of Israel.

6. Submarine detection experiments.

18 JANUARY 1916

Sloane Laboratory, Yale University
New Haven, Connecticut

My dear Rutherford,

A letter which reached Bumstead yesterday and which he showed to me, reminded me (If I had needed a reminder) of the fact that I had not acknowledged the kind letter which I received from you this Autumn. Notwithstanding my apparent indifference to your thoughtfulness, I can assure you that I was very much pleased to hear from you. Your letter to Bumstead was the next best thing to hearing from you directly, because it told me that you were well and gave me some knowledge of your interests and your activities.

I was much interested also in what you wrote in regard to the two young Canadians who are working here in our laboratory. I know both of them well and have talked much with them on the subject of their patriotic duties. I am especially fond of Johnstone,[1] who is a fine, high-strung, manly young fellow, and I should hate to have him sacrifice himself uselessly on the altar of duty. The position of young men of this sort under the existing circumstances is a particularly difficult one and I can only be thankful that I have never been placed in a similar situation. I sincerely hope that some suitable occupation can ultimately be found for both of them; I would not give much for either one of them in the ranks as an ordinary soldier.

Well, the war seems to go on endlessly, without any prospect of improvement in the immediate future. My only desire in connection with it is that it might be stopped before the useless expenditure of lives and resources has progressed any farther. But that is a hopeless wish, as I very well realize when I refer to it. It is very inspiring to think of you in your present capacity of expert adviser to the Navy. It is a great comfort to know that I am not one of the objects of your designs and plannings. I remember so well your natural pugnacious tendencies, and how we used to shock the luncheon parties at the Refectory with our blood-curdling schemes for making war really effective!

Everything here is very much as usual. Our new man, Zeleny, is certainly an addition and having Nichols [2] here next year will certainly possess many advantages. Bumstead is physically much stronger than he was before his last operation. But I think that we all feel the oppression of the conflict in Europe and science must necessarily take a secondary place when so many other greater problems are being worked out to some possible final solution.

You will probably have seen the paper by Miss Gleditsch [3] in which she gets results for the life of radium from growing experiments which are in excellent agreement with those which were obtained by you and Geiger. This brings everything into good accord now and seems to me to settle all previous matters of uncertainty. As usual, your prediction that my separation of ionium was not a complete one has proved to be the true explanation. I am occupied on one or two minor problems just at present, and hope to have something for publication before long.

I wish that when you have the time you would write me and give me some news of people and things at Manchester. I am really hungry for news of my former friends there, the men who were around the laboratory especially. I see from an occasional communication in Nature that Elliot Smith is still at the University, although I would have thought that he might be off on medical service somewhere. What about good old Chaffers and Holland, and how is Pring getting along as a military chemist? What is the news of Lady R's brother, the doctor, who you wrote me last winter was with the Australian contingent? Really, you know, I may not be as sympathetic as some people who are blown before a strong wind in any direction, but I have a strong personal regard and affection for a great many people which is not affected in the least by even a war like the present one. And so, although I may not be as strong a pro-Ally as many of my countrymen, I do not feel that I am guilty of any disloyalty to my friends in my unwillingness to approve of every action of their countrymen. I am constantly recalling the innumerable pleasant occasions which it was my great privilege to enjoy while among you and I remember so many instances of friendship and hospitality. I wish that you might all have the best that there is and I wish it might all be brought about without injustice to anyone.

I can assure you that everyone who knew Moseley must have felt a deep sense of personal loss at the news of his death. Surely everyone familiar with his scientific work must have realized what a loss his death meant to science. I never knew him very well. He came to you the year after I returned to this country. But I met him in the laboratory the following summer when I was making a visit with you, and found him to be a very attractive fellow. I was awfully sorry to hear of the death of young Bragg, especially at the thought of the bereavement to his father and his mother. I had seen them all together at Bolton and at Brussels, and I know what a strong affection existed between them.

Except for a short letter of greeting from Stefan Meyer, I have heard nothing from anyone in Germany or Austria for many months. I do not know what has become of my former acquaintances over there. I have written Meyer and asked him for any news of Hahn or Geiger.

Well, I must close this somewhat long and, I fear, somewhat doleful letter. Here's hoping for better times, anyway. With best wishes and warmest personal regards to yourself, to Lady Rutherford and to Eileen, and with kindest remembrances to my friends, I remain, Yours sincerely,

B. B. BOLTWOOD

1. John H. L. Johnstone received his early training at Dalhousie and then an 1851 Exhibition Scholarship brought him to Yale where he earned his Ph.D. degree in 1916. Following military service in World War I, he returned to Dalhousie where he rose through the ranks to a professorship in physics.

2. Ernest Fox Nichols.

3. Ellen Gleditsch, "The life of radium," *Am. J. Sci., 41* (Jan. 1916), 112–24. Her two separate values for the half-life of radium were 1642 and 1674 years.

21 FEBRUARY 1916

17 Wilmslow Road
Withington, Manchester

Dear Boltwood,

I was glad to hear from you a week or so ago, and to know that you are still alive and kicking notwithstanding your long silence.

I have little to report of interest from the Laboratory. Teaching work of the women and the unfit continues, and there will be a big drop in the first year at the end of this term. Everyone in the Laboratory has attested, but several, excluding the medically unfit, will be retained to carry on the University work and to assist in war investigations. I am very busy in that direction, and practically have no time for my own special work. I go to

London and to the Experimental Station up North pretty often, and am getting rather tired of long railway journeys in winter weather. Apart from a chill last week which kept me indoors two or three days, I have been keeping fit and well, and much interested in my work.

My wife a few weeks ago was rather suffering from overwork and had to spend a week in bed. She is now herself again. Eileen is now quite happy at boarding school, and grows rapidly.

I think I have told you that most of the men you knew here are engaged in military operations, including Pring, Robinson, Florance, and others I do not think you met. Pring has been in the thick of the battle at Loos, and has now a sort of roving Chemical Commission, and is doing special work to liven up our German friends in the future. He has shown considerable originality, and produced some good things. Pring is one of the very few people I have come across who really thoroughly enjoys the chance of a fight at the front. I think he is one of those rare people who do not appreciate what danger is. You probably have heard stories of his rashness in the laboratory, when he apparently preferred to work with his nose against a bomb with a pressure inside of three or four times that for which it was constructed. Robinson comes over at intervals, and has been much improved by his military experiences. He and young Bragg are working together in Flanders.

By the way, I saw the Braggs the other day, and stayed with them in their new home in London. They are, of course, very much cut up by the loss of their younger boy in the Dardanelles. Bragg is a very busy member of the same Committee as I am.

Florance has gone to the East, and is probably in Salonika or Egypt.

You probably saw the German report that the last Zeppelin raid had destroyed Manchester and Liverpool. Fortunately none of the inhabitants at either place either saw or heard a Zeppelin, but I have no doubt they will come our way soon.

They expended a good deal of their time and energy in bombarding a poor inoffensive place called Burton, which, as you know, is one of the chief beer producing places of this country. Unfortunately they failed to hit the breweries. Possibly they thought the Englishman would give in directly they interfered with his beer!

By the way, I think you would be interested to live in this country at the present time. The people have never been so united in their history, and are quite determined to down the Germans, even if it takes another three years. Of course, as you know, the whole country is exceedingly prosperous with such an enormous amount of Government money being expended, and in consequence of the scarcity of labour, a very large number of women are being utilised. Some of the shipping lines are making fabulous profits notwithstanding their losses due to the submarines. Economically it may be very unhealthy, but it certainly does not tend to make people discontented with the present situation. There is very little need of conscription, but as in the case of the American Civil War, it has lead to the voluntary enlistment of the residuum.

I am very much interested in the future to see what is going to happen in the East. We have great forces there, much greater than is usually supposed, and we may expect before long a great change in that situation. I think that Turkey and Bulgaria will be on their last legs within six months.

I forget whether you met my wife's brother, Major Newton, who has been through the Dardanelles, and has kept fit and well throughout. He is now in Egypt, not far from the Canal, and it is quite on the cards that they may come over to France later. I think if they could get the Candians and Australians and New Zealanders together they would give the Germans a livelier time than they have ever had, and I think a million of them would go through the line without much difficulty. Unfortunately their number is not yet half a million, but it is increasing rapidly.

Wilson must be having a pretty difficult time in your country, trying to keep Germany and this country in order and at the same time keeping out of the scrap. It looks as if you will have a pretty difficult time with Germany within the next month or two, as the Germans are apparently determined, if possible, to destroy everything on the sea. I saw in a German paper the statement that the blood goes to the good German's head every time they think of England going where she likes on the sea and the impotence of their own fleet and merchantmen. We trust that the new submarine war will have no greater luck than the old, but I have no doubt they will give us plenty of trouble. The Germans are a vainglorious people, quite obstinate in their way, but they have never in their history tumbled up against any country quite so obstinate as this. You may be quite sure that they will be worn down in the end. It is really interesting to see how unanimous the whole country is on this point.

Re radium, I was of course very glad to hear the period of Ra agrees well with the calculated value. It is very important to have this point settled as it very much fortifies all the other data. I have got a few young women & medically unfit at experiment so as not to completely lose hold of the old subject. Yours very sincerely,

E. RUTHERFORD

My wife sends her remembrances. By the way, my car has been laid up in cold storage the past six months. My consequent savings goes into "exchequer bonds."

ER

4 DECEMBER 1919

Cavendish Laboratory [1]
Cambridge

Dear Boltwood,

I am very anxious to get a reasonable quantity of Meso-Thorium of the order of 10–20 milligrammes. I have written to

Geiger but he tells me there is nothing to be got in Berlin, and is doubtful in any case whether it would be possible to export it.

I thought you would be likely to know whether any of your people in America are turning out Meso-Thorium in quantity. I saw something about it a year ago but have not heard what has been done. Please let me have as soon as you can any information you can give on the matter including probable cost. I have heard several times from Geiger who is working again in Berlin; he tells me he is soon to be married and is somewhat apologetic over the announcement. I suppose that he is under the impression that an extra worry or two does not matter in these days.

I also heard from Von Hevesy who is visiting Bohr in Copenhagen; he also is soon to be married as also is Hönigschmid. There appears to be an epidemic of marriages among the Radioactive people.

I am now pretty well settled down to the work in the Cavendish. We have had a busy time—nearly 600 people in the Laboratory including 50 Naval Officers & as many research people as we can find room for. I am looking for room to extend the old place; we are very congested under present conditions.

We have at last got into our house but the workmen will be with us till nearly Xmas. We had a 5 months strike of the building trades here while our house stood derelict with part of the roof off.

I enjoy life very well here & find I keep pretty lively for an old man. J.J.T. is still energetic but his time is much occupied with Trinity & the Royal Society. I daresay you know Elliot Smith is now at University College & we hope we may be able to get him here ultimately. We are all pretty well & going strong. Give my kind regards to Bumstead & Zeleny. I understand you have now reverted to the chemical side. Yours ever,

E. RUTHERFORD

1. Rutherford was now head of the Cavendish Laboratory, having succeeded his former teacher, J. J. Thomson, who accepted a nonpaying posi-

tion as professor of physics in addition to the mastership of Trinity College.

New Haven, Connecticut

My dear Rutherford,

Your letter of the 4th reached me this afternoon and I can assure you that it was a pleasure to hear from you again. I have no idea how long it is since I last heard from you or how long it is since I last wrote to you? But it certainly seems like a century!

As you have heard, I am now no longer the fabled ass in a lions skin, namely, a chemist in the guise of a physicist, but have taken off the skin and am now "Acting Professor of Chemistry" in Yale College. This is my second year of "acting" and it is beginning to seem natural! I had some hopes of being able to reform the chemists but I am afraid that I am not making much of a success of it! I am not very keen about reforms just at present but I may get more interest in it later.

As a result of having tried to do too much last year I had a rather annoying nervous breakdown last spring. It quite put me out of business for the time being but a long vacation and a more rational basis of living have quite restored me to my former good health. However, I am still taking things a little easy.

I am just leaving town for the Christmas vacation and I have not much time for a longer letter, but I am writing to a couple of people who will be able to tell me about Meso-Thorium and when I have heard from them I will write you what I learn from them. I do not happen to know much about the matter at present, but I think you can get the material you want without much trouble.

It was a matter of great satisfaction to me when I learned that you were going to Cambridge. You will remember that I often told you that you would finally get there! If it were not the time that it is and if the world had not been torn to pieces by the war I am sure that I would be packing my bags and going over to work with you (provided you were willing to have me)! I will often think of you in that delightful old town with such charming surroundings. And you surely will impart some new life to it!

Your new work on the cracking of the nitrogen atom is exceedingly interesting and most suggestive.[1] I hope you may be able to extend it and have every expectation that you will (unless something more exciting presents itself).

Please give my kindest regards to Lady Rutherford and to Eileen. I understand from Bumstead [2] that the latter is going to be (or perhaps is already) an architect. I recall how much she used to be interested in house plans! Also give my best regards to Elliot Smith if you happen to see him and to any other of my former friends you may happen to meet.

With best wishes for a Happy Christmas and a prosperous New Year, I am Yours very sincerely,

B. B. BOLTWOOD

1. ER, "Collision of α particles with light atoms," *Phil. Mag.*, 37 (June 1919), 537–87. In this first deliberately induced transformation of elements, Rutherford bombarded nitrogen with alpha particles and produced oxygen and protons. The reaction may be represented by the equation

$$_7N^{14} + {_2}He^4 \rightarrow {_1}H^1 + {_8}O^{17}$$

where the superscripts are the atomic weights and the subscripts the atomic numbers.

2. Since February 1918, Bumstead had been scientific attaché at the American embassy in London.

26 JANUARY 1920

Cavendish Laboratory
Cambridge

Dear Boltwood,

I am very much obliged for your letter about the Mesothorium and for your kind intentions with regard to Dr. Kelly. The latter is too uncertain to depend upon, so I am sending in an order to Dr. Miner[1] to provide me with £400 worth of Mesothorium.

I quite appreciate that the product will not be cheap but for my purpose time is more important than money.

Many thanks for your trouble. I daresay you know Elliot Smith is now Professor in University College London. There is some prospect that we may get him to Cambridge ultimately.

We are all well at home. Yours sincerely,

E. RUTHERFORD

Pring is back at the old place & has just got married. Dixon (of Chemical Dept) has married again & has started a second family. Chemists are a vigorous lot! I am full of ginger & spending money freely. Prices are awful for scientific apparatus. Prof & Mrs. Hudson were in Cambridge at the week-end. Their boy is studying here—also Elliot Smith's eldest.

1. H. S. Miner, chemist of the Welsbach Light Company, Gloucester City, New Jersey. This company's products included thorium mantles for gas illumination and its chemist had for many years furnished Boltwood with purified materials from their processing plant. To judge from the size of Rutherford's order, this service had evolved from a professional courtesy into part of the business.

5 FEBRUARY 1920

Cavendish Laboratory
Cambridge

Dear Boltwood,

Just a line to inform you that I have rescinded my order to the Welsbach Co. as Dr. McCoy had written to me and generously offered 10 milligrammes of Mesothorium.

I naturally closed with this. I also find that his charges per milligramme are only 2/3rds of those of the Welsbach Co.

Please regard this information as private, but I like to let you know as it was your letter to Kelly, who in turn wrote to McCoy, that led to this offer.

I am very grateful for your kindness in the matter. Yours sincerely,

E. RUTHERFORD

2 JULY 1920

Hancock Point, Maine

My dear Rutherford,

I have been intending to write to you for quite a long time but I had so much to do for the last few weeks in New Haven that I did not get a chance. We have been having quite a lively controversy over the location of a new chemistry laboratory which is to be built in the near future, with money from the Sterling bequest. We expect to spend about a million and a half and although a new laboratory is much needed it seems a shame to put it out beyond the Sloane where it will be out of reach from everywhere. However, our benighted Corporation so voted at their last meeting and we will have to make the best of it! [1] What a pity it was that so many intelligent men were killed in the war and that so many dumb ones escaped it!

You have possibly heard that Bumstead is to be in Washington for the next year, acting as the Chairman of the National Research Council. In a way this seems rather amusing to me, for he always used to be so bitterly opposed to organized research. However, his recent experience in administrative work has increased his interest in that sort of thing and he will probably fill the office very satisfactorily. I shall miss not having them in New Haven.

I had a very pleasant but altogether too short a visit from Elliot Smith some weeks ago while he was making his flying visit to this country. It was fine to see him again and he looked awfully well and comfortable. What a fine thing that gift of the Rockerfeller Foundation will be for him and how glad I am that they have made it.

I had a letter from him when he had returned to London and in it he said that you had just announced some new results which were going to make everybody sit up and take notice. He said that it was perhaps the best thing you had ever done—and that certainly is going some! Before I left New Haven I tried to find out what it was but without success. Wont you be so good as to send me a reprint or something from which I can learn more about what it is all about, for I am terribly anxious to know. It certainly is fine that you have still your old steam and energy.

I left New Haven a week ago today and came with some friends up to this beautiful place on the Maine coast. It is a very simple little settlement of summer visitors on a large bay known as Frenchman's Bay and is within sight of Bar Harbor but resembles it in no other particular. It is a place where I wear out my old clothes and go about in a white shirt and khaki trousers most of the time. I have a small motor boat and we spend a good deal of time on the water. With some friends of mine who have two boys I rent a cottage and we live very simply and comfortably.

I do not suppose you know who John Johnston is, do you? He is a chemist, born in Scotland, who used to be with Arthur Day in the Geophysical Laboratory. We got him to come to Yale last year and he has been a splendid colleague and a most agreeable companion. I see a great deal of him in New Haven and he is a tremendous help in doing things in connection with the chemistry department. He is up here in Maine also not far away in a place called Manset. We expect to get together occasionally and talk things over during the vacation.

Not long ago I gave a man named Leonard a letter of introduction to you. He had asked me to do so as he is expecting to be in Sweden next year on an American Scandinavian Fellowship (the same sort of a one as Miss Gleditsch held). He plans to visit England and if he looks you up do not take any trouble on his account out of consideration for me, please. He is a simple soul who was a student of mine for a short time. I do not think you will find him very exciting.

I understood from Elliot Smith that Eileen was not very well and had been having a rather unpleasant time of it. I hope she is much better now and that she will be able to follow out her ambition to be an architect, if she still has it.

I often think of the wonderful times I used to have with you in Manchester, in Munich and on that trip through Germany. The latter was a fitting ending to the many happy days that I had spent there and I shall always remember it. I do not ever expect to go back there again, after what has happened I have lost all interest in the place and in its people. And I doubt very much whether I ever go to Europe again. The old spirit has departed!

Please give my best regards to Lady Rutherford and to Eileen. With best wishes to you and hearty congratulations, I remain, Yours sincerely,

B. B. BOLTWOOD

1. The Yale Corporation had more foresight than the scientists, for the Sterling Chemistry Laboratory, standing next to the Sloane Physics

Laboratory, is now in the center of the university's large science complex. Both buildings, in fact, were found too small after World War II, and the departments have since expanded into greatly enlarged quarters.

19 AUGUST 1920

Newnham Cottage
Queens' Road, Cambridge

My dear Boltwood,

I was glad to receive your good letter and to hear how you were progressing with the new Chemical Laboratory. I expect it will mean a good deal of work for you to get it started. I myself am busy with a small extension of the Physical Laboratory which will give us a little more room. We are very crowded with students and research people and I am kept pretty busy. I have been buying a great deal of apparatus both for research and teaching purposes, and fortunately there are reasonable funds for this purpose.

I sent you a copy of my Bakerian Lecture [1] addressed to the Laboratory. In case you have not received it I will mention the main results. I have evidence that oxygen and nitrogen are disintegrated by collision with α particles giving rise to an atom of mass 3 and carrying two charges, which should be an isotope of helium. Nitrogen also breaks up another way with the emission of hydrogen atoms. Recently I believe I have found that carbon and possibly fluorine break up in the same way as oxygen, but it will take a great deal of experiment to prove this definitely. Apparently neither sulphur nor aluminium are disturbed by the shocks. I wish I had a live chemist tied up to this work who could guarantee on his life that substances were free from hydrogen. With this little detail set on one side, I believe I could prove very quickly which of the lighter elements give out hydrogen, but it is very difficult to do so without the chemical

329

certainty as the effect is so very small. You will no doubt have seen about Aston's [2] work on isotopes in the Laboratory. I think I told you it is really first-class work and I have the utmost confidence in his main conclusions. You can see that things are moving pretty rapidly on questions of atomic structure. My own work is rather difficult and takes a good deal of time, but I have now got a couple of good counters on whom I can rely. I hope in the next few years to form some idea of the constitution of the nucleus of the lighter atoms, but on account of the impossibility of getting the α particles close to the nucleus of the heavy atoms, I do not think it likely that we shall get much beyond neon. [3]

I met Elliot Smith on his return from America, and he told me of his visit to you. He was looking very fat and rosy and more like an archbishop than ever. It looks as if he will have a really good department and plenty of funds in the future. We have had Sir Arthur Schuster staying with us here for some time. He is on the University Commission which is examining into the dark corners of Cambridge and Oxford; that is officially —in practice I think it comes down to the question of how much money the Government is prepared to give to finance the older institutions. I find Cambridge a very pleasant place to live in and enjoy the change from the darkness of Manchester. My Laboratory is only seven minutes' walk from my home and I never see a tramcar. We have had Lamb with us this week. He is just getting into his new house in Cambridge and has retired from his professorial duties. He has just left us this morning to go into his new house.

I go to the B.A. Meeting at Cardiff this week; then back to Cambridge and motor up to the Yorkshire moors for a fortnight's holiday with Eileen. The latter has been troubled with her eyesight and has been spending three months on the moors, and is, I believe, very much better for the change. She is intending to enter Newnham [4] in October. On September 15th I go over to Copenhagen to deliver a few lectures and to open the

Laboratory for my old friend Bohr. I shall return in time to motor the family down from Yorkshire and to start a new session. I am feeling pretty fit but lazy in this close summer weather. I am very satisfied with the Laboratory and in two or three years I am hopeful to get it into really good shape. We have about 600 students to look after and about 30 research students, so that there is not much chance of getting rusty. I go to dinner in Trinity several times a week and find it a very agreeable change when I am not feeling fit for hard work in the evening. We have got a very nice garden in our new home and manage to grow a fair amount of fruit. My wife is very much interested in the flower garden and in growing chickens of which she has had a very successful year.

I got a note from Geiger this morning. He is married and has got back to his scientific work again. I have already written a long letter to you but have not given half the news. We are all very fit and well here. Yours sincerely,

E.   RUTHERFORD

P.S. I am very interested to hear that Bumstead is going to Washington. I guessed that he rather liked that type of work when he was in England. It has many advantages over running a laboratory.

1. This was the second Bakerian Lecture Rutherford delivered before the Royal Society, the first being in 1904. It has achieved some fame for its prediction of the existence of the neutron. "Nuclear constitution of atoms," *Proc. Roy. Soc.*, *97A* (1 July 1920), 374–400.

2. F. W. Aston received the Nobel Prize in chemistry in 1922 for his discovery, by means of the mass spectrograph he invented, of numerous isotopes of *non*radioactive elements.

3. The nuclei of all atoms repel alpha particles, since they are similarly charged. The heavier atoms, bearing larger total charges, repel the alphas more strongly. But since these particles are ejected from the decaying radioactive atoms with great energy, they are able to overcome this electrostatic or Coulomb repulsion and strike the nuclei of some target atoms. As the repulsive forces get stronger, however, the chances of such contact

diminish. It was for the purpose of bombarding heavier atoms and observing the induced transformations that particle accelerators were developed (cyclotron, Cockcroft-Walton, Van de Graaf, etc.), for these machines impart sufficient energy to the "bullets" to overcome the barriers. And the neutron, discovered at the same time as the first accelerators were constructed, also serves as a probe into the nucleus, for it has no charge and thus suffers no repulsion.

4. Newnham College is one of the few colleges for women in Cambridge University.

13 OCTOBER 1920

New Haven, Connecticut

My dear Rutherford,

Thank you very much for your interesting letter and for the reprint of the Bakerian lecture which was forwarded to me from New Haven. The latter has proved to be particularly useful and valuable since I found when I returned here from the country that none of my colleagues had seen the original and so I have been continually passing it around from one to the other. Everyone is very much impressed by your experiments and your conclusions and it has proved an interesting topic for discussion at a number of informal gatherings. The paper is very suggestive to anyone interested in chemical theory and awakens a number of attractive speculations. I hope soon to write to you concerning some of these when I have had a chance to look into them more thoroughly.

There is just one item, however, which I would like to speak about at this opportunity. Very probably it has already suggested itself to you or has been pointed out by others. I have not the reprint at hand (it is still circulating) so if I am at fault in my quotations you will please excuse me. As I remember you conclude that since helium is the only apparent product of radioactive disintegration (I mean aside from the final atomic residual), and since the mass of the alpha particle corresponds so closely with the density of helium as obtained from the usual sources, it would be desirable to search for the presence of the X_3 isotope in some non-radioactive mineral like Strutt's beryl, for example. What bothers me is this: If X_3 is produced from the disruption of the oxygen atom as your bombardment experiments would seem to indicate and persists as an isotope of helium, why is it not present in very appreciable amounts in helium from radioactive minerals since these minerals contain oxygen as a prominent constituent, and thorianite and the uraninites are essentially oxides of thorium and uranium respectively? In thorianite and uraninite there are as a minimum two atoms of oxygen to each atom of thorium or uranium, the empirical formula for thorianite being ThO_2 and for uraninite UO_2, although the latter is actually more nearly U_3O_8 in its usual occurrence. Would it not be expected therefore that a certain proportion of the oxygen atoms would be disrupted through bombardment by the alpha particles originating from the disintegration of the uranium or thorium and that any X_3 produced would be found mixed with the Helium which accumulates in the mineral?

I would like to inquire also as to any possible connection between your X_3 and the H_3 of J.J.'s earlier experiments on the deflexion of positive rays. I did not find any reference to the latter in your paper although I was constantly expecting it. I suppose I have ignored some perfectly obvious reason why they are utterly unrelated! Will you enlighten me?

It is certainly refreshing to have ones interest in the ultimate nature of things awakened occasionally and to get away from the narrowing drudgery of teaching the youthful mind how to shoot and to hit something. Not but that teaching has its interest and that the contact with the fine type of young man that we have here is not inspiring. But still there is a good deal of hack work about it and a good deal of wasted energy in our present method of college teaching. But notwithstanding all the talk and all the fine phrases, the thing which our American universities and Yale in particular are able and prepared to pay for is the drill of the class room and not the abstractions of a research laboratory. They do not mind buying exotic plants but they want them to submit to the grafting on of nitrogen fixing tubercles. If they do not, then they receive very little water or fertilizer. You would have found that to have been the case if you had come here when they wanted you.

Things have started out comfortably and we have begun the year's work under generally favourable conditions. Unlike many American universities we are not embarrassed by a large increase in our numbers since the war and our classes now are in general smaller than they were formerly. This is due in part to our rather rigid entrance requirements and undoubtedly to other more subtile causes. Under Hadley our administration has been rather consistently rotten and we have lost some ground as a result of shifting policies. They have got to find a new man for president this year as Hadley is resigning and unless they pick a rotten one it will be some improvement.

I passed an exceptionally fine summer vacation in Maine this year and have come back feeling more fit than ever before. Ernest Brown, one of our professors of mathematics is to spend the first half of the year in Cambridge and will probably have arrived there before this letter reaches you. I believe you know him and you will undoubtedly see something of him. He is stopping at Christ's and is a great friend of Shipley. He is a good friend of mine and can give you lots of information about me if you care to have it. You might tell him at the start that I told you that he was inclined to exaggerate. That will make him more careful to be truthful!

With regards and best wishes to yourself and to Lady Rutherford, I remain, Yours sincerely,

B. B. BOLTWOOD

P.S. Did you take Kay[1] down with you from Manchester? I have often wondered about him. I remember him as so efficient and obliging that I hope you have him with you. If such is the case please remember me to him. Do you know what became of Baumbach? He wrote and wanted a position over here but I naturally could not take him although we could easily find a place for a good glassblower.

1. William Kay, Rutherford's laboratory steward at Manchester.

2 NOVEMBER 1920

Cavendish Laboratory
Cambridge

My dear Boltwood,

I got your good letter of October 13th and make haste to reply before I forget about it. First in regard to your postcript. Kay first of all decided to come to me to Cambridge, but his wife was averse to leaving her friends so I advised him to stay where he was, as I did not want a disgruntled wife interfering with his work. I saw him in Manchester a few months ago; he is much the same as ever but has a great deal of work owing to the great numbers of students in Manchester. Baumbach fortunately was not repatriated, but has started business with his father-in-law in Manchester. I got a note the other day saying that they were prepared to do special glass blowing. I was surprised to hear that Ernest Brown was in Cambridge. I have not seen him but no doubt I shall come across him before long.

The amount of the helium isotope in oxygen is not much more than one in ten thousand of the number of α particles and we should consequently not expect to detect it in the helium from radio-active minerals. J.J.T.'s H_3 has been shown by Aston to have the molecular weight of $3H$. I do not consider that the helium isotope has any connection with it, for I imagine the three hydrogens are in exceedingly close combination forming the nucleus analogous to that of ordinary helium. One would anticipate that the mass would be very nearly three in terms of oxygen and less than that of 3H. We are exceedingly busy all round in the laboratory and I do not get much time during the session for my own work; the counting experiments are so difficult and so many are required that it is not easy to make rapid progress. There are innumerable points to look into to make sure of the facts; fortunately I have a few men helping me in the counting which makes it much easier.

We are all well at home. Eileen is resident in Newnham but drops in several times a day; she is very happy in her new life. J.J.T. is very flourishing and I think enjoys his job as Master of Trinity. He is looking after a number of research students and thus relieves me of what would be an intolerable burden. I am getting an extension of the Laboratory made which I hope to inhabit after Christmas.

With kind regards. Yours very sincerely,

E. RUTHERFORD

Send me Bumstead's address—I suppose he is now in Washington. Kind regards to Zeleny.

30 JANUARY 1921

New Haven, Connecticut

My dear Rutherford,

You will undoubtedly have heard of Bumstead's death but possibly you will not have learned of any of the details. There was a general meeting of the A.A.A.S. in Chicago during the Christmas holidays and Bumstead left Washington just after Christmas, together with R. W. Wood and Augustus Trowbridge,[1] to attend this meeting. He stopped with the Millikans while in Chicago and went through the usual round of conferences, meetings and social festivities which are characteristic of these occasions. On the afternoon of December 31st, with Vernon Kellogg who is the secretary of the Research Council, he started back on a night train for Washington. According to Kellogg he was not apparently tired or worn out, but was in his usual health and in good spirits. They had dinner together, sat for a time in the smoking compartment and then turned in to their berths at an early hour. They occupied berths which were directly opposite each other, and rather late next morning, when the "last call" for breakfast was announced, Kellogg got up and called to Bumstead. He received no answer and crossing over the aisle he pushed back the curtains on Bumstead's berth and soon discovered that he was lifeless. He had apparently died very quietly and peacefully some hours before. The body was taken on to Washington and brought to New Haven on the following Tuesday. As no autopsy was performed the cause of death was not definitely established, but there appeared to be every reason to assume that it was due to heart failure.

Mrs. Bumstead with the two children and other members of the family came to New Haven on Tuesday and they were fortunate in having the Bumstead house placed at their disposal. The house had been rented during their absence from New Haven. The funeral services were held on Wednesday morning from the College Chapel and the body was cremated in Springfield. Mrs. Bumstead returned later to Washington where she still is and will be for a short time longer. Then she will go out to Illinois for a few weeks and return here later, probably about the end of February. She naturally feels terribly cut up for she simply doted on Harry and she really spent most of her time in taking care of him. Now that this responsibility is gone she feels quite lost without it. I think she will come around all right in the end, but she is really a much more impressionable and sensitive person than one would think from her general appearance and manner. I think she would undoubtedly appreciate getting a few lines from you and if you have not already done so wont you just send her a note of condolence? If you address it to 45 Edgehill Road, this city, it will be sure to reach her.

Of course Bumstead's death means a lot more to me than it does to most other people. We have been such intimate friends for such a long, long time that it certainly seems queer not to be able to look forward to seeing him again. Of course his having been over in England two years ago and then this year in Washington has made a sort of a break and the change is not so abrupt as would have been if I had been with him more continuously. But, as you must have noticed, he was the sort of a person with whom you could just begin where you had left off and I always looked forward to talking things over with him with so much pleasure. I was not so much surprised as I was shocked when I heard of his death. He has always been so sort of fragile and delicate that the idea of his dropping off at almost any old time has often occured to me. I think that his experience in London was a good deal more of a strain than he ever acknowledged and I think it took something out of him which he did not get back afterward.

Things here in the University are certainly in a fine state of affairs just at present. Our Corporation is labouring to select a successor to our distinguished President—and we underlings are all praying that a mouse may not be born! They do not seem able to decide on anyone who can fill the place and who will accept the job, a necessary requirement if the eggs are ever to be unscrambled! There is much talk of the Reverend Dr. Anson Phelps Stokes, for many years secretary to the University, a time server and a sycophant, but he seems to be a sort of last choice although a very obvious one. Yale, like many of the other endowed universities of the East, is financially on the rocks and the wild and futile gestures of the present pilot are not helping matters. Hadley is simply hopeless these days and reminds one of a decapitated chicken flopping about the barnyard. We have had a dose of so-called reorganization and some how it is not digesting well in our interior. The little Mazarin of the Scientific School is still effectively pursuing his Machiavellian policy of casting the monkey wrench into the machinery. In the chemistry department we are confronted by the necessity of saving less than three thousand dollars on our salary budget on the one hand and of spending a couple of million on the erection of a palatial new laboratory on the other!!

It is a relief occasionally to get out of the Beehive, where one is always getting *stung* for trying to do things, and read a little science. Thank you ever so much for your letter setting me right on that question of the disruption of oxygen in uraninites. I certainly was off on my "order of magnitude" in that case (the kind of a mistake which I deplore more than any other). It is harder than I thought for a chemist to conceive of atoms as "mostly voids" even though he is willing to heartily accept the idea when it has been made clear to him. Can you make any sense out of the papers by Harkins?[2] I have tried to read a number of them and they only make me dizzy. Should I persevere or are they mostly foolishness? Our friend Soddy obtained a lot of notoriety in the American press not long ago because of his alleged refusal to have anything to do with gas warfare! Was he really guilty of reprehensible behavior?

We had a very interesting public lecture here last week given by E. F. Slosson,[3] a man who recently wrote a book on "Creative Chemistry" which has attracted much attention. I wonder if you have read it, the book, I mean, for if you have not you must do so. I once had the pleasure of introducing Slosson to you in Manchester around 1910, when he was in England looking over some of the provincial universities. Do you happen to remember? His lecture here was on the subject of the progress of mankind as related to the second law of thermodynamics. The title was: "The Fall of Energy and the Rise of Man." It was really exceedingly interesting and very entertaining, one of the very best lectures I ever remember having heard. He speaks well and has a very simple way of putting forward scientific facts. He also has a very strong sense of humor. You will be interested to know that he has been put in charge of a sort of news bureau established with a large endowment by the National Research Council. This bureau is to collect, prepare and distribute in a popular form all kinds of scientific information to the press of the country. The idea is the education of the public and the awakening of public interest in science. It is a rather utopian scheme but I think if anyone can put it over it will be Slosson.

You will, I dare say, be interested to know as to what plans are under way for filling the place left vacant by the death of Bumstead. There are nominally two vacancies now in physics in Yale College because of Nichols' withdrawal. So far as I can discover there is no present intention of filling either of these posts, the reasons being first the financial shortage (neither of the professorships is endowed) and second a determination on Chittenden's part to eliminate all science from the College and segregate it in the Scientific School. The first and most obvious step in this plan is to block a new appointment in the College— and this he is doing through the President in a way that is quite effectual. He is, and has for the past three years been, doing his best to get me squeezed out since I am a College representative and am openly opposed to his schemes. But so far I have managed to block him and have even gone directly to the Corporation with a protest against his interference. But if you hear of anyone being approached with a view to their accepting an appointment in physics in this institution, warn them to get a good insight into the various aspects of the situation before making the dive—or they may come to the surface in an altogether strange environment.

Well, I hope things are going well with you and that you have gotten out a lot of new and exciting discoveries since I last heard from you. If that is true then let me hear of them just as soon as you can conveniently do so. I have just recently been reminded of that delightful motor trip through Tyrol with you in 1913 by reading a very entertaining book "Tyrol" by

W. A. Baillie-Grohman with charming illustrations by E. H. Compton. I wonder whether Lady Rutherford has ever seen it, for if she has not and will let me know I shall be glad to send it to her.

With kindest regards and best wishes, Yours sincerely,

B. B. BOLTWOOD

1. Augustus Trowbridge was one of the large number of Americans who received advanced training in Germany around the turn of the century. After several years at Wisconsin, he became professor of physics at Princeton where he remained for the rest of his career.

2. William D. Harkins, professor of physical chemistry at the University of Chicago, is credited with a wide range of significant predictions: existence of the neutron and of heavy hydrogen (deuterium), the whole number rule of atomic masses and the related idea of packing fraction, the concept of a compound nucleus as a step in transformation, the possibility of artificial radioactivity, and the nuclear-shell picture for the structure of the atom's core. For the most part, his views seemed to be ahead of the times, and even when experimental confirmation came later, he was denied real credit. From his efforts to acquire recognition he did acquire the title of "Priority Harkins." In the field of experimental work he again had the ability to see the scientifically significant, and was among the first to achieve nuclear transformations using neutrons.

3. Edwin E. Slosson in 1921 became director of the newly founded Science Service.

28 FEBRUARY 1921

Cavendish Laboratory
Cambridge

My dear Boltwood,

I was very glad to get your long letter, especially the details about poor Bumstead's death. I had, of course, heard of it sometime before and had written to Mrs. Bumstead c/o The University, and I hope she has received my letter. I quite agree with you that Bumstead was an unusually fine fellow and one with whom one always felt in sympathy. I quite agree that he possessed that peculiar power of carrying on one's friendship even after long intervals of separation. I can quite appreciate that Mrs. Bumstead will feel his loss unusually keenly for she had practically devoted herself to looking after his health for the last ten years.

I was very interested to hear about the doings of Yale, but am somewhat surprised that the Mazarin you refer to is still so energetic. I should have thought that his peculiar diet would have interfered with his activity long ago, but possibly the production of bile is an accompaniment of the said diet.

As to ourselves we are all well, and Eileen is enjoying herself at Newnham. She has had some trouble with her eyes but I think this will soon be remedied; she is a very keen student and also a vigorous dancer which will serve to keep the balance even.

By the way you mention a book on the Tyrol by Baillie Grohman; my wife tells me she has not seen it and would be very glad if you could send it to her. She and Eileen are hoping to take a trip in the Italian Lakes this Easter, but my engagements will not allow me to join them. I am going over to the Solvay Conference in Brussels at the end of March where we will discuss the properties of electrons and the structure of the atom. The only German invited is Einstein, who is considered for this purpose to be international. Bohr comes from Copenhagen. Later on he is coming over to Cambridge to give a course of six lectures on his subject and no doubt will stay with us during that period. I happen to know he is just publishing a theory on the 'Constitution of the Atom,' which is much more physical and more general than Langmuir's [1] 'Statical Atom.'

You speak about Harkins. Yes, he writes at great length on every topic but as a whole is moderately sound from my point of view. Actually, however, most of the ideas on which they are based have been common property in this country and especially to myself for the last five years. It is exceedingly easy to write about these matters but exceedingly difficult to get experimental evidence to form a correct decision. The work of Aston and, if I may say so, my own afford the only positive data on which to base a conclusion. However Harkins is a man of intelligence, but I wish he did more experimenting and spent less time in theorising and in endeavouring to cover every possible idea.

You will be interested to hear that I have made some progress on the general question of the disintegration of elements. Chadwick and I have been hard at work and we find that a number of elements like nitrogen, boron, aluminium, fluorine, and phosphorus emit long range particles under an alpha ray bombardment. These particles go much further than ordinary H. atoms under the same conditions, showing that the effect cannot possibly be due to the presence of any hydrogen or hydrogen compound in material under examination. The range of these particles is very great; in the case of aluminium it is at least three times that of the normal H. atom. If these, as they probably are, prove to be hydrogen nuclei their energy of motion is even greater than that of the incident alpha particle. I shall probably publish a brief account of this in *Nature* [2] shortly, but I thought you would be interested to hear about it. Apparently no element whose atomic mass is given by 4n where n is a whole number gives any effect but only those whose masses are given by 4n + 2 or 4n + 3. This is an indication that the 4n elements are built up of helium and the others of helium plus hydrogen nuclei, satellites of the centre nucleus. You also will be interested to hear that Aston and G. Thomson [3] have just shown that lithium has two isotopes 6 and 7.[4] The rush to determine the isotopes goes on apace. Harkins is always saying what he is going to do but apparently no results except statements follow. Dempster [5] of Chicago seems to have done magnesium well.

You will be interested to know that I am now a member of

the University Council and so have a good deal of general business on my hands. However I keep pretty fit and manage to keep my own work going somehow. Yours very sincerely,

E. RUTHERFORD

Kind regards to Zeleny.

1. Irving Langmuir, the Brooklyn-born Nobel Prize winner, received his Ph.D. degree from the University of Göttingen in 1906 before beginning a lifetime association with the General Electric Company research laboratory in Schenectady, New York.

2. ER and Chadwick, "The disintegration of elements by α-particles," *Nature, 107* (10 March 1921), 41.

3. George Paget Thomson, later professor of physics at Aberdeen and then Imperial College of Science and Technology, received the Nobel Prize in 1937 for showing that electrons have wave characteristics. Coincidentally, his famous father, "J. J.," received his Nobel Prize thirty-one years earlier for detecting the particle nature of electrons. In 1952 the younger Thomson was elected master of Corpus Christi College, Cambridge, in which post he served for ten years.

4. F. W. Aston and G. P. Thomson, "The constitution of lithium," *Nature, 106* (24 Feb. 1921), 827–28.

5. Arthur J. Dempster was yet another 1851 Exhibition Scholar from Canada. After receipt of his Ph.D. degree from the University of Chicago in 1916, he joined the faculty there, rising eventually to professor of physics.

14 JULY 1921

Hancock Point, Maine

My dear Rutherford,

Well, here I am out in the country once more with all the dust and heat of New Haven behind me and all the trials and tribulations of the last academic year almost forgotten. I came up here on the 25th of June after an exceedingly eventful year at New Haven.

At last we are free of the sinister influence of Hadley and Stokes! It really seems too good to be true and sometimes I am inclined to pinch myself in order to be sure that I am not only dreaming. Our new president [1] took up his duties on the first of July. You can take my word for it that he is a very different person from his predecessor. He is a plain speaker, a clear thinker, intellectually honest and possessing plenty of moral courage. Any one of these characteristics would serve to distinguish him from the late incumbent of the office. He has a great sense of humor, and is the kind of a man who makes you feel that you know him well when you first meet him.

I have never known greater and more general approval to be expressed over any appointment than over Angell's. Even the old dyed-in-the-wool moss backs of the faculty were pleased and satisfied when the appointment was finally announced and agreed that no mistake had been made in choosing a non-Yale man, since they had selected such a fine one. The faculties were satisfied, the undergraduates were satisfied, the alumni were satisfied and all of the members of rival institutions I have had a chance to talk with seem to think that we have got the best man obtainable. We were led to believe toward the end of the campaign that the choice lay between Angell and Henry Sloane Coffin, a prominent divine of New York, who has had no experience in educational administration and is simply a spellbinder. For some unknown reason, it must have been the intervention of providence, the Corporation showed good judgement and selected Angell. There were many prayers and supplications indulged in by some of us during this period and they certainly were answered.

Stokes dropped out of the running sometime before the end. I was glad to have an opportunity for reducing his chances by talking plainly with a couple of members of the Corporation during the critical period. He was later considered as a candidate for election to the Corporation but I think that this is no longer probable. I trust that we are through with him forever

You must have been amused at all the furor created by the visit of Madame Curie to this country. I have saved up a lot of newspaper clippings which I intend to send you, but I left them in my desk at New Haven. In anticipation of her coming the various scientific societies appointed committees to welcome her. I was appointed for the American Chemical Society to serve on a committee with a number of others. I wrote to the Secretary and respectfully declined the honor (giving a few reasons) but I thought it best to withdraw my resignation later when I found that my action was likely to be misunderstood and to cause some hard feeling. Not long afterwards I was informed that the Madame had expressed a particular desire to visit New Haven and call on me, so I went over to the Secretary's office and informed Stokes that I had no desire to have the honor thrust upon me and that I considered that it was the duty of the institution to entertain her. He then told me that at an earlier meeting the Corporation on the recommendation of a couple of medical men had voted the Madame an honorary degree of Doctor of Science! He seemed very much disappointed when I told him that I thought they had been a little hasty in their action. One might have supposed that they would have consulted some of the people who were supposed to know something about the candidate! [2] That is to say that someone who was ignorant of the way the administration did things might have supposed so.

I saw the Madame first at a luncheon given in her honor in New York shortly after she landed. Then I saw her again at New Haven when she came for Commencement. Kovarik and I had her for a couple of hours at the Sloane Laboratory and I was quite pleasantly surprised to find that she was quite keen about scientific matters and in an unusually amiable mood, although she is in very poor physical condition and was on the verge of a breakdown all the time she was over here. She has learned a lot of English since we saw her in Brussels and gets along quite well in a conversation. She certainly made a good clean up over here and took back a gram of radium and quite a tidy number of thousands of dollars.[3] But I felt sorry for the poor old girl, she was a distinctly pathetic figure. She was very modest and un-assuming, and she seemed frightened at all the fuss the people made over her.

Thank heaven, Yale did not give Einstein a degree. We escaped that by a narrow margin. If he had been over here as a scientist and not as a Zionist it would have been entirely appro-priate, but under the circumstances I think it would have been a mistake. I would have been glad to have seen Weizmann but although he was in New Haven and tried to get into touch with me, I was out of town at the time and so I missed him. I remem-ber him pleasantly because of the Manchester associations.

Our new chemical laboratory is about to be started and I am expecting to hear any day that work has been commenced on the excavation. The plans are complete in all the essential de-tails and I think it is going to be quite a fine plant when it is completed. If we are lucky it will be ready for occupancy in Oc-tober 1922 and we are planning to have quite a ceremony when it is formally dedicated. John Johnston and I have a little scheme which is based on the hope that we may be able to per-suade you to be our leading feature on that occasion, so you must keep the prospect in mind and give it your kind considera-tion. It is time for you to be thinking of visiting this country again where you have so many friends and admirers. If our scheme goes through it will give you the necessary excuse and justification for leaving Cambridge for a few weeks during term time.

Gus Trowbridge is spending the summer here with his fam-ily. He tells me that he saw you in Cambridge this spring. I envy him his good fortune.

I hope that your work is progressing as steadily as ever. I was greatly interested in the details which you gave me in your last letter and I read the communication to Nature with much pleasure. You certainly are opening up a wonderful field of possibilities.

Just before I left New Haven I sent Lady Rutherford the book about the Tyrol which I mentioned in an earlier letter. I hope it has reached her safely.

We are having very hot weather in most of the sections of this country, but here it is always cool and the present season is no exception. I see in the daily papers that England and much of Europe is experiencing a severe drought and am reminded of 1911 when I was over there and it seemed to be as dry as it possibly could be. Is it possible that it is really worse this year?

With regards and best wishes, Yours very sincerely,

B. B. BOLTWOOD

The appointment of Nichols to the head of the Tech.[4] was a surprise to many, myself included! Not exactly a pleasant surprise to some of the Tech. people!

1. James Rowland Angell, a noted psychologist, had earlier been professor and department head, as well as dean and acting president of the University of Chicago. In the two years immediately prior to his appointment at Yale, he was chairman of the National Research Council and president of the Carnegie Corporation.

2. Boltwood was against Yale's award to Marie Curie of an honorary degree because he considered her scientific work not to warrant it. He felt that her creative period had ended about 1903, and that her more recent fame was based on the facts that she was one of the few women in science and had gained much sympathy when her husband was killed in a traffic accident. To this must be added the circumstance that Boltwood knew her only as a relatively nonproductive investigator whose taciturn personality made international cooperation difficult. The Yale Corporation, of course, was merely taking the first opportunity to honor her for *all* her past work. Several other American colleges and universities also bestowed honorary degrees upon Madame Curie, although Yale's great rival, Harvard, for some reason saw fit only to hold a reception for her.

3. On the initiative of the editor of a woman's magazine, approximately $100,000 was collected in the United States to purchase one gram of

radium as a gift to the discoverer of this element. Marie Curie crossed the Atlantic in 1921 to receive this gift from President Harding, and made a triumphant, though exhausting, tour of the country.

4. Ernest Fox Nichols, appointed president of the Massachusetts Institute of Technology.

20 AUGUST [1921]

Dear Mr Boltwood,

You must forgive me for not writing sooner to thank you for the charming book on Tyrol you sent me; the sketches make one long to go back there. I hope we shall some day. I have had a very busy life the last year. Eileen had trouble with her eyes necessitating not using them at all for reading for about 8 months. As she is at Newnham all her work had to be read to her, by a reader & me, & all her sewing. Now she is able to use them but has to be careful—ciliary spasm was the trouble. I dont know if Ernest has told you she is engaged to be married to Ralph Fowler [1] a Fellow of Trinity & a great pal of all of us. It happened in June. I had been very interested in watching it for a couple of months before. At first they planned to be married next June, but have recently decided Xmas is long enough. So now they will be married about Dec 12, go for a ten days honeymoon & then to Switzerland for winter sports with the same party as she went with last year.

R. is a splendid fellow, everyone loves & respects him. He is a mathematician aged 32, about 6 ft 1″ & weighs 15 stone. She is 20½ & about 5 ft 3½, wears her hair bobbed like all the girls now. I enclose a snapshot of them. Ern asked her if R. liked something the other day & she said "If I had a wart on my nose he'd think it was beautiful!" Homes are almost impossible to get, so I am hunting hard. They are away with his people in Wales, & on Monday Ern & I meet them at Grantham in the car, on our way up to Glencoe in Scottish Highlands where R. is one of a climbing party. He is very good at it—I wish he weren't. Also he is a crack golfer. Then we come back & spend a fortnight together in Yorkshire, high up on a heather moor. We love our home here. It is a delightful old house. Ive run out of all but a bad snapshot but will send you a better one for a Xmas card. The trees in the lawn are about 100 years old. It is mainly lawn & trees, flowers dont do well. A pretty veg. garden at the side. When are you coming over to stay with us? Yours very sincerely,

MARY RUTHERFORD

1. Originally a pure mathematician, Ralph Fowler became interested in applied mathematics and theoretical physics and it was in these fields that he did his most significant work. In 1920 he was appointed a lecturer at Trinity College and twelve years later became the first Plummer Professor of Mathematical Physics at Cambridge. He was the recipient of the Adams Prize and other honors, and delivered the Bakerian Lecture in 1935. In 1938 he was appointed director of the National Physical Laboratory, but illness prevented his taking up these duties and the post then went to C. G. Darwin. Though in poor health, Fowler served the government on several committees and missions during World War II, but died a year before the end of hostilities.

8 FEBRUARY [1922]

Dear Mr. Boltwood,

Thank you very much indeed for the delightful little bracelet watch you have given me, I do so like its quaint unusual shape. In fact it is just what I wanted to help me away from formal dinner parties! Again, with many thanks for the charming present.[1] Yours sincerely,

EILEEN FOWLER

1. Boltwood was invited to the wedding of Eileen Rutherford and Ralph Fowler, which took place in the Trinity College Chapel on 6 December 1921, but was unable to attend. The watch was his wedding gift to Eileen. The Fowlers had four children prior to Eileen's early death in 1930.

30 MAY 1922

My dear Boltwood,

I recognise your handiwork in the invitation from Angell to give the Silliman Lectures next year. It is a pity but I cannot go. I am bound to the wheel into my Laboratory, Royal Institution Lectures & prospective President of the British Association at Liverpool in August 1923. I should very much like to be free to spend a few weeks in Yale again & regain some of the enthusiasm of my lost youth, but life for me is very busy in these days & I have to drive the 'boys' along. I am, however, fitter than I have been for years & bear up nobly under the strain. Cambridge suits me well alround & even the presence of the Master of Trinity in the Lab adds a fillip to life. He is as keen as a youngster still & is still searching for a 'bahn-brechende' scientific event as in the old days. I have got a very good group of researchers together—but too many of them—& it is a business to get sufficient apparatus & ideas to keep them going strong. The whole family including Fowler go off for 3 weeks in the Dolomites on June 20 & we hope to have a pleasant holiday. The young people are very keen to go while I am of course quite blasé, but will bring up the tail of the procession with my wife at the head. She does all the work while I like a normal man adopt a passivistic pose.

When are you coming over to England again? You would thoroughly enjoy Cambridge at this time of the year while there would be ample opportunity to refresh your thirst.

As to my own research, we keep going on the counting slowly but other elements prove very coy in yielding up their secrets. We are making much progress in α & β & γ rays & hope to get to know something of the nucleus before long. Give my regards to Zeleny & Kovarik. Yours ever,

E. RUTHERFORD

20 FEBRUARY 1924

Cavendish Laboratory
Cambridge

My dear Boltwood,

I am thinking of buying either Radiothorium or Mesothorium to the value of about £200, to supplement the quantity which McCoy kindly sent me. Can you give me any information whether either of these are now produced in the U.S.A. and whether they can be bought at reasonable prices. I have had quotations for small quantities here, and the price seems much higher than it ought to be considering the short life of these preparations. I suppose McCoy is now entirely out of the business. Can you give me his address?

We are all very well and flourishing, and work is going along in good style. We have been disintegrating a few new elements and will publish the results in due course. I am kept very busy in a multitude of ways but manage to keep fairly fit. We went for a holiday in the Italian Riviera at Xmas, and had a good deal of sunshine. I will be over in Canada early in August and will probably spend a little time in the U.S.A. before my return. I may hope to come across you. You seem to have entirely deserted this side.

The break in the exchange in Paris is the healthiest sign we have seen in Europe for some time for it is the only thing that will bring the French to take a reasonable view of their importance in the world. I have no doubt they will blame us for it, but I imagine it is inherent in their present inability to balance their budget.

As you see, our Labour Government is as mild as milk, and the Conservative party is already purring over the situation. I myself wish they had a little more independence.[1] Yours sincerely,

E. RUTHERFORD

P.S. I am now a grandfather one year old, so an added respect is due on this account. The youngster [2] flourishes.

1. This is one of Rutherford's rare remarks on a political topic. Though liberally inclined, he seems not to have taken much interest in political issues.

2. Peter Fowler, now professor of physics at the University of Bristol.

16 APRIL 1924

My dear Boltwood,

I heard recently from Kovarik, who hopes to come to Cambridge next session, that you had been knocked out for the time & had gone south for a rest. I hope your trouble is not serious & you are fit again by this time. Why don't you take a complete change & come over to England for part of the summer at any rate? We should be delighted to have you here in Cambridge which I think would amuse you & you could study the Laboratory & laboratory people in your spare time. We should be glad to put you up for a few days while you were fixing up comfortable rooms for yourself. I have not seen you since 1917 & you ought to get in the habit of making an annual trek as in the old days.

We—the whole family minus the grandson—go to the B.A. meeting at Toronto. My wife, Eileen & Fowler with some friends then go on to the Rockies for a few weeks & after a stay in Montreal return home. I shall probably attend the Centennial for the Franklin Institute about Sept 17–19. We started off for a motor holiday about a week ago, staying at the Schusters' enroute but my wife went down with 'flu' & a temperature; so I left her there & went on with Chadwick by motor to Somerset &

returned to bring her back to Cambridge to convalesce. Eileen is also ill with the same trouble, so both our households are feeling limp. This has been an unending winter but I try to keep fit in spite of an excess of work. Write & tell me yours news. I believe Mrs. Bumstead is coming to Cambridge in June. Yours ever,

E. RUTHERFORD

The grandson Peter is worth a visit for himself!

7 JUNE 1924

Kenilworth Inn
Biltmore, North Carolina

My dear Rutherford,

Your welcome letter of April 16 reached me in Chapel Hill, N.C., where I have been staying for about five months in order to get away from the New Haven atmosphere and environment. For about six months last year, beginning about the end of June, I had a very rotten time of it due to overwork and the neglect of reasonable precautions to preserve a proper equilibrium of mind and body. For a time I was not very much interested in life, liberty or the pursuit of happiness, but I finally got straightened out and came down South for the winter to regain my composure. Unless I am much mistaken and the indications I notice are deceptive, I have succeeded admirably, and for some time past I have been greatly enjoying myself and making progress in every direction. I was more than fortunate, too, in getting away when I did, for the spring in the North has been exceptionally cold and disagreeable, while here it has been delightful ever since the first of April. Chapel Hill is the seat of the University of North Carolina, but of the inner workings of that institution I saw little and cared less. What I was looking for was a change of surroundings and I succeeded in finding something which was altogether different [in] this community. It is a beautiful locality, there are a good many sights to see and my friend [1] is providing considerable entertainment and diversion. I expect to stay here for about a week longer and shall then wend my way back to New England.

I am planning to sail for your side of the Atlantic on the 12th of July on the Homeric. Just what my plans will be and where I shall go when I get there is very indefinite at the present moment. I am going over particularly to be with some very good friends of mine by the name of Green, who are planning to wander around southern France and the Pyrenees. Mrs. Green sails in June with their three children and Mr. Green sails at the same time as I do, on the Homeric. I sincerely hope that I can disembark at Southampton and get a chance to run up to spend a few days with you at Cambridge, but that possibility can not be decided until I have had a chance to see the Greens and talk matters over. We all return on the Veendam of the Holland American Line on the seventeenth of September.

You can well believe that I have had very little opportunity to pick up the threads of radio-activity and electronics, which have ravelled a good deal since I have been so distracted by other matters, but I have read a little during the winter and among other things looked over the new LEHRBUCH DER RADIO-AKTIVITAT by Hevesy and Paneth. I thought it was exceedingly well done and that the subject was presented in a very novel and lucid manner. In fact, I strongly advised Macmillan to publish an English translation. I feel sure that you have seen it and I wonder what you think of it.

Your earlier letter asking about sources of Mesothorium was finally forwarded to me, and I intended to answer it long ago. I have little doubt but that H. S. Miner of the Wellsbach Company of Gloucester City, N. J., can provide you with what you need at a reasonable figure. There are no other sources that I happen to know of at the present.

I have great difficulty in picturing you as a grandfather, and I have no doubt but that Lady Rutherford would seriously object to my addressing you by that title. She used to think it wasn't proper for me to call you "father!" I hope you maintain a proper dignity in keeping with your responsibilities.

You will perhaps have seen Mrs. Bumstead before you receive this letter. If you see her afterward please give her my very best regards and tell her I am quite myself again.

You will have heard of the death of Nichols which occured under such dramatic circumstances at the meeting of the National Academy.[2] I had seriously considered going up to the meeting and had decided not to at the last minute, but I was very glad I did not go when I learned of what had happened.

When I see you again, which I hope now will not be long, either on this side of the Atlantic or the other one, I shall have a lot to tell you and I hope many things that will amuse you. I have had some rather humorous experiences since we last were together.

With the very best of wishes to all, Yours sincerely,

BERTRAM B. BOLTWOOD

1. Probably Joseph Hyde Pratt, who until 1906 was Boltwood's partner in a mining engineering–consulting chemistry company. At this time Pratt was professor of economic geology at the University of North Carolina.

2. Nichols collapsed and died while giving a paper at the National Academy of Sciences' spring meeting.

23 JULY 1924

Cavendish Laboratory
Cambridge

My dear Boltwood,

I am very sorry to hear that I will not be able to see you on your journey this time, but I hope for better luck another year.

I will be traveling in the Eastern States probably early in September and will finish up at the centennial celebrations in Philadelphia on Sep 17–19.

I then return to Montreal and sail on the 26th, so it just looks as if we would miss one another at both ends.

The family are all very well and I am very busy trying to get things cleared up before I leave. With kind regards, In haste,

E. RUTHERFORD

Appendix: The Radioactive Decay Series

Radioelement	Corresponding Element	Symbol	Radiation	Half-Life
Uranium I ↓	Uranium	^{238}U	α	4.51×10^9 yr
Uranium X₁ ↓	Thorium	^{234}Th	β	24.1 days
Uranium X₂* ↓	Protactinium	^{234}Pa	β	1.18 min
Uranium II ↓	Uranium	^{234}U	α	2.48×10^5 yr
Ionium ↓	Thorium	^{230}Th	α	8.0×10^4 yr
Radium ↓	Radium	^{226}Ra	α	1.62×10^3 yr
Ra Emanation ↓	Radon	^{222}Rn	α	3.82 days
Radium A 99.98% | 0.02%	Polonium	^{218}Po	α and β	3.05 min
Radium B	Lead	^{214}Pb	β	26.8 min
Astatine-218	Astatine	^{218}At	α	2 sec
Radium C 99.96% | 0.04%	Bismuth	^{214}Bi	β and α	19.7 min
Radium C′	Polonium	^{214}Po	α	1.6×10^{-4} sec
Radium C″	Thallium	^{210}Tl	β	1.32 min
Radium D ↓	Lead	^{210}Pb	β	19.4 yr
Radium E ~100% | 2×10^{-4}%	Bismuth	^{210}Bi	β and α	5.0 days
Radium F	Polonium	^{210}Po	α	138.4 days
Thallium-206	Thallium	^{206}Tl	β	4.20 min
Radium G (End Product)	Lead	^{206}Pb	Stable	—

* Uranium X₂ is an excited state of ^{234}Pa and undergoes isomeric transition (§ 10.147) to a small extent to form uranium Z (^{234}Pa in its ground state); the latter has a half-life of 6.7 hr, emitting beta radiation and forming uranium II (^{234}U).

1. Reproduced with the author's and publisher's permission from Samuel Glasstone's *Sourcebook on Atomic Energy* (Third Edition), pp. 152–54; Copyright 1967, D. Van Nostrand Company, Inc., Princeton, New Jersey.

Appendix

THE THORIUM SERIES

Radioelement	Corresponding Element	Symbol	Radiation	Half-Life
Thorium ↓	Thorium	^{232}Th	α	1.39×10^{10} yr
Mesothorium I ↓	Radium	^{228}Ra	β	6.7 yr
Mesothorium II ↓	Actinium	^{228}Ac	β	6.13 hr
Radiothorium ↓	Thorium	^{228}Th	α	1.91 yr
Thorium X ↓	Radium	^{224}Ra	α	3.64 days
Th Emanation ↓	Radon	^{220}Rn	α	52 sec
Thorium A ↓	Polonium	^{216}Po	α	0.16 sec
Thorium B ↓	Lead	^{212}Pb	β	10.6 hr
Thorium C 66.3% | 33.7%	Bismuth	^{212}Bi	β and α	60.5 min
Thorium C′	Polonium	^{212}Po	α	3×10^{-7} sec
Thorium C″	Thallium	^{208}Tl	β	3.1 min
Thorium D (End Product)	Lead	^{208}Pb	Stable	—

Appendix

Radioelement	Corresponding Element	Symbol	Radiation	Half-Life
Actinouranium ↓	Uranium	^{235}U	α	7.13×10^8 yr
Uranium Y ↓	Thorium	^{231}Th	β	25.6 hr
Protactinium ↓	Protactinium	^{231}Pa	α	3.43×10^4 yr
Actinium 98.8% | 1.2%	Actinium	^{227}Ac	β and α	21.8 yr
Radioactinium	Thorium	^{227}Th	α	18.4 days
Actinium K	Francium	^{223}Fr	β	21 min
Actinium X ↓	Radium	^{223}Ra	α	11.7 days
Ac Emanation ↓	Radon	^{219}Rn	α	3.92 sec
Actinium A ~100% | ~5 × 10⁻⁴%	Polonium	^{215}Po	α and β	1.83×10^{-3} sec
Actinium B	Lead	^{211}Pb	β	36.1 min
Astatine-215	Astatine	^{215}At	α	$\sim 10^{-4}$ sec
Actinium C 99.7% | 0.3%	Bismuth	^{211}Bi	α and β	2.16 min
Actinium C'	Polonium	^{211}Po	α	0.52 sec
Actinium C''	Thallium	^{207}Tl	β	4.8 min
Actinium D (End Product)	Lead	^{207}Pb	Stable	—

Index

Aachen, Technische Hochschule, 140 n 6

Aberdeen University, 32 n 4, 344 n 3

Abraham, Max, 193, 197 n 5

Académie des Sciences (France), 90, 243, 244 n 6

Accelerators, 11, 331 n 3

Actinium, 15, 59, 77, 80, 89, 108, 110, 147, 153, 165, 202, 239, 240; series position, 15, 17, 20, 64 n 1, 89, 142-55 passim, 160 n 3, 163 n 3, 185, 188, 193, 206, 265; discovery, 25, 83 n 8, 160 n 2, 168 n 5; activity, 62-65, 84, 88, 90, 91 n 1, 120, 122, 148; treatment, 80, 158, 166-67, 172-73, 177-78, 246-48

Active deposit, 45, 65, 175, 246, 264-65

Adelaide, University of, 92 n 3

Admiralty Laboratories (Great Britain), 315 n 5

Aeschynite. See Minerals

Air, radioactivity of. See Atmospheric radioactivity

Alberta, University of, 222 n 3

Allanite. See Minerals

Alpha ray or particle. See Radiation

American Association for the Advancement of Science, 336

American Chemical Society, 67 n 1, 87, 191, 346

American Journal of Science, 33, 46, 74, 75, 82, 100, 106 n 4, 122 n 1, 129, 134, 138, 139 n 3, 143, 180, 182, 183, 232, 269

American Physical Society, 108, 113, 114, 115, 134, 135 n 4, 139 n 3, 149-51, 191, 196, 228, 232

American Scandinavian Foundation, 285, 328

Ames, Joseph Sweetman, 191, 197 nn 1, 2

Anderson, Carl, 237 n 5

Andrade, Edward Neville da Costa, 5, 293, 295 n 2, 301, 302, 307, 310

Angell, James Rowland, 345, 348 n 1, 351

Antonoff, George, 243, 244 n 7, 250

Appleton, Edward Victor, 11

Arrhenius, Svante, 205, 208 n 3

Aston, Frederick W., 330, 331 n 2, 335, 343

Atmospheric radioactivity, 25, 36, 38, 89 n 2, 116 n 1, 154, 272

Atomic mass, 343

Atomic number, 268 n 11

Atomic physics, 8, 21. *See also* Atomic structure

Atomic structure, 2, 7, 10, 21, 85-86, 197 n 7, 220, 235, 242, 244 n 3, 246, 247 n 2, 268 n 10, 292, 330, 331 n 3, 339, 341 n 2, 342, 351

Atomic weight, 158, 259 n 4, 268 n 11, 286 n 2, 310

Index

Bronson, Howard L., 68, 69 n 1, 84, 88, 136, 139, 140, 157, 183, 184, 206

Brooks, Harriet, 300, 301 n 1

Brown, Ernest, 298, 300 n 2, 334, 335

Brown University, 183 n 7, 298

Bryn Mawr College, Pa., 113 n 5, 228, 230 n 18, 307, 307 n 2, 310

Budapest, University of, 267 n 4

Bumstead, Henry Andrews, 77, 108, 113 n 5, 132, 136-40 passim, 146, 150, 160, 165, 169, 171, 181, 184, 202, 215, 228, 237, 244, 246, 267, 280-82 passim, 298, 303, 311, 314, 315, 322, 324, 354, 356; biographical, 12, 141, 193, 210, 231, 233 n 2, 260-62 passim, 274, 295, 316, 324 n 2, 336-38, 341-42; Yale activities, 12, 15, 60-61, 64, 69 n 1, 74, 75, 115, 121, 122, 218, 220, 305, 340; miscellaneous scientific activities, 25, 36, 58, 76 n 2, 82, 86, 89, 113, 124, 195, 196, 232, 240, 327, 331

Bureau of Standards (United States), 67 n 1

Cairo Government Medical School, 219 n 1

California, University of, at Berkeley, 140 n 1

California Institute of Technology, 230 n 18

Callendar, Hugh L., 155 n 7

Cambridge University, 9, 86 n 5, 105 n 1, 116 n 1, 152 n 1, 256 n 4, 267 n 2, 307, 312, 324, 325, 330, 332 n 4, 334, 342, 344, 350

n 1, 351, 353. *See also* Cavendish Laboratory

Campbell, Norman R., 179, 224, 224 n 5

Canterbury College, New Zealand, 9

Cardiff, University of, 267 n 2

Carnegie benefactions, 50 n 2, 89 n 4, 213, 246, 348 n 1

Carnotite. *See* Minerals

Cassel Cyanide Co., Glasgow, 272 n 2

Cathode rays, 2, 3, 5, 283 nn 1, 3, 4

Cavendish Laboratory, 9-11, 32 n 2, 58, 76 n 2, 86, 86 n 5, 89, 113 n 5, 140, 152 n 1, 205, 209, 237, 265, 268 n 10, 303 n 2, 322, 322 n 1, 329, 331, 336, 351

Century Dictionary, 217

Chadwick, James, 10, 11, 303-5 passim, 303 n 2, 343, 353

Chemical Society (Great Britain), 158, 159, 169, 214, 283 n 1

Chemisches Central-Blatt, 94

Chicago, University of, 42, 273 n 2, 341, n 2, 343, 344 n 5, 348 n 1

Chittenden, Russell H., 60, 61, 62 n 6, 339-42 passim

Christ's College, Cambridge, 301 n 4, 334

Clark University, Mass., 273 n 1

Cockcroft, John, 11

Colgate University, New York, 113 n 4

Collège de France, Paris, 259 n 2

Collie, John Norman, 282, 283, 283 n 2

Colorado, University of, 197 n 6

Columbia University, 113 n 4, 135 n 4

Index

Index

Index

Radium Institute, Paris, 37 n 7

Radium Institute, Vienna, 99 n 2, 193, 285

Ramsay, William, 32 n 4, 57 n 1, 158, 224, 249, 266, 272 nn 1, 3, 283 n 2; criticized, vii, 19, 23, 79, 81, 83 n 4, 87, 88, 101, 103, 109, 162, 174, 175, 186-88, 188 n 1, 190, 191, 213, 236, 240-41, 243, 271, 278, 282, 283, 289; discovery of radiothorium, vii, 56, 57, 60, 72, 80, 81, 90, 94, 95 n 2; miscellaneous scientific activities, 1, 214, 215 n 2, 217, 218, 222, 264, 267, 270, 283 nn 1, 2; relationship with Hahn, 73 n 3, 132-34, 132 n 1; alleged emanation products, 158, 159, 160 n 4, 162-64, 169, 180-82, 184, 186, 187, 190, 191, 196, 202 n 2, 283 n 4; shares radium with Rutherford, 170 n 1, 175, 180; emanation spectrum, 184, 185 n 2, 187, 198, 199, 204, 234

Rare earths, 13, 47, 80, 104, 105, 109, 110

Rayleigh, Fourth Baron. *See* Strutt, R. J.

Rayleigh, John William Strutt, Third Baron, 1, 32 n 2

Rayless change, 34, 37 n 2, 52, 88, 136

Recoil, 213 n 5, 226, 242, 265, 275

Regener, Erich, 205, 208 n 7

Relative activity, 62 n 4; actinium series, 15, 62-65 passim, 84, 89, 120, 135, 135 n 4, 143-48 passim, 183; thorium series, 62-63, 65, 136, 137, 162, 183, 184, 217; uranium-radium series, 62-90 passim, 96-100 passim, 119, 135-38 passim, 143-48 passim, 165, 168 n 6, 173, 174, 192, 217

Remsen, Ira, 191, 197 n 2

Richards, Theodore W., 259, 259 n 4, 286 n 2

Richardson, O. W., 176 n 2, 256 n 4

Riecke, Eduard, 226, 229 n 8

Righi, Augusto, 226, 229 n 11

Robinson, Harold R., 264, 267 n 2, 307, 312, 319

Rockefeller Foundation, 327

Röntgen, Wilhelm Conrad, 2

Röntgen Society, 242

Rosa, Edward B., 232, 233 n 7

Rossi, R., 276, 277 n 2

Rowland, Henry, 197 n 1, 276

Royal Academy of Science, Stockholm, 208 n 2

Royal College of Science, Ireland, 188 n 1

Royal College of Science, London. *See* Imperial College

Royal Institution of London, 92 n 3, 182, 295 n 6, 351

Royal Military Academy, London, 140 n 7

Royal Society of London, 32 n 1, 57 n 2, 136 n 1, 158, 169, 170, 170 n 1, 175, 185 n 2, 202, 203, 215 n 2, 236-49 passim, 295 n 6, 322, 331 n 1

Royds, Thomas, 5, 61 n 2, 198, 199, 202 n 3, 203, 210, 236, 303 n 1

Rubens, Heinrich, 205, 208 n 4

Rümelin, Gustave, 140, 140 n 6

Russell, Alexander S., 255, 256 n 1, 262, 265, 276, 277 n 2

Rutherford, Eileen (daughter of Ernest R.), 169, 174, 185, 196,